A
PEOPLE
APART

Ethnicity and the Mennonite Brethren

A
PEOPLE
APART

John H. Redekop

Kindred Press

Winnipeg, MB, Canada   Hillsboro, KS, U.S.A.

PREFACE

The completion of this interdisciplinary analysis of several questions associated with Mennonite ethno-religiousity in Canada was facilitated in many ways. Wilfrid Laurier University provided extensive computer and computer related services. I am grateful to WLU and, in particular to Bob Ellsworth, for the extensive support. The Research Office of Wilfrid Laurier University also made available a manuscript preparation grant.

The funding to undertake the national survey, to assist with some travel, and to cover various other costs, was provided by the Board of Spiritual and Social Concerns of the Canadian Conference of the Mennonite Brethren Churches. I am grateful to the Board and particularly to its chairman, Rudy Boschman.

In a special way I am indebted to Debbie Kohlruss who, armed with her trusty word processor, transformed my reams of manuscript into final form. Though facing imminent deadlines, and responsible for the usual secretarial tasks in an academic setting, she persevered cheerfully. Her diligence, dedication, and patient acceptance of seemingly endless revisions and insertions, as well as her willingness to work long hours, much beyond the call of duty, are hereby gratefully acknowledged. She has helped me much in writing this assessment of Mennonites in Canada.

Noteworthy secretarial assistance was also provided by Catherine Shank, Deborah Cox, Joy Gleeson (Martens), Arvis Oxland and Helen Paret. Karen Craigen helped to prepare the graphs and Mike Strathdee researched some journals for me. Their assistance is also gratefully acknowledged.

For cooperation and support in helping me to survey student views, I thank the participating faculty members and students at the University of Alberta, the University of Calgary, the University of Winnipeg, the University of Manitoba, the University of Waterloo, Wilfrid Laurier University, Columbia Bible College, Mennonite Brethren Bible College, Canadian Mennonite Bible College, Bethany Bible Institute, Winkler Bible Institute, Mennonite Educational Institute, Mennonite Brethren Collegiate Institute, and Niagara Christian College. I am equally grateful to the 600 Mennonite Brethren church members who responded, and especially to the 130 or more pastors who helped to expedite the Mennonite Brethren component of the survey. I am sorry that the scores of pages with compiled comments from the various categories of respondents could not presently be included.

To my family, especially Doris, I am grateful for putting up with the disruptions, absences, late nights, and frustrations which accompany such a weekend and after-hours undertaking. I promise that the next Christmas holidays will be different.

In working with Kindred Press, especially Ethel Goertzen, who did some final manuscript corrections, and Gilbert Brandt, Managing Editor, I experienced again the joys of joint service in the family of faith. One could not ask for a more understanding, supportive and patient publisher.

Finally, I want to thank Miriam Warner for permitting me to quote at length from her doctoral dissertation.

John H. Redekop
Waterloo, Ontario
February 20, 1987

This research project was undertaken by Dr. John H. Redekop under the auspices of the Board of Spiritual and Social Concerns of the Canadian Mennonite Brethren Conference which commissioned him to study the issue of ethnicity and the Mennonite Brethren. Upon receiving the report, the Board agreed that the findings needed a wider forum for discussion and debate.

It is with this in mind that the Board of Spiritual and Social Concerns authorized the publication of *A People Apart*.

FOREWORD

The question of how to relate ethnicity to faith has in recent decades become an important one for Mennonite Brethren, especially in North America. The challenge, while not unique to Mennonite Brethren, is particularly central and consequential for conferences, such as most Mennonite church associations, which include the ethnic designation in their official name.

This study presents findings and observations based on wide-ranging investigation. It makes no claim to be an exhaustive treatment of the subject or to provide a comprehensive analysis of the scholarly literature on ethno-religious dynamics. Such a review, while clearly useful, would take us much beyond the time and space constraints set in the preparation of this volume.

Many readers will be familiar with much of the material presented. Many details are, indeed, very well known. The systematic and inclusive depiction of Mennonite ethnicity, however, will probably help many of us, both Mennonites and non-Mennonites in our congregations, to see our identity in a new light. Some readers will agree that ethnicity has become an important question which needs to be addressed. Others, even if they accept the evidence as presented, will insist that there is no serious problem. Some will see no problem because the familiar ways are accepted as natural and normative.

It can be argued that Mennonite Brethren in North America presently face three fundamental problems, all of which relate to identity and mission. First, we face a theological question. We need to clarify and then reaffirm our theology. In this connection some knowledgeable observers have suggested that the general category of Mennonite theology and theological emphasis has become so broad and so diluted that we should reevaluate our conference name for that reason. A thorough investigation of that issue would be timely.

Second, we need to address the urgent matter of conference and congregational policy. Our practices have been changing and not always for the better. Most of us still call ourselves Mennonite Brethren but we have tended to adopt many procedures and practices which differ markedly from those of our founders. As many of our congregations have struggled to define themselves in multi-ethnic terms, they have set aside some very beneficial anabaptist ways of worshipping, fellowshipping, ministering, serving, evangelizing, selecting leaders, and generally functioning as a community of believers. We need to ask ourselves why we have been so quick to move away from proven "brotherhood" ways of doing things. We need to reappropriate many facets of the Biblically-rooted polity which is part of our valued heritage.

Third, we need to clarify and then deal with some problems associated specifically with our Mennonite ethnicity. In addressing this question we must avoid all tendencies to deny our identity. Rather, we must restate who we are and what we believe. In doing so, we have the duty to clarify priorities.

We should note, in passing, that these three problems, while distinct, also intersect. Theology provides an integrating framework for all of life, a framework which overlaps with many ethnic interests. It also guides us in developing church polity. The development and utilization of a Biblically-based church polity, in turn, helps us to process wisely various concerns, including vital theological and ethnic questions. It also facilitates the achievement of mutual accountability. Our forefathers left us a sound legacy in such matters and we sell ourselves short if we abandon it. Ethnicity, as we well know, can be used to sustain as well as convey faith and to influence church polity.

This volume, while dealing briefly with theology and touching marginally on polity, deals mainly with ethnic concerns. It consists of two parts. The first part includes the six chapters which focus on the evidence, and chapter seven which outlines the major kinds of response. The second part consists of chapter eight, which sets forth a personal proposal; chapter nine, which addresses some common questions; and chapter ten, which is a brief summary and conclusion.

If this book has any unique quality it would probably be the combination of calling for a greater emphasis on Biblical Anabaptism while at the same time suggesting that in the church we place less emphasis on Mennonite ethnicity and culture. Such an approach recognizes the powerful and positive role that ethnicity can play as a sustainer and vehicle of faith traditions. Nowhere does this book suggest that ethnicity should be suppressed. It argues only that all ethnicity should be subordinated to Christian faith and that more recognition and acceptance should be extended to persons from other ethnicities. This perspective holds that, where appropriate, Mennonite ethnicity should still be consciously affirmed in our churches and our conference provided that the ethnic identity of sisters and brothers with other heritages also be affirmed.

If this study helps us as Mennonite Brethren, with or without the retention of an ethnic designation, to be more accepting of people from other backgrounds, then the effort put into this book will have been worthwhile. If, as a conference, we also commit ourselves more unitedly and more thoroughly to a Biblically-based Anabaptist theology, then it will have been doubly worthwhile.

John H. Redekop

CONTENTS

Chapter 1.   Introduction

    1. WHY STUDY THE QUESTION OF ETHNICITY? 1
    2. TERMS AND DEFINITIONS 2
    3. RESEARCH METHODS 6
    4. ARE WE TRULY OPEN-MINDED? 7
    5. AUTHOR'S PERSONAL STANCE AND
       COMMITMENT 8
    6. THE SCOPE OF THE STUDY 9

Chapter 2.   Questions, Assumptions, Hypotheses

Part A. The Basic Questions 11

Part B. Some Key Assumptions 12

    1. THE TERM "MENNONITE" HAS A POSITIVE
       CONNOTATION 12
    2. THE MENNONITE BRETHREN CONFESSION
       OF FAITH MUST BE RETAINED 13
    3. THE RETENTION OF THE EVANGELICAL-
       ANABAPTIST DISTINCTIVENESS IS NOT
       NECESSARILY RELATED TO THE RETENTION
       OF THE NAME "MENNONITE" 15
    4. IF MENNONITE BRETHREN DO NOT TAKE
       CORRECTIVE ACTION, RETENTION OF
       ANABAPTIST THEOLOGY WILL BECOME
       PROBLEMATIC 17
    5. MENNONITE BRETHREN SHOULD BE
       GUIDED BY OUR UNDERSTANDING OF
       GOD'S WORD 17
    6. THE PRESENT GENERATION HAS A
       RESPONSIBILITY TO DO WHAT NEEDS
       TO BE DONE 18
    7. THE STRONG ARGUMENTS ARE NOT ALL ON
       ONE SIDE 18
    8. THERE IS NO OPTION WHICH WILL PLEASE
       EVERYONE 19
    9. IT IS POSSIBLE TO DEAL WITH THIS TOPIC
       AND MAINTAIN UNITY AND GOOD WILL 19
   10. WE COMMIT OURSELVES TO CONSIDER ALL
       EVIDENCE FAIRLY 19
   11. UNLESS THERE ARE COMPELLING REASONS,
       THERE SHOULD BE NO CHANGE 19
   12. IT IS MORE IMPORTANT TO AGREE ON GOALS
       THAN ON INTERPRETATION OF PAST
       OR PRESENT 19

Part C. The Basic Hypotheses 19

Chapter 3. Religion and Ethnicity: A National Survey

    I. INTRODUCTION 22

    II. EXPLANATION CONCERNING THE
        QUESTIONNAIRE 25

    III. LIFE SITUATION RESPONSES (NATIONAL
         SAMPLE) 26

    IV. COMPARISON OF OPINIONS AND
        PERCEPTIONS 27

    V. CONCLUSION 54
      QUESTIONNAIRE 55

Chapter 4. Are Mennonites Ethnic?

    1. IS ETHNO-RELIGIOUS ETHNIC? 57

    2. MENNONITES LISTED AS ETHNICS 58

    3. TEACHING ABOUT MENNONITES IN
       SCHOOLS 58

    4. THE MENNONITE PRESS 59

        Mennonitsche Rundschau 59
        Mennonite Mirror 60
        Festival Quarterly 61
        Mennonite Reporter 61
        Mennonite Brethren Herald 62

    5. MENNONITE CULTURE 65

        Mennonite Names 69
        Mennonite Clothing 70
        Mennonite Quilts 71
        Mennonite Painting 71
        Mennonite Music 72
        Mennonite Drama and Film 73
        Mennonite Literature 74
        Mennonite Language; Low-German 74
        Mennonite Food 75
        Mennonite Religion 77
        Mennonite Museums 78
        Mennonite Relief Sales 79

    6. VIEWS OF "NEW" MENNONITES 81

    7. MENNONITES AS TOURIST ATTRACTIONS 84

    8. MENNONITES IN THE MEDIA 86

    9. STATEMENTS BY MENNONITES ABOUT
       MENNONITES 87

    10. VIEWS OF MENNONITES WHO HAVE LEFT
        THE MENNONITE CHURCH 90

    11. DESCRIPTION OF MENNONITES IN
        SCHOLARLY LITERATURE 92

    12. FIELD RESEARCH DEALING WITH
        MENNONITE ETHNICITY 95

13. STATEMENTS BY GOVERNMENTAL AND
    OTHER OFFICIALS CONCERNING MENNONITE
    ETHNICITY 97
14. CONCLUSION: MENNONITES ARE ETHNIC 112

Chapter 5. Are Mennonite Brethren Ethnic?

1. THE PRESENT SITUATION 119
2. THE SAN JOSE SURVEY 122

Chapter 6. Mennonites and Ethnicity; Some Religious and
            Historical Considerations

1. ETHNICITY AS A PROBLEM IN CHURCH
   MINISTRIES 131
2. WHAT DOES THE BIBLE SAY ABOUT ETHNICITY? ... 132
3. WHAT DID THE EARLY ANABAPTISTS SAY ABOUT
   ETHNICITY? 135
   THE DEVELOPMENT OF ETHNICITY 137

Chapter 7. Coming to Terms with Ethnicity: The Options

1. FUSING MENNONITE ETHNICITY AND
   ANABAPTIST CHRISTIANITY 143
2. SEEING THE ANABAPTIST CHURCH AS PART
   OF THE MENNONITE ETHNIC GROUP 144
3. SEEING THE MENNONITE ETHNIC GROUP AND
   THE ANABAPTIST CHURCH AS OVERLAPPING
   COMMUNITIES 144
4. VIEWING THE MENNONITE ETHNIC GROUPS
   AND THE ANABAPTIST CHURCH AS DISTINCT
   ENTITIES BUT STILL CALLING BOTH
   MENNONITE 145
5. TRYING TO REFORM AND REVISE
   MENNONITE ETHNICITY 146
6. DENYING MENNONITE ETHNICITY 146
7. DENYING MENNONITE ETHNICITY AND
   REJECTING ANABAPTIST THEOLOGY 147
8. PARTIALLY SEPARATING MENNONITE
   ETHNICITY FROM ANABAPTIST THEOLOGY
   AND AFFIRMING BOTH 148

Chapter 8. A Modest Proposal

1. CONCERNING ATTITUDE 152
2. CONCERNING ACTIONS 152
3. CONCERNING THE NAME 153
   SOME IMPORTANT ISSUES:
   (1) HOW SERIOUS IS THE EROSION OF
       ANABAPTIST THEOLOGY? 154
   (2) MUST WE TAKE ACTION NOW? 155

(3) SHOULD WE "RISK" A NAME CHANGE? 156

(4) HAVE THERE BEEN OTHER NAME
CHANGES? 160

(5) IS "EVANGELICAL ANABAPTIST" THE
BEST ALTERNATIVE? 160

Chapter 9.   Questions Commonly Asked

1. WHY TALK ABOUT MENNONITISM? THERE
IS NO PROBLEM. 167

2. WOULD A NAME CHANGE CONSTITUTE A
BETRAYAL OF OUR ANABAPTIST TRADITIONS
AND BELIEFS? 168

3. WOULD A FORMAL NAME CHANGE CREATE
A LOSS OF IDENTITY? 169

4. "BUT I DON'T WANT A NAME CHANGE!" 173

5. DOES MENNONITE DIVERSITY IN THE GLOBAL
SCENE NOT PROVE THAT "MENNONITE"
DOES NOT MEAN A PARTICULAR
ETHNICITY? 173

6. WOULD A CHANGE OF NAME CONFUSE
PEOPLE? 175

7. IS NOT THE SITUATION ALREADY
IMPROVING? 175

8. WHAT'S WRONG WITH BEING AN ETHNIC
CHURCH? AREN'T ALL PEOPLE ETHNIC? 176

9. ARE NOT THE ETHNIC CHURCHES IN
NORTH AMERICA GROWING RAPIDLY? 177

10. WOULD ANY OTHER NAME NOT PRODUCE
THE SAME PROBLEMS? 177

11. CAN'T WE EDUCATE THE PUBLIC? 177

12. HOW WOULD A NAME CHANGE AFFECT OUR
RELATIONSHIPS WITH OTHER MENNONITE
CONFERENCES AND INTER-MENNONITE
AGENCIES? 178

13. HOW WOULD A CANADIAN CONFERENCE
NAME CHANGE AFFECT OUR MISSION
WORK OVERSEAS? 178

14. HOW WOULD THE PROPOSED NAME
CHANGE AFFECT OUR DENOMINATIONAL
INSTITUTIONS? 179

15. WOULD MENNONITE BRETHREN CEASE
TO BE MENNONITE BRETHREN? 179

16. WOULD A CONFERENCE NAME CHANGE
NOT MAKE US APPEAR TO BE DISHONEST? 179

17. COULD A NAME CHANGE BE UNDERTAKEN
WITHOUT A SIMILAR CHANGE OCCURRING
IN OUR SISTER MB CONFERENCE IN
THE U.S.? 180

18. WOULD KEEPING THE NAME MENNONITE
     NOT HELP US TO RETAIN OUR
     THEOLOGICAL DISTINCTIVES? 180

Chapter 10. Conclusion

     Concluding comments 181

Chapter 11. Postscript

     Answering early responses 185

SUBJECT INDEX 189

NAME INDEX 197

CHAPTER ONE

INTRODUCTION

1. *Why Study the Question of Ethnicity?*

One can cite numerous reasons for undertaking such a task. Perhaps the most obvious one is that increasingly Mennonite Brethren congregations are not calling themselves Mennonite Brethren. We have no records of earlier years but by 1981, the first year that more or less accurate congregational names were included in the *Yearbook of the Canadian Conference of Mennonite Brethren Churches*, about 53 out of 147 congregations did not use the Mennonite Brethren designation. The more accurate recording in the 1983 *Yearbook* indicates that 57 out of 158 congregations had chosen other names. Although there was slight movement in the opposite direction, it is surely very significant that, according to the 1986 *Yearbook*, the net growth of 15 congregations, 158 to 173, from 1983 to 1986, was matched by a similar 15-church net increase in use of a non-MB name, 57 to 72.

The trend continues. *The Mennonite Brethren Herald* of September 5, 1986, carried a news item about one of Canada's long-standing, supposedly traditional, Mennonite Brethren congregations. "Ebenezer Mennonite Brethren Church in Dalmeny, Sask., also known as Dalmeny Mennonite Brethren Church, officially changed its name July 19 to Dalmeny Community Church."[1] The practice of not designating a Mennonite Brethren church as an MB church, apparently began in Canada with the acceptance of the 25-member Mountainview Gospel Chapel (near Mission, BC), on July 1, 1963, during a national conference session at Herbert, SK. It continues at a fast speed. In recent years about 75% of new congregations do not call themselves Mennonite Brethren. Nor does the trend affect only recent, new, or small churches. Indeed, the two largest congregations in Canada, which together account for 7% of the total Canadian membership, have in recent years both eliminated

1

"Mennonite Brethren" from their letterhead — in the 1986 *Yearbook* they are, however, still designated as Mennonite Brethren.

A second reason involves a growing awareness of ethnic identity in Canada, partly as a result of the unrest and the emphasis on self-awareness which characterized Canadian society during the 1960s and to some extent still does, but also because of a major governmental emphasis on multiculturalism, a national policy officially announced by Prime Minister Pierre Elliott Trudeau in the House of Commons, October 8, 1971. The increasing celebration of racial, ethnic, and cultural diversity in Canada, indeed, in much of the world, has impacted Canadian Mennonite Brethren in a major way.

A third reason, one warranting extensive research in its own right, is that Canada in general, and the Mennonite Brethren Conference in particular, is, in fact, becoming more multicultural. The acceptance in 1984 of the Quebec churches as a provincial conference underscored that fact for all Canadian MBs. Increasingly, new Canadian MBs, not only those in Quebec, raise questions about the meaning of Mennonitism. The recently-formed Quebec conference is the only MB conference not primarily Russo-Mennonite in ethnicity which cannot easily be isolated geographically or socially. Therefore it forces us to face new issues.

A fourth reason involves the Third World. Mennonite Brethren spokespersons from various foreign countries have raised questions. Now that they are coming to North America in significant numbers, and are frequently studying here and reading North American periodicals, they note that "Mennonite" has several meanings and therefore they now ask penetrating questions about what it means to be a Mennonite.

A fifth reason grows out of the research known as the 1982 "Mennonite Brethren Church Membership Profile" study. Virtually all relevant indices indicate declining identification with the denomination.[2] The traditional glue which holds the conference together has lost some effectiveness. Significantly, the North American MB Board of Reference and Counsel has repeatedly discussed the "Erosion of Mennonite Brethren identity...." It was deemed a sufficiently important problem to request the entire brotherhood to make it a prayer concern.[3]

The sixth reason involves a troubling shift in theological emphasis. In some "Theological Reflections" on the 1982 profile study, John E. Toews, academic dean of the denomination's seminary, writes that, "What is happening to the Mennonite Brethren Church theologically? The data suggest that the Mennonite Brethren church [in North America], especially in the United States, is giving up its Anabaptist-Mennonite Brethren heritage...."[4] In summation he adds, "The Profile suggests that the Mennonite Brethren Church is at a critical moment in history. The trends identified in the Profile point toward the loss of a particular theological identity...."[5]

A seventh reason arises from the increasing difficulty in relating Anabaptist theology to the well established Mennonite/Mennonite Brethren lifestyle and culture in North America. Leaders and laymen ask many questions and academics have begun to zero in on the topic in a major way, even though virtually no practical guidelines have been generated thus far. At least there has been some important analysis. For example, from May 28 to 31, 1986, Conrad Grebel College in Waterloo hosted a major consultation involving 120 academics from across Canada and the US, and even some representation from Europe, to deal with the theme, "Toward a Mennonite Self-Understanding." Media reports stated that the purpose of the gathering was to undertake "A critical self-examination of Mennonite experience, identity, and task, especially as it pertains to the North American context." During November 14 and 15, 1986, another large contingent of mainly Mennonite academics met in Winnipeg to discuss, "Dynamics of Faith and Culture in Mennonite Brethren History."

The eighth reason is that Canadian Mennonitism is increasingly expressing itself as culture alongside other cultures and in the public arena. Thus the perception of Mennonitism is becoming more blurred and needs to be clarified.

The ninth reason relates to the results of my own 1985 national Canadian opinion survey. (The results are presented and discussed in Chapter 3.) The data substantiate what I had surmised. They indicate that many widely held MB assumptions may not be valid. In fact, a host of assumptions, many unexamined, need to be investigated. The data, especially Graphs 1-3, also show that a large majority of MBs as well as of the non-MBs sampled perceive Mennonites as ethno-religious or ethnic. Perhaps most importantly, as indicated in Graphs 8 and 9, 75% of the combined MB sample believe that "Mennonite ethnicity" is either a minor or a major "Denominational Problem" for Mennonite Brethren and 68% want "the leadership of our conference" either "to study the matter of ethnicity as it relates to our conference" or to "actively address the matter of ethnicity as it relates to our conference." Reviewing the quantitative as well as the extensive written response to the questionnaire it becomes evident that in addressing the questions of identity and ethnicity we are dealing not merely with problems in perception but with problems in reality.

Not everyone sees it that way. In an undated document prepared for a Canadian MB Conference board a few years ago, David Ewert wrote:

> Numerous churches in our conference have not adopted the name Mennonite Brethren from the outset; others have dropped it for some reason or another. The argument given usually is that it hinders evangelism. To me that argument sounds very strange. Other denominations such as Baptists, the Evangelical Free Church, the Christian and Missionary Alliance (to mention but a few) do not seem to have the same identity problem as we do, and do not seem to be hindered in their outreach because of a denominational label.[6]

In his assessment David Ewert reflects the traditional Mennonite perspective on ethnicity. This perspective holds that while Mennonites need to be open to ethnic diversity, there is no particular or inherent problem. Thus, for example, the generally inclusive, four-volume, *Mennonite Encyclopedia* of 1959 has no entry for "ethnicity" or "culture" and, of course, not for "multiculturalism." Similarly, no index reference to any of these terms can be found in such standard works as *An Introduction to Mennonite History,* Cornelius J. Dyck, editor,[7] *Smith's Story of the Mennonites,*[8] or Frank H. Epp's *Mennonite Exodus*[9]. Even the standard Mennonite Brethren denominational history by John A. Toews has no index reference to ethnicity. Chapter 19, "Facing Cultural Change," deals with diverse issues such as support for Hitler, language change, urbanization, and the wearing of a beard, but nowhere can I find any reference to ethnicity. Apparently it is not seen as a Mennonite Brethren problem or even a fact.[10] However, at one point he notes that in Prussia, "The constant identification of true Mennonitism with German language and culture created serious problems for the faith and mission of the church."[11] Typical of Toews' treatment of the ethnic issue is the statement which he attributes to B.B. Janz, "Never use the gospel-horse to pull the culture-wagon; but hitch culture to the gospel...."[12] Generally Toews defines culture in terms of language and ethical values; nowhere does he even mention ethnicity.

Many writers and spokesmen, I suggest, see no problem because they have not been asking the right questions or they have not been asking them of the right people. To consider mainly the satisfaction level of comfortable ethno-religious traditional Mennonites, as some writers and speakers seem to do, is like asking residents in Whitehorse if it is too cold in the Yukon to live there. The answers will be predictable and inadequate.

We have been slow to recognize the problems related to ethnicity and reluctant to describe or discuss them candidly. If, as seems to be the case, the survey results as presented in Chapter 3 indicate for the first time that most Canadian Mennonite Brethren think that we have a serious "ethnic" problem, then this is new information because this is apparently the first time that Canadian Mennonite Brethren have been asked the question.

Until recently Mennonite Brethren have not written much about ethnicity. John A. Toews observes that "throughout the history of the M.B. Church faith and culture have often been in conflict."[13] But conceptually he does not take us very far. During the last decade, however, some writers have recognized the existence of a problem and have set a new agenda. Even so the question has rarely been analyzed in a specific, practical way. History and Biblical theology have proven to be safer than practical theology.

At a national convention at Three Hills, Alberta, in 1978, the present writer publicly raised some of the basic issues in a study paper, "The Mennonite Brethren as a Believers' Church: Past, Present and Future."[14] In Strassbourg, France, at the 1984 Mennonite World Conference, John E. Toews and Hugo Zorilla addressed the topic. Analyzing the question, "Who are God's People?" (I Peter 2:4-10), they asked,

> What does our text mean for Mennonites with long ethnic traditions and family ties that define the meaning of being Mennonite? The critical issue facing Mennonite peoplehood today is the question of Mennonite identity.... Ethnocentrism of all forms and varieties is sin. The new Mennonite reality calls for a Mennonite identity

that is profoundly Jesus-centred and genuinely universal.... Clarity about identity is prior to any task in the kingdom.... Our text calls us to a Jesus-centeredness and to an ethno-religious inclusiveness.... Our mission means the rejection of all ethnocentrism....[15]

The points made by Toews and Zorilla must be given full attention even if the arena in which they made them may not have been the crucial one. The main ethnic problem, I suggest, is not found in the multi-ethnic Mennonite World Conference, but in some national conferences, as in North America, where "Mennonite" has taken on a second meaning.

In a less theological manner Paul Toews, at a November, 1986 Winnipeg consultation, raised some of the same issues. "The current discussion of the faith and culture question largely hinges on the issue of ethnicity. It is the question of whether Mennonite Brethren are an ethnic group and whether ethnicity has anything to do with Biblical faith. The discussion is surely appropriate for an ethno-religious tradition."[16]

In brief, that is the answer to the question posed at the outset, "Why study the question of ethnicity?" It needs to be studied because it is a problem and to understand the problem is to become involved in trying to resolve the problem. The core of the problem, especially the Canadian problem, has, to date, perhaps not been adequately explained. This essay is an attempt to explain that problem and to suggest that there are answers and that there are ways to deal with the problems positively.

A key point must be emphasized. The intent is not that Christians should avoid having problems in and with a non-Christian society, but that Christians should not have problems for the wrong reasons or face obstacles of their own creation.

2. *Terms and Definitions*

The word "Mennonite" has several definitions. William Klassen has proposed that "we define a Mennonite simply as someone who conscientiously participates in the life of a Mennonite congregation.... But what makes us Mennonites is that we share an understanding of the church...."[17] Wally Kroeker echoes a similar view. "Remember that to be a Mennonite is to believe a certain way."[18] Elsewhere I have, in a preliminary manner, explained that the situation is more complex.[19] A central concern of this essay is to shed more light on that question.

"Ethnicity" is a second key term. We need to clarify the meaning at the outset. It may have several shades of meaning but we will follow the definition developed by Donald Kraybill. Accepting Talcott Parsons' statement that an ethnic group has a "distinctive identity which is rooted in some kind of a distinctive sense of its history,"[20] he suggests that, "A common history, a collective biography, a transgenerational cultural legacy and a shared fate constitute the ethnic glue which fuses Mennonites together above and beyond the religious experience...." Indeed,

a powerful tribal memory recalls that 'we were in this together'.... Ethnic identity is the symbolic process by which a group answers the question, 'Who are we?' Distinctive symbols, belief systems, and cultural practices are the collective answer to the identity question:

'we are the people who....' Ethnic traditions and identities fused with experience over the centuries have an amazing resilience to change when legitimated and empowered by religious symbols.[21]

Another expert in the area, Leo Driedger, highlights six "identification factors," namely, identification with some territory, for North American Mennonites that would be mainly Russia and parts of some other European countries but also regions in North America such as Lancaster County, Waterloo County, Coaldale, Yarrow, Hillsboro, Virgil, Goshen, Reedley, and Steinbach; identification with an ethnic culture; identification with ethnic institutions; identification with historical symbols; identification with a political or religious ideology; and identification with charismatic leadership, past or present or both. For Mennonites, suggests Driedger, Menno Simons served as a key charismatic leader and continues to do so symbolically.[22]

For additional excellent analyses of ethnicity, especially as it relates to religion, consult *Religion and Ethnicity*, Harold Coward and Leslie Kawamura, eds., which investigates the Canadian scene[23], and *Ethnicity in Canada: Theoretical Perspectives*, by Alan B. Anderson and James S. Frideres.[24] Anderson and Frideres cite four key ethnic identification factors: (1) ethnic origin, which may be traced to immigration to North America with "descent represented in a family name typical of the group"; (2) mother tongue, i.e., a language traditionally spoken by members of the group; (3) ethnic-oriented religion; and (4) folkways, i.e., the practices of certain customs unique to the group.[25] The authors observe that "Religion has frequently been used to bolster ethnic consciousness and perhaps language maintenance."[26] I am reminded of the valiant efforts of "Das Kommittee fuer die deutsche Sprache" (The Committee for the German Language), sponsored for many years by Mennonite Brethren in Canada. "Many of the functions of religion," write Anderson and Frideres, "are oriented toward the preservation of ethnic identity...it promotes social integration; it attempts to validate a people's customs and values; it inculcates values through socialization; it affirms the dignity of the ethnic group members...; it tends to be a pillar of conservatism; and it often encourages social isolation from outsiders."[27] In this connection G.W. Allport makes an important point. Among ethnic groups religion "usually stands for more than faith — it is the pivot of the cultural tradition of a group.... The clergy...may, often do, become defenders of a culture...."[28]

In discussing ethnicity we must be careful to distinguish between two uses of ethnicity. Christianity is always transmitted through a language and a culture but Christians were specifically enjoined by the Founder of their faith from wedding that faith to any one race or ethnic group.

3. *Research Methods and Approach*

As already indicated, this research project incorporates several modes of inquiry. The major field study of opinion generated important new data. Scores of interviews and extensive correspondence added insights. Much time was also spent reading primary and secondary sources in textbooks, monographs, and scholarly literature. Mennonite periodicals provided much useful information as did various non-Mennonite media sources.

The research involved in investigating this general topic included reading materials which dealt with the topic from many perspectives. It would have been possible, I suppose, to include summaries of everthing that I read, to incorporate all possible perspectives. That would have produced a much larger volume. Instead, I utilized an approach common in the social sciences. On the basis of preliminary analysis, I spelled out 12 hypotheses. These are listed in chapter 2, Part C. Then I set out to determine whether these hypotheses were valid. Thus it was not a matter of deciding in advance what the conclusions would be and then selecting only evidence which supported a pre-determined conclusion, rather, it was a matter of clearly stating hypotheses and then undertaking research to see wheter these hypotheses were valid. In later sections of this book I have indicated my evaluation of the evidence. Readers will, naturally, form their own conclusions.

4. *Are We Truly Open-Minded?*

A very important preliminary question must be asked. Are we, in truth, prepared to discuss the matter of ethnicity? Are we willing to bring an open mind to this agenda or are we closed-minded? Several spokespersons, representing various views, have told me that they do not want to discuss the issue. Some say that they are quite comfortable with the situation and that they see nothing to discuss, at least not to discuss as a problem. Others state that the best way to deal with this controversial problem is to ignore it.

For me the key question in this regard is not whether we want to put the identity/ethnicity question aside, but whether there is a problem to be addressed. If, as various experts suggest, Mennonite Brethren, especially in North America, are experiencing an identity crisis, then we need to address it. A reversal of identity loss, after all, cannot be achieved simply by wishing for it.

In pursuing the topic we should avoid the perennial temptation to trivialize or marginalize, or even "emotionalize" the issue. Nor dare we caricature those who disagree with us.

We must, rather, dialogue. I'm not sure that it's possible to dialogue about such central values. I hope that it is. I hope that people will consider the evidence carefully even when controversial propositions need to be considered. And, in the final analysis, I trust that we are prepared to follow insight wherever that may lead us. Or will we back off with the excuse that the most logical option is too formidable to contemplate?

I expect some negative reaction, not only from some people who see no major problems but also from some who opt for other solutions. That's fair. All I ask is that we trust one another, that we read the entire analysis, that we read it with an open mind, and that we do not attribute negative motives.

I am fully aware that by presenting reality, as I see it, I may be disturbing a surface tranquility which will not readily be re-established. My justification, if one is needed, is that all other options, in the long run, have less desirable outcomes.

5. *My Personal Stance and Commitment*

Readers have a right to know where I stand. I shall spell out my basic hypotheses in Chapter 2 and my "Modest Proposal" in Chapter 8. For now let the following suffice.

I struggle. A part of me says, "Affirm your ethnicity more strongly. It's the only one you have. Express it with your faith." Another part of me says, "As long as ethnicity and theology are fused for your denomination you have a problem."

Integrity requires me both to acknowledge and address a problem, a problem which for several reasons I would just as soon ignore. To a considerable degree I am emotionally and intellectually comfortable with the traditional MB orientation in Canada. To a large degree my own identity involves a fusion of faith and ethnicity. Besides, I do not want to create confusion, alienation, or division.

And yet I must speak, I must say what I believe. I must speak because I agree with Delbert Wiens' observation that, "Ironically, we heirs of the Anabaptists are among the last to experience the abstraction of faith and ethics from an older ethos." [29] I must speak to say that I am puzzled that evangelical Mennonites have not seen the obstacle and error of fusing ethnicity with faith for what it is. (I am equally puzzled why the majority of Christians in Canada, including many MBs, miss Jesus' peace teaching and some want to abandon it altogether.)

Some critics of earlier writings have suggested that I am trying to deny my Mennonite roots and identity. How wrong they are! The religious past is precisely what I am committed to retain and reinforce. Everything that's Biblical should be kept. Nor am I attacking ethnic traditions. Contrary to what some people might think, I do not wish to see the decline of ethnic Mennonitism. Specifically, I merely want to separate the official and central, and only the official and central, ethnic component from the religious faith and then I want both ethnicity and faith to thrive.

I stand firmly with those founders who in the first Mennonite Brethren Confession of Faith (1902) wrote that they wanted to recover the biblical concept of the church, "as it was in the beginning — in the apostolic church." I find the Biblical concept of the church best expressed in traditional anabaptist emphases and I am whole-heartedly committed to the nurture and dissemination of that emphasis.

Some sections of this analysis will raise a few eyebrows. If there is evidence that my assessment is faulty, I shall be very willing to adopt a different perspective. (Sometimes I wish that my assessments on ethnicity would turn out to be wrong — it would be easier.)

Conviction forces us to address certain issues which we believe to be very important. Integrity requires all of us to state exactly that which we believe.

I wish to emphasize one further qualification. The most important part of this report involves the analysis. My own "Modest Proposal" for a name change, itself part of a three-part recommendation for improvement, must stand or fall on its own merits as a separate, though related, agenda item. For several reasons I felt compelled to include it. First, many respondents to my 1985 national survey requested that some alternative be provided, at least as a basis for comparison and further thought. Second, numerous sisters and brothers with whom I discussed this research venture felt that it would be enhanced if I presented not only the problem but also a possible solution.

6. *The Scope of this Study*

This investigation deals mainly with the Canadian Mennonite Brethren experience but it also draws heavily from the similar American Mennonite Brethren experience. Beyond that, in keeping with the evidence that most people do not distinguish between Mennonite Brethren and other Mennonites, it also deals with Canadian Mennonites in general.

Chapter 1 — FOOTNOTES

1. *Mennonite Brethren Herald*, September 5, 1986, p. 24.
2. See the abbreviated statistical report in *Direction*, 14, 2, Fall, 1985, esp. pp. 15 and 16.
3. *Rejoice*, September, 1985, p. 60.
4. John E. Toews, "Theological Reflections," *Direction*, 14, 2, Fall, 1985, p. 60.
5. *Ibid.*, p. 68.
6. The two-page document entitled, "Issues That Need To Be Addressed" was probably written in June or July, 1983.
7. Cornelius J. Dyck, *An Introduction to Mennonite History* (Scottdale, PA:Herald Press, 1967), p. 324.
8. C. Henry Smith, *The Story of the Mennonites* (Newton, KS: Mennonite Publishing Office, 1950), pp. x, 856.
9. Frank H. Epp, *Mennonite Exodus* (Altona, MB:D.W. Friesen & Sons, 1962), pp. xix, 571.
10. John A. Toews, *A History of the Mennonite Brethren Church: Pilgrims and Pioneers* (Fresno, CA: Board of Christian Literature, General Conference of Mennonite Brethren Churches, 1975), pp. xxi, 513.
11. John A. Toews, p. 14.
12. *Ibid.*, p. 341.
13. *Ibid.*, p. 338.
14. *1978 Yearbook of the Canadian Conference of Mennonite Brethren Churches* (Winnipeg: Christian Press, 1978), pp. 142-158.
15. *Program and Information: Mennonite World Conference* (Lombard, IL: Mennonite World Conference, 1984), pp. 95-96. A slightly edited version of the paper can be found in *The Christian Leader*, August 21, 1984, pp. 2-5.
16. Paul Toews, "Faith in Culture and Culture in Faith: Mennonite Brethren Entertaining Expansive, Separative and Assimilative Views About the Relationship," a paper read at the Mennonite Brethren Bible College in Winnipeg, MB, November 15, 1986, pp. 17-18.
17. "What did Anabaptist-Mennonites believe? An outline of their faith," *Mennonite Reporter*, February 16, 1981, p. 5.
18. *The Christian Leader*, July 23, 1985, p. 4.
19. "Three Kinds of Mennonites," in John H. Redekop, *Two Sides: The Best of Personal Opinion, 1964-1984* (Winnipeg: Kindred Press, 1984), pp. 112-114.
20. "Some Theoretical Considerations on the Nature and Trends of Change of Ethnicity" in N. Glazer and D. Moynihan, (eds.), *Ethnicity, Theory, Experience* (Cambridge: Harvard University Press, 1975), pp. 56-57.

21. Donald B. Kraybill, "Modernity and Identity: The Transformation of Mennonite Ethnicity," a paper read at Conrad Grebel College, May, 1986, pp. 7-9. For an excellent bibliography on the topic see pp. 30-32.

22. Leo Driedger, "Ethnic Identity in the Canadian Mosaic," in Leo Driedger, (ed.), *The Canadian Ethnic Mosaic: A Quest for Identity* (Toronto: McClelland and Stewart, 1978), pp. 14f. For additional bibliographic sources see pp. 37-39.

23. Harold Coward and Leslie Kawamura, (eds.), *Religion and Ethnicity* (Waterloo, ON: Wilfrid Laurier University Press, 1978), p. 181.

24. Alan B. Anderson and James S. Frideres, *Ethnicity in Canada: Theoretical Perspectives* (Toronto: Butterworths, 1981), p. 334. This monograph contains excellent bibliographies.

25. *Ibid.*, pp. 36f.

26. *Ibid.*, p. 41.

27. *Ibid.*

28. G. W. Allport, *The Nature of Prejudice* (Garden City, NY: Anchor/Doubleday, 1954), pp. 415-416.

29. Delbert Wiens, "The Moralities of the Mennonite Brethren," a paper read at the Mennonite Brethren Bible College in Winnipeg, November 15, 1986, p. 24.

CHAPTER TWO

QUESTIONS, ASSUMPTIONS, HYPOTHESES

PART A. THE BASIC QUESTIONS

The next step in our analysis is to spell out our basic questions. We shall deal with twelve although some will get relatively less attention than others.

1. What are the author's assumptions? Assumptions can be very important. Knowing the author's assumptions tells the reader where the author is coming from. Some assumptions were described in Chapter 1. Additional key assumptions will be explained in PART B.

2. What is the author's basic thesis? The author's thesis, or hypothesis, will be stated in PART C.

3. Are Mennonites ethnic? Here we encounter one of the most important questions. We will investigate the matter thoroughly. If it turns out that in Canada the term "Mennonite" has an ethnic connotation — the readers will decide for themselves — then we must agree to accept that fact and not keep acting as if the fact has not been established. If it turns out that "Mennonite" in Canada is not primarily an ethnic label, then that fact must, of course, be accepted as well.

In ascertaining whether "Mennonite" means ethnic we will consider the views of Mennonites, selected non-Mennonites, and public perceptions generally. We must also remind ourselves that the question is not whether every congregation or even every Mennonite denomination is ethnic but what is the general situation. There is a related matter. The question is not whether Mennonite refers to conferences or churches — that fact everyone acknowledges. The question is whether the word "Mennonite" also refers to something else, with the result that the designation "Mennonite" sends a dual, blurred, and confusing signal.

4. Are Mennonite Brethren ethnic? Here we enquire whether, even if Mennonites generally are seen as having a distinctive Mennonite

ethnicity, Mennonite Brethren can nevertheless be seen as not having a distinctive Mennonite ethnicity.

5. Does ethnicity constitute a problem for Mennonite Brethren, especially in evangelism and other church ministries? Assuming there are some ethnic problems, we want to ascertain to what extent they relate to attitude, to the Mennonite name, to both, or to something else. In this connection we do well to remind ourselves of the extent to which Mennonite Brethren churches no longer use their MB identity. We must note the trends and contemplate the long-term consequences.

6. What does the Bible say about ethnicity? Since we want to be thoroughly Biblical in dealing with this matter we will identify at least the main texts and note the Biblical guidelines.

7. What did the early and the later Anabaptists say about ethnicity?

8. If Canadian Mennonite Brethren, in fact, possess a distinctive Mennonite ethnicity, how did such a situation evolve?

9. What are Mennonite Brethren options concerning ethnicity in Canada?

10. Has the designation "brethren" outlived its usefulness? Katie Funk Wiebe has said that "We need a stronger teaching on the theology of peoplehood coupled with a deliberate effort to discard terms such as 'brotherhood' and maybe even 'brethren', which are clearly 19th century terms and have changed meaning in our time."[1] Many people who responded to the questionnaire raised the same point even though no question touched on the issue. We will assess a proposed solution.

11. Assuming that Canadian Mennonite Brethren have an ethnic problem, what is the best solution? Chapter 8 sets forth a specific proposal. In this connection we will also ask ourselves whether the term "Mennonite" has become a denominational liability? In what ways is it still an asset? How do the pros and cons of retaining it compare?

12. How can one answer fellow Mennonite Brethren who raise seemingly major and valid objections to the proposed solution? We will address all major criticisms.

PART B. SOME KEY ASSUMPTIONS

The following twelve assumptions both shape and explain the subsequent analysis.

1. *The term "Mennonite," generally speaking, has a positive connotation.* It was not always thus in Canada, for example, during World War II when Mennonites encountered widespread animosity: partly because of anabaptist pacifism, partly because many Mennonites spoke German, and in some regions because hard-won economic success had produced jealousy. But today the reaction is generally positive and well it should be. Many very fine organizations call themselves Mennonite: Mennonite Central Committee, Mennonite Disaster Service, Mennonite Economic Development Associates, and MCC Selfhelp are four examples. We should note, however, that not all of the positive connotations have to do with Christian matters, let alone specifically Anabaptist values. Thus, to the

extent that "Mennonite" is used as meaning "thrifty person," "hard-working farmer," "good tradesman" or something similar it has a positive but not particularly Christian meaning. Not everything positive is Christian. Not everything positive is good enough. We are called to become transformed and to lead holy lives, not just noble, honourable and praiseworthy lives.

2. *The Mennonite Brethren Confession of Faith with all of its Biblically-based anabaptist distinctives, must be retained.* We must always remember, of course, that Confessions of Faith reflect our understanding of the Word at the present time. Further, although it seems expedient to analyze the question of ethnicity, such an examination should not be construed as a re-examination of our basic precepts except in the sense of learning more about them and re-affirming them.

Unfortunately some MBs, including some leaders, with or without a formal review of the ethnic aspects, have decided to put aside part of our historic Gospel. I call upon them, not in the name of history or tradition but in the name of Biblical truth, to embrace the whole counsel of God. We are not being faithful if we embrace and proclaim only a truncated Gospel.

We do well to remind ourselves briefly what anabaptism means, especially at a time when many Christians from other persuasions are coming to see and accept the fullness and Bible-centeredness of anabaptist theology. We need to become convinced why it would be foolish of us to set aside our rich theological heritage.

Thomas G. Sanders reminds us that Christians of the anabaptist tradition "belong to one of history's most misunderstood religious groups;" today we must add that many so-called anabaptists also misunderstand it. He continues: anabaptism "is as distinctive as Lutheranism, Calvinism, and Anglicanism." [2] We need to rediscover the fact that in a profound sense, since January 21, 1525, anabaptism has constituted a unique third option for at that time a new understanding of the Christian faith and the Christian church appeared. For members of a small, dissenting group, the full first-century qualities of the church had again been accepted as normative. In his succinct analysis, *Anabaptism: Neither Catholic nor Protestant*, Walter Klaassen has portrayed the distinguishing characteristics of this rediscovered Biblical way. [3]

We can identify eight essentials of biblical anabaptism.

(i) It is Jesus-centered. "Anabaptism means a profound commitment to take Jesus seriously in everyday life." In the 20th century, as in the 16th, such a view runs counter to the notions that the demands of Jesus are too difficult for ordinary people and that Jesus' significance lies mainly in providing heavenly salvation. [4] Authentic anabaptism also insists that there can be no true "shalom" apart from Jesus' atonement.

(ii) It has a high view of the Bible. While not worshipping the Bible itself, for that would be bibliolatry, anabaptists affirm that "As the inspired Word of God, the Bible is the infallible and inerrant rule of faith and life for us and for all mankind." [5]

(iii) It stands for a believers' church. This means that the church consists of "adult" believers who have joined voluntarily and that this individual choice is taken very seriously. True anabaptism stresses both praying the sinner's prayer of repentance and committing oneself to walk in the full newness of life.

(iv) It sees the church as a visible counterculture, a covenant community. The church is not simply a place where God's truth is preached but a united fellowship of people distinct and profoundly different from the rest of society and, of course, the state. As a separated people, the church has one over-riding, singular loyalty — to Jesus as Lord.

(v) It sees the church as a fellowship without divisions in the sense that all racial, ethnic, class, and gender differences yield to the unity of the Body.

(vi) It assumes and insists that the church is a missionary church. "Precisely because the Anabaptists rejected both infant baptism and the marriage of church and state," they defined all of society as a mission field. If infants are baptised and people generally undergo such a ceremony, and if that is deemed to make them Christian, then there is no need for evangelism.[6]

The church, anabaptism asserts, "can be missionary only if it is a prophetic minority. When the church no longer sees itself as a missionary minority it has become identified with the citizens and powers of the state."[7] It has then forfeited its Christian calling. This criterion holds true as much in 20th century North America as in 16th century Europe.

(vii) It emphasizes the New Testament. Anabaptists make a clear, functional distinction between the Old and the New Testaments. "They read the Bible as the story of God's movement for and among His people which reached its high point in the life and work of Jesus, and which sees His continuing work in the life of His disciple community."[8] Thus anabaptists see an old and a new covenant, they read the old from the perspective of the new, they see the new as the fullfillment of the old, and derive their ethics from the love ethic of the new.

(viii) It embraces the biblical teaching concerning peace. Here anabaptists part company with the so-called Christian fundamentalists who tend to see the peace position as optional or even as theologically liberal. Where Christian fundamentalists have in error fused the cause of the Christian church with the cause of their country, Christian pacifism is also seen as unpatriotic.

Anabaptists, taking Jesus' life and teaching as fully relevant for all of His followers at all times, see peace and reconciliation as cardinal to the Christian message. God gave this ethic to His followers not as a point to consider but as a command to obey. This emphasis on peace involves costly discipleship. It did so for Jesus and it may well do so for His committed followers.[9]

In reflecting on these eight essentials we should note the following. Virtually all church-related Mennonites today stress discipleship but not all stress decision. Some emphasize an obedient discipleship but one without a beginning. But, surely, it is never proper to separate discipleship from decision. Jesus didn't, the 16th century anabaptists didn't, and we shouldn't either. That's one reason why we need to distinguish between Mennonitism and anabaptism. I want a strong peace emphasis but not at the expense of the call to salvation. There need not be such a trade-off and I, for one, refuse to make it.

Jesus came as the Prince of Peace. What does that mean? [10] It means that He came to bring about peace, first between man and God and then, as a consequence, between man and man to the extent that individuals and groups in society accept His ethic. True anabaptists, however, do not believe that if peace between man and man is pursued with enough diligence, such an undertaking will produce, or in itself be evidence of, peace with God. Important though it may be, the central anabaptist concern is not the absence of war but the absence of alienation from God.

Unfortunately some Mennonites seem to make more of Jesus as the model of peace than as the means of peace. The result may be a gospel of relief and rehabilitation without a Gospel of redemption. We do not accept such an emphasis nor that which equates Christian obedience with social activism.

In providing even a cursory overview of anabaptism, two other items must be stressed. The biblical peace emphasis, as taught by Jesus, does not deal only or even mainly with the military question. We recall that no one in Jesus' Jewish audience was permitted to undertake any military involvement. Jesus was describing a way of life, based on love, valid for men and women of all ages and in any calling or situation. "Non-resistance," thus, is really an inadequate, negative, label. "Limitless love" might be better.

Similarly, defining the peace emphasis in terms of the avoidance of modernity or withdrawal from society is also inappropriate. [11] Christian pacifism is positive, assertive, and activist.

I have described anabaptism at some length to help clarify my stance. When I subsequently question the emphasis on Mennonitism in the church, it shall be abundantly clear that I am not questioning the importance of Biblical anabaptism.

3. *The retention of the evangelical-Anabaptist distinctives is not necessarily related to retention of the term "Mennonite."* The concepts and designations "anabaptist" and "Mennonte" are related but they are not synonymous.

Certain "givens" must be stated clearly. For centuries after its initial usage, and in many parts of the world even today, the word "Mennonite" has had a profoundly significant religious meaning. But for many of us the situation has changed. "It is ironic that the emphasis on ethnicity rejected by the early Anabaptists should have become a special characteristic of their descendents. For an outsider to become a member of a Mennonite church has often implied the contradiction of accepting a totally different ethnic identity as well." Writing about a decade ago, Walter Klaassen, an internationally recognized expert on anabaptism adds, "It is no wonder that the various centennial celebrations of these years evoke little enthusiasm among Mennonites of other than white Germanic background." [12]

We have spent much time during the past 40 years rediscovering, although not always reappropriating, New Testament anabaptism. That process must continue. But simultaneously we must re-examine the meaning of Mennonitism. As Klaassen states in the quotation above, many fellow church members in Mennonite churches do not identify with Mennonitism — and for good reason. They do not share the same ethnic heritage. [13]

But even the above does not tell the whole story. Not only are not all contemporary anabaptists Mennonites, but also, as shall be demonstrated later, not all present Mennonites in North America are anabaptists.

Consider this analogous situation. According to Rabbi Howard Hoffman of Shalom Synagogue in London, Ontario, Canada presently has some 320,000 Jews. But of these only "about 60%" practice Jewish religion.

The data for Canadian Mennonites is as follows. The Mennonite World Conference office, in the 1986 update, comes up with a total of 104,033 Mennonite and Brethren in Christ members. (The US figure is 243,667.) [14] My own incomplete survey suggests that at least another 70,000 "Mennonites" belong to "other" denominations and, on the basis of available evidence, it seems that at least 50,000 adult "Mennonites" do not belong to any religious group. That adds up to a total of some 224,000. If we add a figure of 50,000, a low estimate, for children who have not become members and 25,000 for Mennonite adults who attend Mennonite churches but who have not joined, also a conservative estimate, then we have about 300,000 Mennonites in Canada or about 1.15% of the population. According to these figures, slightly more than 1 person out of every hundred in Canada is somehow part of the Mennonite sector. Interestingly, the 1981 Census which, of course, allowed respondents to identify themselves as they saw fit, produced a figure of 189,370 Mennonites in Canada, an increase of about 12.6% from the 1971 figure of 168,151. During that decade the Canadian population increased by 12.9%. In 1981 Manitoba had 63,490 Mennonites and British Columbia had 30,895. These figures include only Mennonites, with children, who claim a Mennonite religion. [15]

Currently, increasing numbers of people of non-Mennonite ethnic background are attending our congregations. Many are strongly anabaptist. The task of making all of these non-Mennonites — as well as all those we still want to reach — into Mennonites is so monumental that it boggles the mind. Fortunately, it is not necessary, theologically. Our task is less ominous; it is to work together towards a full acceptance of the total gospel. We keep in mind that a true anabaptist is simply a Christian prepared to accept and obey the whole counsel of God. Nothing more and nothing less. Such full acceptance has nothing to do with a person's background. Thus everyone, all who respond to Christ's invitation, can become anabaptist.

But there may still be some who say that, by and large, Mennonite and anabaptist mean the same thing. If the meanings are, in fact, still similar, then why do writers in Mennonite periodicals, both scholarly and popular, increasingly use either the hypenated or some other fusion of Mennonite/Anabaptist when they refer to the Christian aspect of Mennonitism?

Beyond that, of course, one can point to the Brethren in Christ. Are they anabaptist? Of course they are? Are they Mennonite? Obviously not.

In sum, one does not have to be a Mennonite to be an anabaptist.

4. *If the Mennonite Brethren denomination does not take corrective action soon, the retention of anabaptist theology will become very problematic.* As we have seen in Chapter 1, Mennonite Brethren congregational identification with the term "Mennonite" is weakening. If "Mennonite" and "anabaptist" continue to be treated as if they mean the same thing, then, as Mennonitism declines, so will the anabaptist orientation.

The anthropologist, Jacob A. Loewen, is right, when he states,

> When we look at the MB's in regard to the peace stance per se — one of the original Mennonite distinctives which MB's have consistently reaffirmed — we see that loyalty to this Anabaptist bedrock has been greatly weakened, and in many cases, totally lost.
>
> ....This erosion of the peace stance has progressed to the degree that today in Western and Central USA, it seems to me, many MB's probably would feel more drawn to Moral Majority and Militarism than even to mainstream evangelicalism. [16]

Vital Anabaptist biblical distinctives are eroding. Where have we as leaders been? Why are we allowing this to happen? Some important elements of acculturation are proceeding rapidly and, not willing to separate the theological from the ethnic, many of us who are leaders stand by as observers. [17]

The status quo is not an acceptable option. If we do not decide soon and act forthrightly, then the trend will soon become irreversible and within a generation or less, we will still be clinging proudly to our Mennonite name but it will designate an empty shell. The anabaptist theology will essentially be gone. The result of continued drift is all too predictable.

The other option involves separating ethnicity from anabaptism, affirming both, but stressing mainly anabaptism in the church. In either case there will be some loss. Some members, maybe even some congregations, will decide to go their separate way. But I strongly assert that the loss will be less if we soon separate the two than if we opt for drift. That decision involves a judgement call but our experience during the past quarter century and the present evidence support such a judgement call.

It is time for denominational renewal and we do not have much time to do it. [18]

5. *Our Mennonite Brethren action or inaction on the issue of ethnicity should be guided primarily by our understanding of God's Word.* I'm assuming that we have no disagreement on that point. It is not enough to please oneself or others, we must seek to please God. We deal with the matter at hand because that is the right thing to do. The ethnic/cultural problem also bedeviled the New Testament church and that church dealt with it. [19]

In the pamphlet, "The Story of the Mennonite Brethren church," [20] we read, "The open Bible, then, is the great distinctive of the Mennonite Brethren Church today." [21] Let us covenant to abide by that norm rather than be unduly influenced by emotions, tradition, or personal preference.

6. *The present generation of Mennonite Brethren, especially congregational and conference leaders, has a responsibility to review the current situation and to do what needs doing.* Our task is made a bit easier by the fact, clearly demonstrated in GRAPH B9 in Chapter 3, that most Canadian MBs want us to deal with the ethnic issue. Leaders, precisely because they have knowledge, opportunity, and ability, must also shoulder responsibility. We cannot avoid ulimate accountability.

Some critics will surely say, "But such an undertaking has never happened before!" They are right. And why has it not been done sooner? In part because the time was not ripe. Until the language transition was virtually complete in Canada, the Mennonite Brethren Conference was basically a church within an ethnic group. In some localities that ethnic situation persists but the MB church, by and large, is changing. Since 1980 six major developments have occurred:

(i) the number of MB churches not choosing, or setting aside, an MB designation has become an avalanche.

(ii) the French-speaking Quebec MB conference has joined the Canadian MB conference.

(iii) Mennonite Brethren schools, especially the seminary, have consolidated an anabaptist orientation.

(iv) substantial numbers of people with non-Mennonite backgrounds have joined Mennonite Brethren churches.

(v) almost all MB churches have switched to English or at least adopted English as a second language.

(vi) the number of congregations, outside of Quebec, not using English or German, has reached at least ten.

Thus we find ourselves faced with a particular confluence of historic factors and opportunities. Earlier generations would have had a difficult time trying to refocus the conference's orientation; later generations will not have the opportunity. The present leadership, broadly defined, must sieze this opportunity.

The present leadership must speak prophetically and act energetically. We must work at building a broadly based consensus but we should not wait for unanimity. On questions of ethnicity and anabaptism, unanimity will always be elusive. Of course, in all matters we should be very sensitive to the sentiments of a dissenting minority, especially if it involves older sisters and brothers.

7. *The strong arguments are not all on one side.* There are major reasons why we should act but there are also some advantages in maintaining the status quo. The question is, what is the net effect? Merely having pointed to some advantages does not constitute a convincing case. Obviously ethnic emphasis can be useful. "Ethnic communities perform a valuable function in adjusting immigrants to the ways of their adoptive country." [22]

8. *There is no option, including the option of doing nothing, which will please everyone.*
9. *It is possible to study this topic while maintaining unity and good will.* Where there is love, diversity of viewpoints will not drive people apart.
10. *In dealing with this question we commit ourselves to consider all of the evidence and arguments openly, honestly, and fairly.*
11. *Unless there are compelling reasons for change, there should be no change.*
12. *It is much more important to agree on common goals than to agree on a common interpretation of the past or a common description of the present.* It is hard to critique objectively familiar values, emphases, and names in which we have invested heavily. In our analysis we must also acknowledge that the situation varies from place to place.

On the basis of these twelve assumptions, six of which have been developed somewhat, I set forth the following hypotheses and eventually, having weighed the evidence, make my "modest proposal."

PART C. THE BASIC HYPOTHESES

The twelve assumptions described in PART B were presented as affirmations about which there was, presumably, general agreement. We turn now to my basic hypotheses. While evidence supporting some of these hypotheses has already been presented, I do not assume that there is general agreement on their validity. Having stated these twelve fundamentally important hypotheses in this section, I shall then, in chapters 3 to 9, present the evidence which has convinced me that they are, indeed, valid.
1. Mennonites in Canada, and in several other countries, are correctly perceived as being an ethnoreligious people.
2. The perception of Mennonites in Canada as an ethno-religious people will continue at least for several generations.
3. The ethnic element in Mennonite ethnoreligiosity in Canada is very prominent and in some important respects actually increasing.
4. There is overwhelming evidence that the actual ethnic element in Mennonite ethnoreligiousity in Canada will survive, even flourish, at least for several generations.
5. As part of the larger Mennonite community in Canada, Mennonite Brethren, in actual fact and in public perception, function largely as an ethno-religious group with a prominent ethnic element. Also, most people do not see Mennonite Brethren as being significantly different from other Mennonites in Canada.
6. In Canada, and in several other countries, the word "Mennonite" has taken on a double meaning. It refers to ethnic reality as well as to religious reality. The double meaning creates confusion for Mennonites as well as non-Mennonites. Also, the two meanings of "Mennonite" are contradictory and create specific problems for Mennonite church ministries.
7. It is impossible for Mennonite Brethren to educate the Canadian public so that Mennonite Brethren, still officially known as Mennonite

Brethren, are perceived as a religious rather than as an ethnic or ethno-religious group. Mennonite Brethren waste much time and energy trying to achieve that goal.

8. In part the Mennonite Brethren ethnic problem involves unchristian attitudes and habits. This part of the problem can be corrected only by a major effort to change these attitudes and habits.

9. In part the Mennonite Brethren ethnic problem involves the usage of the ethnic or ethno-religous term "Mennonite." This part of the problem can be corrected only by replacing the term "Mennonite" with something else.

10. By itself, neither a change of attitudes and habits nor a change of name will get us very far in dealing with the Mennonite Brethren ethnic problem. In order to make significant progress we must do both. Each of the changes is necessary but by itself neither is sufficient. Undertaking both changes will not guarantee that we will resolve our ethnic problem but will, at least, make it possible. If we do not undertake both changes, then we cannot solve our ethnic problem.

11. It is possible for Mennonite Brethren to deal successfully with their ethnic problem while still holding to, indeed, strengthening, anabaptist theology. Resolving the ethnic problem will make it easier for non-Mennonites as well as members and leaders of Mennonite Brethren churches to affirm anabaptist theology. It will also eliminate the argument of some Mennonite Brethren leaders that they feel compelled to drop the Mennonite name, and with it also the fused anabaptist theology, in an attempt to resolve the ethnic problem locally. For those Mennonite Brethren who have dropped the Mennonite Brethren name because they do not like anabaptist theology, and there are some, the issue will then be clearly drawn in theological terms. Such cases can then be dealt with as church or denominational issues, unencumbered with ethnic issues.

12. The resolution of the Mennonite Brethren ethnic problem does not require Mennonite Brethren to reject any ethnic heritage. In fact, once it is clear that the denomination is no longer formally and officially fused with a particular ethnic heritage, namely, the traditional Mennonite ethnic heritage, then it will be easier for all ethnic heritages, including the largely dominant Mennonite heritage, to flourish in the various congregations and to be used in diverse ways to enhance and to advance Christian ministries. Such an approach more closely incorporates Biblical teaching than does our present situation.

Chapter 2 — FOOTNOTES

1. Katie Funk Wiebe, "The New Mennonite Brethren: In But Still Out." A paper read at the Mennonite Brethren Bible College in Winnipeg, MB, November 15, 1986, p. 12.

2. Thomas G. Sanders, *Protestant Concepts of Church and State* (New York: Holt, Rinehart and Winston, 1964), p. 75.

3. Walter Klaassen, *Anabaptism: Neither Catholic nor Protestant* (Waterloo, ON: Conrad Press, 1973).

4. For a concise discussion of this point, and several others, I am indebted to John E. Toews, "Where to, Mennonite Brethren...?" *The Christian Leader*, January 6, 1976, pp. 2f.

5. *Yearbook, General Conference of Mennonite Brethren Churches* (Hillsboro, KS: Mennonite Brethren Publishing House, 1978), p. 12. For the complete statement see pp. 12 to 15.

6. *Ibid.*

7. *Ibid.*

8. *Ibid.*

9. For a particularly useful discussion of this aspect see John Howard Yoder, "The Heart of our Heritage," *The Christian Leader*, July 5, 1966, pp. 3-5.

10. See John H. Redekop, "Peace-Six expressions," *Mennonite Brethren Herald*, February 21, 1986, p. 12.

11. See John H. Redekop, "When Anabaptism Isn't," *Mennonite Brethren Herald*, August 15, 1986, p. 8.

12. Walter Klaassen, "The Meaning of Anabaptism," *The Christian Leader*, March 4, 1975, pp. 3-4.

13. See also John H. Redekop, "Three Kinds of Mennonites," *Mennonite Brethren Herald*, February 12, 1982, p. 12.

14. *Courier*, vol. 1, no. 4, Fourth Quarter, 1986, p. 9.

15. *Mennonite Mirror*, September, 1984, p. 19.

16. Jacob A. Loewen, "The German Language, Culture and the Faith," a paper read at Mennonite Brethren Bible College, Winnipeg, MB, November 15, 1986, p. 20.

17. See John H. Redekop, "Why is Christian 'nonresistance' weakening among Mennonite Brethren?" *Mennonite Brethren Herald*, November 14, 1986, p. 10.

18. See John H. Redekop, "At issue: Integrity and Unity," *Mennonite Brethren Herald*, October 17, 1986, p. 12.

19. See Acts 6: 1-7.

20. "The Story of the Mennonite Brethren Church," (Winnipeg, MB:Kindred Press, n.d.)

21. *Ibid.*, p. 5.

CHAPTER THREE

RELIGION AND ETHNICITY; REPORT OF A NATIONAL SURVEY

Section I. INTRODUCTION

As part of a research project to acquire information about Mennonites and ethnicity in Canada, a questionnaire entitled, "Questionnaire on perception or experience of Mennonite religion and ethnicity" was administered between July and November, 1985. The questionnaire was sent to all Canadian Mennonite Brethren pastors of record as of June, 1985, to all other members of the Canadian Council of Boards, and to 565 selected additional church members. Each (senior) pastor had been requested to submit the names of two ethnic and two non-ethnic church members selected at random; an interim assumption was made concerning the propriety of distinguishing between ethnic Mennonites and other church members. Significantly, all of the MB pastors apparently knew what I meant by "ethnic." They all selected precisely the kinds of respondents I had in mind. The final sample consisted of 242 pastors, either "single" or additional full-time, and 565 other members, about 51% ethnic and 49% non-ethnic.

TABLE 1. *Mailing and Response Percentages*

	Returned/ Sent	Response Percentage	Percentage of Total Mailing	Percentage of Total Response
BC	181/239	75.7%	29.4%	30.2%
AB	74/103	71.8	12.7	12.3
SK	101/144	70.1	17.7	16.8
MB	124/174	71.3	21.4	20.7
ON	94/118	79.7	14.5	15.7
Quebec & other	26/35	74.3	4.3	4.3
TOTAL	600/813	73.8	100	100

Note: After the December 6 cut-off date, when 600 completed questionnaires had been received, only two additional completed questionnaires were returned.

Question B10 asked the respondent to indicate whether the person was a pastor or part of a local leadership team, or whether the person was not a pastor or part of a local leadership team. The 321 who identified themselves as leaders included about 85% of the 242 pastors who received the mailing, about 80% of the non-pastoral members of provincial executives and the Canadian Council of Boards, as well as about 75 persons who considered themselves part of a local leadership team by virtue of holding some other leadership position (e.g. ordained and active minister not designated by the congregation as a pastor.) A few of the leadership respondents, especially in some small congregations, indicated that they were parttime or interim leaders.

All factors considered, it seems reasonable to assume that the 321 respondents who identified themselves as leaders not only constitute about 80% of the actual congregational and denominational leadership, but are a representative sample of the entire leadership group.

Concerning the 226 who identified themselves as not being leaders, it should be noted that while the initial selection was not totally a random sample, that group, both in its ethnic and non-ethnic components, probably constitutes a representative sampling of non-leadership conference members. An additional 53 respondents did not indicate whether they were part of the leadership team; virtually all of these 53 indicated that they held some "lower level" church office other than pastor or moderator.

TABLE 2. *Leadership/Membership Response*

	Total	Percentage
Leadership	321	53.5%
Non-leadership	226	37.7
Not indicated	53	8.8
Total	600	100

If this national survey reflects any bias it is a weighting in favour of those people who are in leadership. The bias was intentional because a major purpose was to ascertain as accurately as possible the views of those persons who have been entrusted with leadership, who are the most important decision-makers and who are likely the best informed. For all charts, of course, separate data for leadership and non-leadership groups are provided. The 53 respondents who did not indicate any leadership or laity status are not included in either category but are included in "MB combined."

In addition to the national Canadian Mennonite Brethren sample of 600, two other broad categories of respondents were established: university students and students in Mennonite schools. Questionnaires were administered to selected and thus at least partially representative classes as follows.

TABLE 3. *University Sample*

	Percentage of Total University Sample	Sample Size
University of Alberta	7.5%	26
University of Calgary	10.8	37
University of Winnipeg	15.4	53
University of Manitoba	16.8	58
University of Waterloo	13.0	45
Wilfrid Laurier University	36.5	126
Total	100	345

For most of the questions the responses from the six universities were similar and therefore, for much of the analysis, the university students will be treated as a single group. Combining the university data makes it more reliable. Additional responses were received from Mennonite schools as indicated below.

TABLE 4. *Responses from Mennonite High Schools*

Mennonite Educational Institute, Clearbrook, BC	110
Mennonite Brethren Collegiate Institute, Winnipeg, MB	76
Eden Christian College, Niagara-on-the-Lake, ON	46
Total	232

The high school responses come from the grade 12 students.

TABLE 5. *Responses from Institutes and Colleges*

Winkler Bible Institute, Winkler, MB	99	
Bethany Bible Institute, Hepburn, SK	116	
Columbia Bible Institute, Clearbrook, BC	145	
		360
Mennonite Brethren Bible College, Winnipeg, MB	56	
Canadian Mennonite Bible College, Winnipeg, MB	77	
		133
Total		493

The responses from each institute or college are a representative or virtually complete sample with one exception, the MBBC responses come from first-year students only. It should be noted that since the questionnaire was administered at CBI, that inter-Mennonite school has been renamed Columbia Bible College. It is treated here as a non-degree granting institute because that is what it was when the questionnaire was administered. CMBC was included for comparative purposes.

In this report the data from high schools and institutes are included in totals only. Data from the two colleges are listed separately.

The total survey consists of the following responses:

National Canadian Mennonite Brethren (by mail)	600
Six Canadian universities	345
Eight high schools, institutes, and colleges	725
Total number of responses	1670

Section II. EXPLANATION CONCERNING THE QUESTIONNAIRE

Part A ellicited general demographic and identity questions. The ten items generated no major problems. Although questions 6 and 7 provide space to identify "other" religious persuasions specifically, option (9), for computing purposes such specific designation was ignored. Question 8 forced respondents to identify with one of three levels of familiarity and also assumed that respondents who considered themselves to be Mennonite had considerable knowledge about Mennonites. Given the purpose of the questionnaire, the term "Mennonite" was not defined in the question; each respondent had to indicate a response according to his own definition. Very few respondents indicated that they had difficulty knowing whether or not they were Mennonite. As we shall see, some members of Mennonite Brethren churches do not consider themselves to be Mennonites. Question 9 also required respondents to assume some functional definition of "Mennonite." Again, no significant problems were evident. Question 10, as already intimated, allowed for some self-identification in terms of leadership role.

Part B consisted of ten questions which required respondents to make some difficult judgements. The options were not always mutually exclusive: respondents were simply expected to select the best of the available answers. As assumed, most respondents have their personal views although, especially concerning questions 1,2,3 and 6, some respondents, according to their comments, gave idealistic rather than realistic answers.

For all 10 questions in part B the answers were arranged in such a way that if respondents were slightly inclined to check off the answer which they read first, then the answers would be biased towards religion rather than ethnicity. Consequently, if there is a questionnaire-related bias in the responses it is one which tilts away from the pro-ethnic responses.

Question 5 in Part B created some problems. Some respondents insisted that neither of the available answers was acceptable. Answer (1) assumed that the Old Order (and other "uniformed" segments) constitute an ethnic group and suggested that they, together with other Mennonites, were generally thought of by "the average person" as "collectively forming one of society's ethnic groups." Answer (2) suggested that there were "significant differences among the various branches of Mennonites." Checking answer (2) meant that the respondent believed that the average person tended not to think of all Mennonites as ethnic or that even though there might be a perception of all Mennonites as being ethnic, the more important factor was the presence of "significant differences."

Section III. LIFE SITUATION RESPONSE; FREQUENCY AND PERCENTAGE

(NATIONAL SAMPLE OF MENNONITE BRETHREN)

A1. Age:
(1)	Under 30	9%	(55)
(2)	30 to 55	65%	(391)
(3)	Over 55	26%	(154)

A2. Urban/rural residence:
(1)	City (more than 10,000)	55%	(328)
(2)	Town (1,000 to 10,000)	20%	(122)
(3)	Village or rural	24%	(144)
	No reponse	1%	(6)

A3. Residence by region:
(1)	British Columbia	30%	(181)
(2)	Alberta	12%	(74)
(3)	Saskatchewan	17%	(101)
(4)	Manitoba	21%	(124)
(5)	Ontario	16%	(94)
(6)	Quebec and other	4%	(26)

A4. Sex:
(1)	Female	27%	(162)
(2)	Male	73%	(436)
	No response		(2)

The preponderance of males reflects the massive majority of males in the leadership group.

A5. Education:
(1)	High school not completed	13%	(76)
(2)	High school	16%	(95)
(3)	At least 2 years post-sec.	14%	(86)
(4)	College or university	27%	(164)
(5)	Graduate degree	30%	(179)

The high percentage in categories (4) and (5) reflects the large leadership segment.

A6 and A7.

These questions dealt with church membership. Of the 600 respondents three indicated that they were not church members. This figure may reflect membership in transit, associate membership, or some other factor. The pastors had been asked to submit names of members. An additional nine respondents, presumably associate members, persons who had or thought they had dual membership, or persons whose membership transfer had not yet been processed, indicated that they held membership in non-MB churches.

A8. Knowledge of Mennonites:

It seems reasonable to assume that all 600 MB respondents, or at least the 588 who indicated church membership, would check item 4, but that was not the case. Surprisingly, 3 respondents apparently were not aware of the fact that they were members of a Mennonite Brethren church.

(1) Very little knowledge		(2)
(2) Some general impressions	12%	(70)
(3) Never heard of Mennonites		(3)
(4) Consider myself a Mennonite	84%	(504)
No response	4%	(21)

A9. Parents:

(1) One parent a Mennonite	3%	(19)
(2) Both parents Mennonites	67%	(401)
(3) Neither parent a Mennonite	29%	(172)
No response	1%	(8)

A10. Church position:

(1) Pastor or part of a local leadership team	53%	(321)
(2) Not a pastor or part of a local leadership team	38%	(226)
No response	9%	(53)

The large leadership component skews the total responses somewhat in the "B" section of the questionnaire but that is not a problem. The non-leaders, by themselves, constitute an adequate response group representing the general Mennonite Brethren membership. The large leadership sample and the high response rate provide a reliable reading of Mennonite Brethren leadership perceptions and opinions concerning the issues at hand. The comparisons between leadership and non-leadership groups, as provided in Section IV, is informative.

Section IV. COMPARISON OF OPINIONS AND PERCEPTIONS; FREQUENCY AND PERCENTAGE

The responses to the ten questions are given by percentages and frequency. The percentages are also presented in bar graphs. Although we have no random sample from the general public, it is useful to compare the combined and separated Mennonite Brethren responses to the combined and separated university undergraduate responses. While space limitations do not permit a detailed demographic portrayal of the university sample, the following data should be noted.

TABLE 6. *Anabaptist segment among university students sample*

	Mennonite Brethren percent	Mennonite Brethren number	Other Anabaptist percent	Other Anabaptist number	sample size
U. of Alberta					26
U. of Calgary	3%	(1)			37
U. of Winnipeg	17%	(9)	40%	(21)	53
U. of Manitoba	2%	(1)	2%	(1)	58
U. of Waterloo			13%	(6)	45
Wilfrid Laurier U.	____	___	1%	(3)	126
Combined Universities	3.2%	(11)	9%	(31)	345

Because questions 7 to 10 were addressed specifically to Mennonite/Anabaptist respondents, the students were not expected to answer them and 85% to 90% did not. Thus university data are provided only for the first six questions. The University of Winnipeg sample included a class in Mennonite Studies and therefore had a relatively high percentage of Mennonites; this fact clearly affects the response distribution for the university sample. If we eliminate the Mennonite university students, then the indicated differences between "MB combined" and "univ. comb." would be a least several percentage points greater for most responses.

TABLE 7. *University students knowledge about Mennonites*
(Question A.8)

	U. of Alta.	U. of Calg.	U. of Winn.	U. of Man.	U. of Wat.	WLU	Univ. Comb.
(1)*	42% (11)	60% (22)	4% (2)	43% (25)	20% (9)	18% (22)	26% (91)
(2)*	58% (15)	32% (12)	26% (14)	55% (32)	64% (29)	80% (101)	59% (203)
(3)*		5% (2)	2% (1)				1% (3)
(4)*		3% (1)	66% (35)	2% (1)	16% (7)	2% (3)	14% (47)
(n)*			2% (1)				(1)

*(1) = Very little knowledge   *(4) = Consider myself Mennonite
*(2) = Some general impressions   *(n) = No response
*(3) = Never heard of Mennonites

Two explanations must be made. In Table 7, some of the 47 MB/Anabaptist student respondents identified themselves as non-church member Mennonites. Second, the inclusion of a class in Mennonite Studies at the U. of Winnipeg, already reflected in Table 6, probably skewed the awareness of Mennonites as represented in Table 7. It should be noted, however, that high percentages of having "some impressions" are also found at the U. of Alberta, U. of Waterloo, and Wilfrid Laurier University.

B1. "The word 'Mennonite' refers to: a religious group or denomination____(1); an ethnic group____(2); both a religious group and an ethnic group____(3); neither a religious group nor an ethnic group____(4)." The following figures represent the percentage and actual numerical responses as depicted in the bar graphs.

	MB Comb.		Univ. Comb.		U. of Alta.		U. of Calg.		U. of Winn.		U. of Man.		U. of Wat.		W.L.U.	
(1) relig.	34%	(204)	30%	(103)	23%	(6)	51%	(19)	32%	(17)	28%	(16)	15%	(7)	30%	(38)
(2) ethn.	3%	(21)	4%	(14)	4%	(1)	5%	(2)			3%	(2)	7%	(3)	5%	(6)
(3) both	60%	(361)	64%	(222)	73%	(19)	38%	(14)	68%	(36)	69%	(40)	78%	(35)	62%	(78)
(4) neither	1%	(4)		(1)			5%	(2)							1%	(10)
No Response	2%	(10)	1%	(5)											2%	(3)

GRAPH B1. *Definition of "Mennonite"*

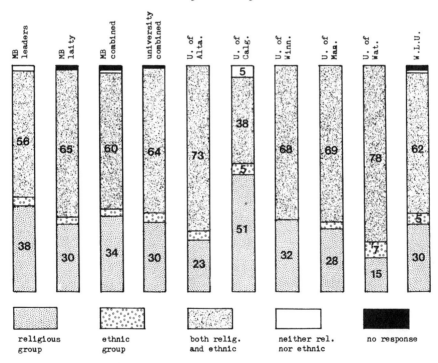

Graph B1 warrants several observations. The overall consistency is amazing with only the Calgary group deviating from all of the others in a major way. One explanation for that deviation may be the fact that the Calgary sample, and only the Calgary sample, involved primarily students in a religious studies course. The low "religious" percentage for the University of Waterloo, as contrasted with

WLU which is also located in Waterloo, may stem from the fact that U. of W. has proportionately more students coming from farther away and whose impressions of Mennonites may be based largely on the horse and buggy Mennonites they see in and near Waterloo.

Significantly, both the MBs and the students agree, and both at the high percentage of 94%, that Mennonites are religious. However, they also agree, at 63% and 68% respectively, that the word Mennonite refers to an ethnic or an ethnic-religious group. It seems evident, from these data, that the problem which causes many MBs to minimize the word "Mennonite" may not be ethnicity itself but the use of the same name for both a religion and an ethnic group. Certainly the responses support the view that in Canada, in the 1980s, the word "Mennonite" has a double meaning, namely an ethnic meaning and a religious meaning.

In general it is noteworthy that a largely non-evangelical and perhaps non-christian student national sample has a perception of Mennonites, in general, which is almost identical to that which MBs have of themselves. The similarity of "MB combined" and "university combined" underscores that very important point.

In all graphs N/R means "no response" and N/A means "not applicable." "Not applicable" was not on the questionnaire but it was often written in.

B1(a) "The word 'Mennonite' refers to: a religious group or denomination____(1); an ethnic group____(2); both a religious group and an ethnic group____(3); neither a religious group nor an ethnic group____(4)."

	MB Comb.		Univ. Comb.		High S. Comb.		Inst. Comb.		MBBC		CMBC	
(1) relig.	34%	(204)	30%	(103)	27%	(62)	26%	(94)	23%	(13)	25%	(19)
(2) ethn.	3%	(21)	4%	(14)	5%	(11)	8%	(30)	2%	(1)	1%	(1)
(3) both	60%	(361)	64%	(222)	67%	(155)	63%	(226)	75%	(42)	74%	(57)
(4) neither	1%	(4)		(1)	1%	(2)	1%	(4)				
No Response	2%	(10)	1%	(5)	1%	(2)	2%	(7)				

GRAPH B1(a) *Definition of "Mennonite"; Sector Responses*

Concerning Graph B1(a) one notes an impressive similarity among the various groups. Students in the Bible Institutes give a slightly higher rating to "ethnic" while both colleges, in virtually identical fashion, give a lower rating to "ethnic" and a significantly higher rating to "both." It is worth noting that there is virtually no difference between the MB-dominated MBBC and the Conference of Mennonites-dominated CMBC.

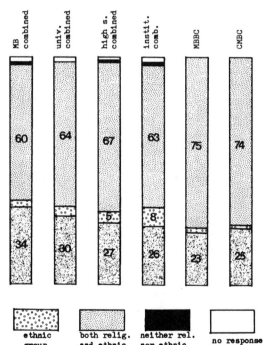

religious group   ethnic group   both relig. and ethnic   neither rel. nor ethnic   no response

31

B2. "Becoming a Mennonite is determined by personal choice____(1); by birth into a Mennonite family____(2); by a combination of birth into a Mennonite family and personal choice____(3)."

	MB leader	MB laity	MB comb.	Univ. comb.	U. of Alta.	U. of Calg.	U. of Winn.	U. of Man.	U. of Wat.	W.L.U.
(1) choice	56% (181)	50% (113)	53% (319)	17% (60)	4% (1)	30% (11)	38% (20)	7% (4)	18% (8)	13% (16)
(2) birth	6% (20)	7% (17)	7% (40)	19% (67)	15% (4)	11% (4)	6% (3)	24% (14)	36% (16)	21% (26)
(3) comb.	35% (114)	40% (90)	38% (227)	59% (204)	77% (20)	49% (18)	55% (29)	60% (35)	44% (20)	65% (82)
N/R	2% (6)	3% (6)	2% (14)	4% (14)	4% (1)	11% (4)	2% (1)	9% (5)	2% (1)	2% (2)

GRAPH B2. *Becoming a Mennonite*

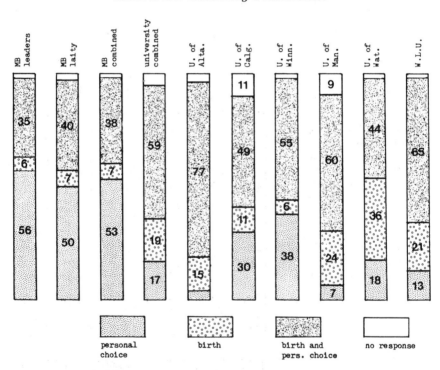

personal choice   birth   birth and pers. choice   no response

Graph B2 documents a major difference between MB views and university student views. While 53% of MB respondents believe that becoming a Mennonite is based on personal choice, only 17% of the students share that view. And the 17% would be even lower if one removed the Mennonites from the student sample. It would be about 15%. Since by definition only non-Mennonites can become Mennonites, the 17% (15% is the more important figure.) MBs and other Mennonites wishing to proselytize, to draw in non-Mennonites, face a truly formidible hurdle, at least among this student sample. A substantial 19% believe that birth into a Mennonite family is the key factor and, much more importantly, another 59% apparently believe that becoming a Mennonite means being born into a Mennonite family and then deciding whether or not to commit oneself to Mennonite values. The main point made by this graph is that about 80% of the students assume that non-Mennonites typically or logically cannot and do not become Mennonites.

Almost as important as the student perception is the fact that a full 45% of MBs share the view that becoming a Mennonite involves either birth into a Mennonite family or birth into a Mennonite family together with subsequent personal choice. Only 50% of MB laity and slightly more than half of the MB leaders believe that personal choice, by itself, is how one becomes a Mennonite.

How does residence in an area having a large Mennonite population affect student responses? It is noteworthy that 36% of the University of Waterloo student sample and 24% of the University of Manitoba sample checked "birth." The WLU response of 21% follows that trend. The substantial deviation at the University of Winnipeg, where the response approaches the MB levels, is doubtless affected by the fact that 57% of the University of Winnipeg sample identified themselves as Mennonites.

The proximity of large numbers of Mennonites obviously does not enhance the "personal choice" response rate by students. Observing Mennonites in the community apparently does not create the impression that non-Mennonites can and do readily become Mennonites.

B2(a). "Becoming a Mennonite is determined by personal choice____(1); by birth into a Mennonite family____(2); by a combination of birth into a Mennonite family and personal choice____(3)."

	MB Comb.		Univ. Comb.		High S. Comb.		Inst. Comb.		MBBC		CMBC	
(1) choice	53%	(319)	17%	(60)	33%	(77)	35%	(128)	46%	(26)	53%	(41)
(2) birth	7%	(40)	19%	(67)	11%	(25)	14%	(51)	2%	(1)	1%	(1)
(3) comb.	38%	(272)	59%	(204)	55%	(127)	50%	(180)	46%	(26)	46%	(35)
N/R	2%	(14)	4%	(14)	1%	(3)	1%	(2)	5%	(3)		

GRAPH B2(a). *Becoming a Mennonite; Sector Responses*

Graph B2(a) indicates that the predominance of Mennonites at the various Mennonite schools produces in those schools results similar to those found among MBs generally. Presumably the figures tilt slightly toward the University results because not all of the students in Mennonite schools are Mennonite. Interestingly the two Mennonite colleges produced almost identical responses.

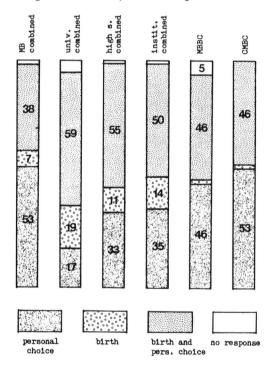

| personal choice | birth | birth and pers. choice | no response |

34

B3. "For a non-Mennonite Christian it is just as easy to join a Mennonite church as it is to join some other church whose theology is also acceptable. Yes____(1); No____(2)"

	MB leader	MB laity	MB comb.	Univ. comb.	U. of Alta.	U. of Calg.	U. of Winn.	U. of Man.	U. of Wat.	WLU
(1) Yes	65% (207)	69% (156)	66% (398)	39% (136)	35% (9)	46% (17)	55% (29)	35% (20)	49% (22)	31% (39)
(2) No	33% (106)	29% (65)	31% (184)	50% (174)	54% (14)	41% (15)	36% (19)	50% (29)	42% (19)	62% (78)
N/R	2% (8)	2% (5)	3% (18)	10% (35)	11% (3)	13% (5)	9% (5)	15% (9)	9% (4)	7% (9)

GRAPH B3. *Ease in Joining Church*

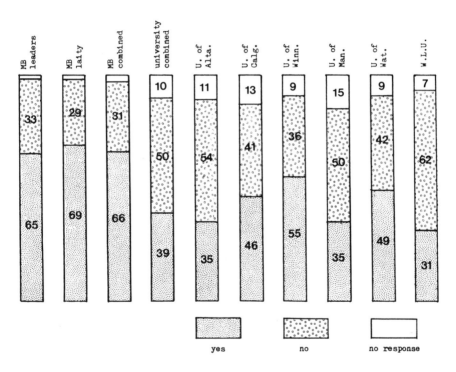

yes   no   no response

The thrust of question B3 is similar to that of B2 with two important differences. First, the question involves actually joining a church. As many respondents noted, most Mennonite churches would welcome a non-Mennonite who wished to join, even though, according to the responses given to question B2, that transition does not happen very extensively. Many respondents apparently related "easy" at least partly to the decision of the church and not only to the decision of the person wishing to join.

The second qualification involves the phrase, "whose theology is also acceptable." The focus in this question thus is theology and church, not simply "Mennonite." Further, acceptance of the theology in itself constitutes a move toward a Mennonite position. Many of the "yes" respondents indicated that they were thinking of people who found everything associated with Mennonites as "acceptable."

Whatever the significance of the various parts of the question, only 39% of the students believe that it is as easy to join a Mennonite church as it is to join any other, if both have acceptable theologies. One might argue that in terms of religion by itself, the 39% should be 100%. After all, joining other churches with acceptable theologies would also involve some sort of transition and adjustment. The comparison of Mennonite churches, we must tell ourselves, is with other churches, not with perfection.

The main point to be noted is that at the outset Mennonite churches have most non-Mennonites, at least in this student sample, tilted against them. The fact that 31% of MBs, a slightly higher percentage for leaders, indicate a similar perception serves to reinforce the existence of a serious problem.

At this point the Questionnaire stated:

"NOTE: If you have checked 'yes' for Question #3, then go to Question #5."

B3(a). "For a non-Mennonite Christian it is just as easy to join a Mennonite church as it is to join some other church whose theology is also acceptable. Yes___(1); No___(2)"

	MB comb.		Univ. comb.		High S. comb.		Inst. comb.		MBBC		CMBC	
(1) yes	66%	(398)	39%	(136)	79%	(183)	84%	(303)	75%	(42)	62%	(48)
(2) No	31%	(184)	50%	(174)	18%	(43)	15%	(54)	23%	(13)	36%	(28)
N/R	3%	(18)	10%	(35)	3%	(6)	1%	(4)	2%	(1)	1%	(1)

GRAPH B3(a). *Ease in Joining Church; Sector Responses*

The data in Graph B3(a) indicate that university-age students in Mennonite colleges have substantially different views on this question than do university students. CMBC students are significantly more like university students, on this question, than are MBBC students. High school and Bible Institute students lean very heavily towards the "yes". Presumably, given the "MB combined" data, their thinking will change as they encounter reality in adult years.

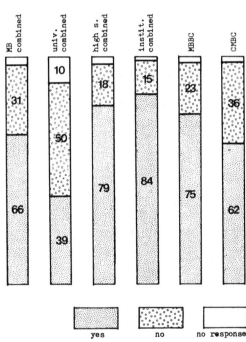

yes   no   no response

B4. "The reason why it is not as easy for a non-Mennonite Christian to join a Mennonite Church as it is to join some other church whose theology is also acceptable is that: Mennonite/Anabaptist theology or/and lifestyle are too demanding____(1); Mennonite/Anabaptist theology is peculiar____(2); Mennonite/Anabaptist churches tend to be too ethnic____(3)."

	MB leader	MB laity	MB comb.	Univ. comb.	U. of Alta.	U. of Calg.	U. of Winn.	U. of Man.	U. of Wat.	WLU
(1) demand.	4% (12)	3% (6)	3% (20)	28% (98)	27% (7)	27% (10)	6% (3)	22% (13)	20% (9)	44% (56)
(2) pecul.	1% (3)	2% (5)	1% (8)	8% (27)	8% (2)	5% (2)		14% (8)	7% (3)	9% (12)
(3) ethn.	28% (89)	24% (53)	26% (153)	14% (47)	15% (4)	8% (3)	28% (15)	14% (8)	16% (7)	8% (10)
N/R	1% (2)	(1)	1% (3)	1% (2)	4% (1)		2% (1)			
N/A	67% (215)	71% (161)	69% (416)	50% (171)	46% (12)	60% (22)	64% (34)	50% (29)	58% (26)	38% (48)

*The questionnaire stated: "NOTE: If you have checked "yes" for Question #3, then go to Question #5." If we eliminate the N/A, as we probably should, then, for example, under Univ. Comb. the 28% becomes 56%, the 8% becomes 16%, and the 14% becomes 28%.

GRAPH B4. *Difficulty in Joining Church*

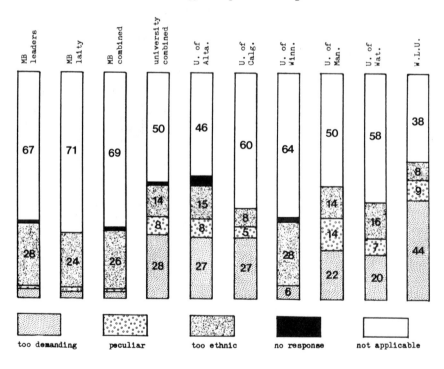

too demanding   peculiar   too ethnic   no response   not applicable

38

The responses in question B4, once we have allowed for slight variations in response rate and consistency, tell us the extent to which joining a Mennonite church is considered not as easy as joining some other church whose theology is equally acceptable. In other words, those who said "no" to question B3, have an opportunity here to identify reasons.

The answers are revealing. The MB total percentage of responses to the three options provided is substantially below the university percentage and virtually the entire "problem" is ascribed to ethnicity. The situation for the University of Winnipeg sample is similar, probably because of the Mennonite presence in that sample and the Winnipeg situation. While ethnicity is of some consequence for all university groups, it generally ranks well behind "theology or/and lifestyle are too demanding." Perhaps this question was not focused very clearly. From the comments it appears that many respondents zeroed in on "lifestyle" which, according to the written explanations, includes everything from "horse and buggy" to "Biblical ethics." Theological "peculiarity" also plays a part. The written answers make it clear that most university students do not easily differentiate Mennonite theology from perceived Mennonite lifestyle, particularly the more conservative and Old Order lifestyle.

If it is, in fact, the case that a demanding theology constitutes a major obstacle, then our concern must be to make sure that our theology is, indeed, Biblical and that we present it with clarity and tact.

We must interpret the data carefully. However, in light of the fact that 26% of the students said that they had "very little" knowledge about Mennonites (TABLE 7), and that 78% of the students say that becoming a Mennonite requires that a person is born into a Mennonite family (Graph B2), it seems reasonable to conclude that ethnicity is seen as a major factor and that many students believe that even if they got past the ethnicity hurdle, a Mennonite theology or/and lifestyle would be too much to accept. We must remember, of course, that partly because of the widespread ethnicity perception, some of these largely non-Christian students may not encounter the theology or, more important and more likely, they focus on visibly peculiar Mennonites and assume that the peculiarity in dress, ethics, and even horse and buggy usage is theology and is too demanding. After all, the question referred to "theology or/and lifestyle."

B4(a). "The reason why it is not as easy for a non-Mennonite Christian to join a Mennonite Church as it is to join some other church whose theology is also acceptable is that: Mennonite/Anabaptist theology or/and lifestyle are too demanding____(1); Mennonite/Anabaptist theology is peculiar____(2); Mennonite/Anabaptist churches tend to be too ethnic____(3)."

	MB Comb.		Univ. Comb.		High S. Comb.		Inst. Comb.		MBBC		CMBC	
(1) demand	3%	(20)	28%	(98)	3%	(7)	2%	(7)	2%	(1)	1%	(1)
(2) pecul.	1%	(8)	8%	(27)	2%	(5)	1%	(3)			4%	(3)
(3) ethn.	26%	(153)	14%	(47)	12%	(27)	10%	(37)	21%	(12)	31%	(24)
(4) N/R	1%	(3)	1%	(2)	4%	(10)	3%	(11)	4%	(2)	1%	(1)
(5) N/A*	69%	(416)	50%	(171)	79%	(183)	84%	(303)	73%	(41)	62%	(48)

*See note in B4.

GRAPH B4(a). *Difficulty in Joining Church; Sector Responses*

Graph B4(a) suggests, as did Graph B3(a), that students in Mennonite high schools and Bible Institutes have not yet encountered society in the way that the older general church membership has. The relatively high "ethnic" response for CMBC is noteworthy.

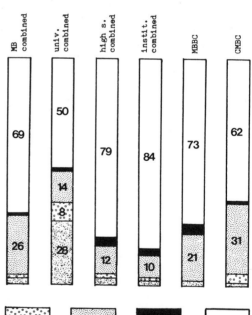

 too demanding peculiar too ethnic no response not applicable

40

B5. "In general, the average person tends to think of the various branches of Mennonites as collectively forming one of society's ethnic groups____(1); the average person tends to see significant differences among the various branches of Mennonites____(2)."

	MB leader	MB laity	MB comb.	Univ. comb.	U. of Alta.	U. of Calg.	U. of Winn.	U. of Man.	U. of Wat.	W.L.U.
(1) one	84% (281)	81% (183)	83% (498)	68% (234)	73% (19)	60% (22)	72% (38)	72% (42)	64% (29)	67% (84)
(2) dif.	9% (30)	12% (28)	10% (63)	21% (72)	12% (3)	13% (5)	15% (8)	19% (11)	24% (11)	27% (34)
N/R	6% (20)	7% (15)	7% (39)	11% (39)	15% (4)	27% (10)	13% (7)	7% (5)	11% (5)	6% (8)

GRAPH B5. *Mennonite Similarity/Diversity*

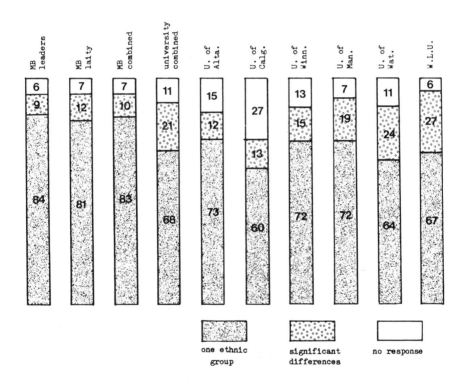

The data in B5 inform us with impressive consistency that "the average person" does not distinguish between "the various branches of Mennonites." Although the MBs may have over-stated the case (I say "may" because the comparison sample is students rather than general public), the fact remains that 68% of the students believed that the average person sees all Mennonites as forming one ethnic group while only 21% believe that significant differences are seen.

The great significance of this data for MBs is that the oft-repeated statement about making sure that society distinguishes between Mennonites and Mennonite

41

Brethren involves whistling in the dark. The vast majority, it seems, do not make such a distinction; rather, "Mennonite Brethren" is perceived to be a sub-category of Mennonite.

B5(a). "In general, the average person tends to think of the various branches of Mennonites as collectively forming one of society's ethnic groups____(1); the average person tends to see signficant differences among the various branches of Mennonites____(2)."

	MB Comb.		Univ. Comb.		High S. Comb.		Inst. Comb.		MBBC		CMBC	
(1) one	83%	(498)	68%	(234)	71%	(165)	73%	(265)	84%	(47)	87%	(67)
(2) diff.	10%	(63)	21%	(72)	22%	(50)	21%	(75)	11%	(6)	9%	(7)
N/R	7%	(39)	11%	(39)	7%	(17)	6%	(21)	5%	(3)	4%	(3)

GRAPH B5(a). *Mennonite Similarity/Diversity; Sector Responses*

In Graph B5(a) we see again that students in Mennonite high schools and Bible Institutes have somewhat different perceptions from those of college students and the older MB membership. The overall similarity in response is noteworthy.

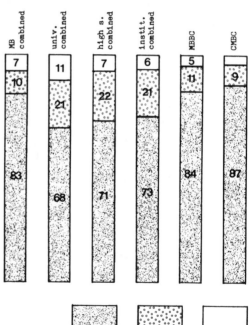

one ethnic group   significant differences   no response

B6. "There is a significant difference in meaning between the terms 'Mennonite' and 'Mennonite Brethren' Yes____(1); No____(2)."

	MB leader	MB laity	MB comb.	Univ. comb.	U. of Alta.	U. of Calg.	U. of Winn.	U. of Man.	U. of Wat.	WLU
(1) Yes	76% (243)	67% (151)	72% (431)	41% (143)	54% (14)	32% (12)	43% (23)	36% (21)	53% (24)	39% (49)
(2) No	20% (63)	28% (63)	23% (136)	39% (135)	27% (7)	22% (8)	43% (23)	43% (25)	36% (16)	44% (56)
N/R	5% (15)	5% (12)	5% (33)	19% (67)	19% (5)	46% (17)	13% (7)	21% (12)	11% (5)	17% (17)

GRAPH B6. *Mennonite versus Mennonite Brethren*

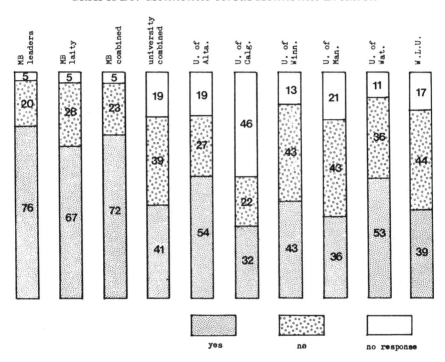

yes   ne   no response

What was implicitly revealed in B5 becomes more explicit in B6. Question B5 dealt with "the average person"; question B6 dealt with the respondents themselves. When asked whether there is a significant different between the terms "Mennonite" and "Mennonite Brethren," 72% of MB respondents (but only 72%!) said that there was. Importantly, only 41% of the students agreed with such a view. This means that even among our educated young adults (and 9% of our university sample declared themselves to be Mennonites!), well below half make the kind of distinction which must be made if Mennonite Brethren are to be perceived as a distinctive Christian denomination. It appears that MBs in general, and MB leaders in particular, will need to adjust their assumptions to take account of reality. And then MBs will have to address that reality.

The other key point that must be stressed about this graph is that even for those who believe that there is a difference in meaning, we have no evidence to conclude that the term Mennonite Brethren is perceived as being less ethnic. In fact, the data in Graph B5 suggests precisely the contrary. At least 68% of our university sample, with its 9% Mennonite component, (which keeps that percentage from being even higher), believe that the average person thinks of all Mennonites as forming one ethnic group. Only a replication of a survey such as this, some years hence, can tell us whether the passing of time will improve perceptions or whether use of the label Mennonite will continue to bring with it a mainly ethnic connotation.

B6(a). "There is a significant difference in meaning between the terms 'Mennonite' and 'Mennonite Brethren'; Yes____(1); No____(2)."

	MB comb.		Univ. comb.		High S. comb.		Inst. comb.		MBBC		CMBC	
(1) Yes	72%	(431)	41%	(143)	45%	(105)	45%	(161)	53%	(30)	40%	(31)
(2) No	23%	(136)	39%	(135)	49%	(114)	47%	(170)	36%	(20)	52%	(40)
N/R	5%	(33)	19%	(67)	6%	(13)	8%	(30)	11%	(6)	8%	(6)

GRAPH B6(a). *Mennonite Versus Mennonite Brethren; Sector Responses*

It appears, according to GRAPH B6(a), that, of the groups surveyed, majorities in only adult MB members and, to a lesser extent, MBBC students believe "That there is a significant difference in meaning between the terms 'Mennonite' and 'Mennonite Brethren'."

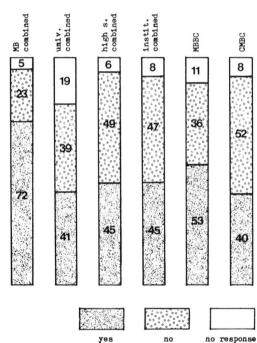

yes   no   no response

"NOTE: If you belong to, or are associated with, a Mennonite/Anabaptist church, then please answer questions 7, 8, 9, and 10; otherwise proceed to the NOTE at the bottom of this page." (The NOTE thanked the respondent and gave mailing instructions.)

B7. "In my opinion Mennonite ethnicity: is no problem for my local church____(1); is a minor problem for my local church____(2); is a major problem for my local church____(3)."

	MB leaders		MB laity		MB comb.	
(1) No	33%	(105)	42%	(95)	36%	(218)
(2) Minor	52%	(167)	46%	(103)	49%	(296)
(3) Major	12%	(38)	8%	(19)	10%	(63)
N/R	3%	(11)	4%	(9)	4%	(23)

GRAPH B7. *Is Mennonite Ethnicity a Problem Locally?*

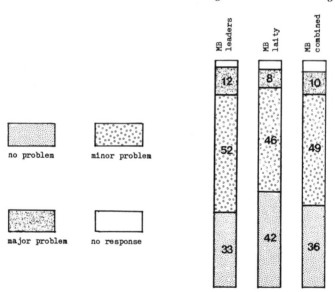

no problem   minor problem

major problem   no response

Graph B7 tells us that about 59% of MBs consider Mennonite ethnicity to be a problem, minor or major, at the local level. For MB leaders the figure rises to 64%.

Since human nature tends not to acknowledge immediate, local, or domestic problems very readily, it seems reasonable to accept these figures as valid.

B7(a). "In my opinion Mennonite ethnicity: is no problem for my local church____(1); is a minor problem for my local church____(2); is a major problem for my local church____(3)."

	MB Comb.		High S. Comb.		Inst. Comb.		MBBC		CMBC	
(1) No	36%	(218)	38%	(89)	42%	(151)	45%	(25)	22%	(17)
(2) Minor	49%	(296)	25%	(59)	32%	(117)	39%	(22)	56%	(43)
(3) Major	10%	(63)	3%	(6)	6%	(20)			16%	(12)
N/R	4%	(23)	34%	(78)	20%	(73)	16%	(9)	6%	(5)

GRAPH B7(a). *Is Mennonite Ethnicity a Problem Locally?*
Sector Responses

In GRAPH B7(a) we should note the understandably high abstention rate among high school respondents. Institute and MBBC student responses do not differ markedly from the high school response, while the CMBC students see things differently. A full 72% of CMBC students see Mennonite ethnicity as a problem, minor or major, for "my local church."

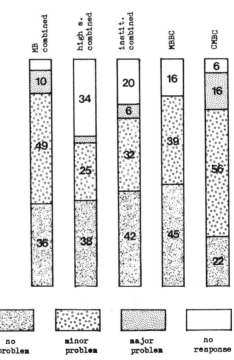

no problem   minor problem   major problem   no response

B8. "In my opinion Mennonite ethnicity: is no problem for my denomination____(1); is a minor problem for my denomination____(2); is a major problem for my denomination____(3)."

	MB leaders		MB laity		MB comb.	
(1) No	16%	(50)	20%	(46)	18%	(106)
(2) Minor	61%	(197)	56%	(127)	60%	(357)
(3) Major	18%	(58)	14%	(32)	15%	(92)
N/R	5%	(16)	9%	(21)	7%	(45)

GRAPH B8. *Is Mennonite Ethnicity a Denominational Problem?*

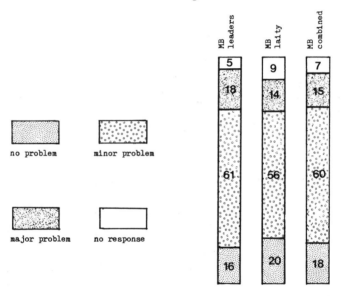

No less than 79% of MB leaders believe that Mennonite ethnicity is a problem, minor or major, at the denominational level. No less than 70% of non-leaders agree. Significantly 7% did not respond, presumably because they were undecided, which means that only 18% of leaders believe that there is no problem and only 14% of laity. The perceptions reflected in Graph B8 coincide with the data found in Graphs B1, B2, B3, B5, B6, and B7.

B8(a). "In my opinion Mennonite ethnicity: is no problem for my denomination____(1); is a minor problem for my denomination____(2); is a major problem for my denomination____(3)."

	MB Comb.		High S. Comb.		Inst. Comb.		MBBC		CMBC	
(1) No	18%	(106)	32%	(74)	36%	(128)	43%	(24)	29%	(22)
(2) Minor	60%	(357)	29%	(67)	36%	(131)	32%	(18)	48%	(37)
(3) Major	15%	(92)	6%	(13)	6%	(23)	9%	(5)	17%	(13)
N/R	7%	(45)	34%	(78)	22%	(79)	16%	(9)	6%	(5)

GRAPH B8(a). *Is Mennonite Ethnicity a Denominational Problem?*
Sector Responses

In GRAPH B8(a) we note again the high abstention rate among high school seniors and, to a lesser extent, also among Institute and MBBC students. Again we note a marked difference between CMBC and MBBC students. Either the CMBC students have experienced or observed more ethnicity-related problems or they are simply more perceptive. The written comments suggest the latter.

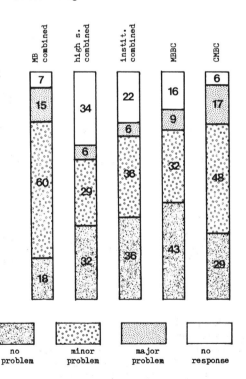

no problem | minor problem | major problem | no response

49

B9. "In my opinion the leadership of our conference should: ignore the matter of ethnicity___(1); study the matter of ethnicity as it relates to our conference___(2); actively address the matter of ethnicity as it relates to our conference___(3)."

	MB leaders		MB laity		MB comb.	
(1) ignore	25%	(82)	20%	(45)	22%	(135)
(2) study	31%	(98)	41%	(92)	35%	(210)
(3) address	37%	(120)	29%	(66)	33%	(199)
N/R	6%	(21)	10%	(23)	9%	(56)

GRAPH B9. *Leadership Response to Ethnic Issue*

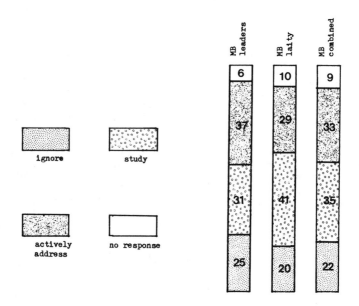

The evidence thus far suggests that ethnicity is a problem for Mennonites, in this case MBs. But that fact was not documented when question B9 was phrased; hence the reference is to "matter," not a problem. Although only 25% of MB leaders and 20% of MB laity indicated that the matter should be ignored, even that figure may be misleading. Many who checked off "ignore" added a comment to the effect that ignoring ethnicity, not talking about it, etc., was a good way to deal with a very real problem. The 68% who want the matter studied or actively addressed, clearly look to MB conference leadership to pursue the matter further.

B9(a). "In my opinion the leadership of our conference should: ignore the matter of ethnicity____(1); study the matter of ethnicity as it relates to our conference____(2); actively address the matter of ethnicity as it relates to our conference____(3)."

	MB Comb.		High S. Comb.		Inst. Comb.		MBBC		CMBC	
(1) ignore	22%	(135)	13%	(31)	12%	(43)	5%	(3)	3%	(2)
(2) study	35%	(210)	34%	(79)	42%	(151)	52%	(29)	56%	(43)
(3) address	33%	(199)	17%	(40)	23%	(84)	23%	(13)	35%	(27)
N/R	9%	(56)	35%	(82)	23%	(83)	20%	(11)	6%	(5)

GRAPH B9(a). *What To Do About The Ethnic Issue; Sector Responses*

GRAPH B9(a) indicates that of all the Mennonites/Anabaptists responding, only among the adult "MB Comb." does the percentage suggesting that ethnicity should be ignored reach 20%. It is clear that in all categories a majority wants the question studied. Among those with an opinion on the matter the percentage is 70% or higher. Even among the students who tended not to perceive a problem, almost all of those with an opinion on the matter want the question studied. Evidently, the CMBC students, while not really associating the ethnic problem with the name "Mennonite," see graph B10(a), are easily the most aware of a major ethnic problem.

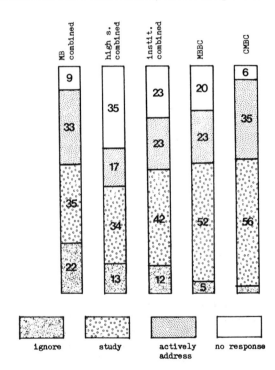

ignore   study   actively address   no response

B10. "In my opinion the word "Mennonite," as part of the official conference name: should definitely be retained by our denomination____(1); should be de-emphasized by our denomination____(2); should be dropped by our denomination____(3)."

	MB leaders	MB laity	MB comb.
(1) keep	55% (176)	57% (130)	55% (329)
(2) de-emph.	30% (97)	29% (66)	30% (181)
(3) drop	10% (32)	7% (15)	9% (52)
N/R	5% (16)	7% (15)	6% (38)

GRAPH B10. *The Name*

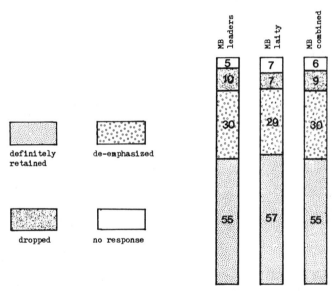

definitely retained

de-emphasized

dropped

no response

Graph B10 informs us that most M.B. respondents presently opt for the label "Mennonite." About 55% indicated that they definitely wanted the word "Mennonite" retained, although many commented that they checked the first option because they couldn't think of anything better and many others said that they were stressing the theology, not the name. Although very many respondents qualified their answers, both the "yes" and the "no," 9% indicated that they want the term dropped and 30% want it de-emphasized.

B10(a). "In my opinion the word "Mennonite," as part of the official conference name: should definitely be retained by our denomination____(1); should be de-emphasized by our denomination____(2); should be dropped by our denomination____(3)."

	MB Comb.		High S. Comb.		Inst. Comb.		MBBC		CMBC	
(1) keep	55%	(329)	48%	(112)	51%	(184)	66%	(37)	87%	(67)
(2) de-emph	30%	(181)	15%	(35)	24%	(86)	14%	(8)	8%	(6)
(3) drop	9%	(52)	2%	(5)	4%	(15)	4%	(2)	1%	(1)
N/R	6%	(38)	35%	(80)	21%	(76)	16%	(9)	4%	(3)

GRAPH B10(a). *The Name; Sector Responses*

GRAPH B10(a) makes it clear, even if one allows for high abstention rates in some groups, that while a very large majority want "the matter of ethnicity" studied or actively addressed, only a very small percentage are presently ready to drop the name "Mennonite." Many respondents, perhaps half of those who checked "retain," stated that we should stress that Mennonite means Christian. They thus voted more for a hope than for the reality documented in this volume. Re-reading the comments I get the impression that if the actual situation were known, the percentages would be quite different.

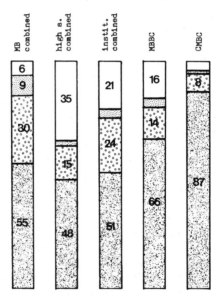

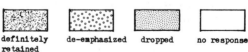

definitely retained   de-emphasized   dropped   no response

53

Section V. CONCLUSION

In large part the data speak for themselves. The overwhelming thrust of the responses to this Canadian survey indicates the following:

1. The term "Mennonite" is widely perceived, by Mennonites and others, as having a dual meaning. The term has a strong ethnic and a strong religious connotation.

2. In general the ethnic connotation of Mennonite looms larger than does the religious connotation. Birth into a Mennonite family is seen as the "usual" way by which one becomes a Mennonite.

3. The data gathered in this survey do not include responses from those who may have the greatest problem with the double usage of the term "Mennonite," the large number who have for that reason left the Mennonite church.

4. To the extent that Mennonites wish to penetrate the community with the church's message, the major ethnic connotation constitutes a considerable problem.

5. The long-standing attempt to sharpen the distinction between the terms "Mennonite" and "Mennonite Brethren" seems not to have been successful and appears not to be very promising for the future.

6. The comments, in particular, suggest that most Mennonite respondents know that there is a problem concerning the role of Mennonite ethnicity, but they do not know what to do about it. Therefore they resign themselves to live with the problem and make the best of it.

7. Some Mennonite respondents, a very small minority, were very upset that such a survey was undertaken. They said that it drew attention to "the Mennonite problem." They and some others, perhaps 25% of the total, suggested that we should ignore ethnicity and get on with more important things. Maybe they are akin to the woodchopper who rejected the idea of sharpening his dull axe because he had more important things to do, such as chopping wood.

8. The vast majority of MB leaders and laity believe that Mennonite ethnicity constitutes a problem, either minor or major, at both local and conference levels for Mennonite Brethren in Canada.

9. MB respondents have indicated, especially in their comments, that they acknowledge the nature of the problem but seem unable or unwilling to undertake basic corrective action. Most are not prepared to take their analysis to its logically and theologically appropriate conclusion.

10. The vast majority of MB leaders and laity want conference leadership to study or actively address the problem of ethnicity.

11. Although the survey results must inform our strategy, the guiding principle must always be, "Is it right?", not "Is it popular?" Leaders convince others to do what is right?

This interdisciplinary research questionnaire is part of a study of public perceptions of Mennonites. Your cooperation in answering these questions is greatly appreciated. The results will be publicized. On behalf of all who are involved in this project, I thank you kindly. Professor John H. Redekop, Wilfrid Laurier University,
Waterloo, Ontario, Canada

QUESTIONNAIRE ON PERCEPTION OR EXPERIENCE OF MENNONITE

RELIGION AND ETHNICITY

INSTRUCTIONS: Please place a check mark (√) in the appropriate space.

A. Life Situation.

1. My age is: under 30 ____(1); 30 to 55 ____ (2); over 55 ____ (3)

2. I live in: a city (more than 10,000) ____ (1); a town (1,000 to 10,000) ____ (2); a village or rural area ____ (3)

3. Residence by region. I live in Canada: B.C. ____ (1); Alta. ____ (2); Sask. ____ (3); Man. ____ (4); Ont. ____ (5); Eastern provinces or the North____(6); or, in the U.S.: West ____ (7); Midwest ____ (8); South ____ (9); East, North East ____ (10)

4. Sex. Female ____ (1); Male ____ (2)

5. Education. I did not complete high school ____ (1); I completed high school ____(2); I have completed at least two years of post-secondary education ____(3); I have completed college or university ____(4); I have completed a graduate degree ____(5)

6. I am a church member. Yes ____(1); No ____(2)
   If you have checked "Yes", then please check one of the following: (then go to #8)
   Mennonite Brethren ____(3)   Protestant "Mainline" ____(7)
   Conference of Mennonites (GC)____(4) Name_____
   Other Mennonite/Anabaptist ____(5)   Non-Mennonite Evangelical ____(8)
   Name_____   Name_____
   Roman Catholic ____(6)   Other (Name)_____(9)

7. Although I am not a church member, I associate with one of the following:
   Mennonite Brethren____(3)   Protestant "Mainline"____(7)
   Conference of Mennonites (GC)____(4) Name_____
   Other Mennonite/Anabaptist___(5)   Non-Mennonite Evangelical____(8)
   Name_____   Name_____
   Roman Catholic____(6)   Other (Name)_____Or none (9)

8. Knowledge about Mennonites. I have heard about Mennonites but know very little about them____(1); I have some general impressions about Mennonites ____(2); I have never heard of Mennonites____(3); I consider myself a Mennonite____(4)

9. Parents. One of my parents was/is a Mennonite____(1); both of my parents were/are Mennonites____(2); neither of my parents were/are Mennonites____(3)

10. I am a pastor or part of a local church leadership team. Yes____(1); No____(2)

B. Opinions and Perceptions.

1. The word "Mennonite" refers to: a religious group or denomination____(1); an ethnic group____(2); both a religious group and an ethnic group____(3); neither a religious group nor an ethnic group____(4)
   Comment:_____

2. Becoming a Mennonite is determined: by personal choice____(1); by birth into a Mennonite family____(2); by a combination of birth into a Mennonite family and personal choice____(3)
   Comment:_____

3. For a non-Mennonite Christian it is just as easy to join a Mennonite church as it is to join some other church whose theology is also acceptable. Yes____(1); No____(2)
   Comment:_____

(please turn the page)

NOTE: If you have checked "Yes" for Question #3, then go to Question #5

4. The reason why it is not as easy for a non-Mennonite Christian to join a Mennonite church as it is to join some other church whose theology is also acceptable is that:
   Mennonite/Anabaptist theology or/and lifestyle are too demanding____(1)
   Mennonite/Anabaptist theology is peculiar____(2)
   Mennonite/Anabaptist churches tend to be too ethnic____(3)
   Comment:_____

5. In general, the average person tends to think of the various branches of Mennonites as collectively forming one of society's ethnic groups____(1); the average person tends to see significant differences among the various branches of Mennonites____(2)
   Comment:_____

6. There is a significant difference in meaning between the terms "Mennonite" and "Mennonite Brethren". Yes____(1); No____(2)
   Comment:_____

NOTE: If you belong to, or are associated with, a Mennonite/Anabaptist church, then please answer questions 7,8,9 and 10; otherwise proceed to the NOTE at the bottom of this page.

7. In my opinion Mennonite ethnicity: is no problem for my local church____(1); is a minor problem for my local church____(2); is a major problem for my local church____(3)
   Comment:_____

8. In my opinion Mennonite ethnicity: is no problem for my denomination____(1); is a minor problem for my denomination____(2); is a major problem for my denomination____(3)
   Comment:_____

9. In my opinion the leadership of our conference should: ignore the matter of ethnicity____(1); study the matter of ethnicity as it relates to our conference____(2); actively address the matter of ethnicity as it relates to our conference____(3)
   Comment:_____

10. In my opinion the word "Mennonite", as part of the official conference name: should definitely be retained by our denomination____(1); should be de-emphasized by our denomination____(2); should be dropped by our denomination____(3)
    Comment:_____

General Comments: _____
_____
_____
_____

Date the form was completed_____ 19____

NOTE: Thank you for your time and your cooperation. If you received this questionnaire by mail, then please return it in the enclosed, stamped envelope as soon as possible. If you wish to do so, you may sign this form but no identification is required. All signatures will be kept confidential.

_____ (optional)

CHAPTER FOUR

ARE MENNONITES ETHNIC?

We will consider the evidence and the arguments under thirteen headings and, in some cases, various sub-headings. In some respects this section, together with the survey data, constitutes the very heart of this monograph. If it should be established that there is something which we must call "Mennonite ethnicity," then it follows that churches and conferences which call themselves Mennonite must either be prepared to be an ethnic church, with all the constraints and limitations which such a designation and reality brings with it, or they must do something about the problem.

1. *Is ethno-religious really ethnic? How does ethnicity fit into religion, especially in a covenant community-emphasizing, anabaptist church?*

Ethnic need not mean secular. Religion can be a major component of ethnic identity. So it is with Mennonites in North America. "The abundant sociological evidence makes it virtually impossible to argue that the Mennonite phenomenon is merely a religious one devoid of ethnic expressions."[1] Discussing Mennonites Donald Kraybill states, "Ethnic traditions and identities fused with experience over the centuries have an amazing resilience to change when legitimated and empowered by religious symbols."[2] An ethnic orientation can be substantially religious but still mainly ethnic. We're not in a "zero sum" situation. It's not the case that the more important the religious component, the less important the ethnic. They can be fused and they can reinforce each other.

The Jews have largely fused ethnicity and religion although, as in the case of the Mennonites, there are many, about 40% in Canada, who consider themselves Jewish ethnically but not religiously. For them it is no great problem because they do not actively proselytize or evangelize. But Christians cannot be comfortable with such a fusion because to be a Christian means to carry out the Great Commission. Thus it is simply wrong for Christians, having fused the faith with a particular culture in their own experience, to institutionalize and perpetuate such fusion and exclusion. By institutionalizing the fusion we reinforce ethno-religious distancing.

Of course, there are small minorities in Mennonite churches, including some in the Mennonite Brethren conference, who do not share in the full ethno-religious identity but they have not noticeably affected the general Mennonite experience nor the public perception and stereotypes of Mennonites.

2. *Mennonites listed as ethnics in books and journals.*

The library shelves are full of books, journals, etc., which list Mennonites together with other ethnic groups. For example, *Cultures in Canada*, by Jack Bavington and others,[3] lists Mennonites together with 27 other groups such as Chinese, Inuit, Polish, Ukrainian, Portuguese, Italian, and Dutch. No religious groups are mentioned. *The Ethnic Almanac*, by Stephanie Bernardo, mentions or discusses Mennonites in six places.[4] *Ethnic Information Sources of the United States* also includes the Mennonites.[5] Historians, sociologists, geographers[6] constantly cite Mennonites as ethnic.

Popular books, including glossy coffee table pictorial volumes, make the same assessments. The widely acclaimed, *A Day In The Life of Canada*,[7] has a two-page spread of a man with a horse and buggy. The description reads: "A Mennonite farmer drives across his farmland near Elmira, Ontario. Only recently some of the younger Mennonites have purchased black automobiles."[8] The fact that the comment is an exaggeration does not change the perception of Mennonites as ethnics.

Those Mennonites and others who say that Mennonites are not an ethnic group will have to take on the top experts. Thus Ron Rempel, editor of the *Mennonite Reporter*, insists that there is no particular Mennonite ethnicity.

Recent sensitivity to ethnic exclusiveness is to be commended. But when this sensitivity creates new hybrids such as "non-ethnic" Mennonites, then it has gone too far. There is no such creature as a "non-ethnic" Mennonite. There are, however, Mennonites with a great variety of ethnic backgrounds.[9]

Concerning North America and a few other regions, Rempel is superficially right but fundamentally wrong. I would sooner go with the analysis of the *Harvard Encyclopedia of American Ethnic Groups*. Not only does this huge and definitive volume provide a detailed description of Mennonite ethnicity but it also provides comparative analysis of various subgroups such as Amish, Germans from Russia, etc.[10] "Mennonite" is listed in as bold a heading as any other ethnic group.[11]

In many cases Mennonites and Hutterites are lumped together. Often the Doukhobors are added as well.[12]

One could go on at great length detailing the examples but that should not be necessary. Sources to be cited later provide ample documentation. Any remaining skeptic needs only to visit any sizeable public library.

3. *Teaching about Mennonites in Schools.* Several surveys indicate that the study of Mennonites as ethnics is increasing substantially, especially as school boards exercise local options. One standard text is Charlotte

Sloan Cooper's, *The Mennonite People,* part of the "People of Our Land Series," widely used at about the grade 4 level.[13] The explanatory "Editor's Note" is instructive. "The people of Canada have many different ethnic origins. Each group has its own colorful history and customs which have influenced and enriched Canadian society.... *The Mennonite People,* written by Charlotte Sloan Cooper, is the second book in this series."[14] Other titles include: *The Hutterite People, The Ukrainian People, The Native Indian People,* etc.

Significantly, Mennonites are themselves promoting the study of Mennonites as ethnics. The April 15, 1985 *Mennonite Reporter* described the preparation of "An educational package complete with filmstrip, sound recording and teacher's manual" to augment school tours of Steinbach's Mennonite Museum. The museum manager "commented that with more and more school tours coming to the museum...he as well as the museum's cultural committee felt it was time to have a kit to supplement the standard tour." Not surprisingly the venture was funded by the multicultural program of the Canadian Secretary of State.[15] The kit is intended "for the grade 6 Social Studies curriculum in Manitoba."[16]

Similar ventures exist in other parts of Canada. A Fraser Valley, BC, paper reported that, "The valley's multi-cultural background will be a major theme of a [teachers] spring professional development day being organized by Fraser Valley College.... Sessions include perspectives on native Indians, East Indians, Mennonites, Dutch Canadians and other groups." The lunch featured "national dishes."[17]

As we proceed in our analysis we must repeatedly remind ourselves that the purpose of this section is to demonstrate that in Canada, Mennonites, by and large, function as an ethnic group and are perceived as an ethnic group. This section specifically is not intented to criticize Mennonites for being ethnic. No people should be criticized for being what they are.

4. *The Mennonite press.* To do justice to the extensive Mennonite press, a vigorous press which reflects and influences Mennonites, including Mennonite Brethren, would take many pages. I can permit myself only to comment briefly on five periodicals. Again, my intent is not to provide a general analysis of the Mennonite press, which is generally of high quality, but to ascertain how assessing the Mennonite press will help us to answer the question about Mennonite ethnicity.

(a) *Mennonitsche Rundschau.* This paper stands in a long and noble tradition of the German language Mennonite press. I chose to examine it, rather than *Der Bote,* because it is now published by the Mennonite Brethren conference and still functions as one of its major organs.

Since 1877 this impressive periodical has served Mennonite people with much success. In general, as my study of many issues of the paper indicates, it concentrates mainly on religious affairs. However, it also assumes and reflects ethnic elements of Mennonite life as the following recent items attest. In earlier times the *Rundschau* carried extensive ethnic news and analysis.

(i) The issue of November 27, 1986 carried a full-page advertisement, in German, promoting "Multiculturalism Canada." This advertisement, in various languages, was placed in many ethnic periodicals across Canada by the "Minister of State for Multiculturalism, Hon. Otto Jelinek."[18]

(ii) The following news item was carried in December, 1985. I shall provide an English translation.

The ethnic diversity in Canada is evident in the Canadian census undertaken every decade....

The 51 ethnic Members of Parliament belong to 15 different language groups. Eight indicated German as their mother tongue; tied for second place were Jewish, Ukrainian, and Scandinavian MPs at six each. Next in line were five Italians, four Mennonites, four Hollanders, and two Poles. Six additional ethnic groups had one MP each.[19]

(iii) In March, 1986 the *Mennonitische Rundschau* carried another full-page ad for Multiculturalism Canada. This time the Hon. Otto Jellinek was promoting a "Multiculturalism and Business Conference" emphasizing tourism, news exchange, investment opportunities, and high technology. Prime Minister Mulroney was scheduled to speak at the the closing banquet.[20]

(iv) The October 1, 1986 issue carried a noteworthy "Pastoral Letter." Significantly, this feature article originally appeared in *Licht auf dem Weg* (Light Along the Way), the official publication of the South American Mennonite Brethren Conference. I shall translate some excerpts. Having discussed the necessity of spiritual renewal and noting the dominant trends, the leadership article states:

The most obvious development involves our growing ethnic diversification. Historically we were a people (Volk) with a common ethnic and cultural background. This ethnic background served as a bond which held us together and still holds us together now.
But because of evangelization and missions the situation is changing somewhat.

What keeps us united now is no longer our common background, not our names, but a much stronger bond, namely, unity and love which unites the family of God. Thus we need a new and broadened understanding of the "holy fellowship of the saints."

...Our unity lies in Christ, not mainly in a specific culture.

...We consider ourselves to be a strongly anabaptist- evangelical church, but concerning that matter, there seems to be no clarity.

...The result is that we do not know exactly what it means to be the Mennonite Brethren church.

...On the other hand, many congregations are still bound to tradition, ethnicity, and self-development.[21]

Thus a fine periodical, steeped in ethnicity and religion, seeks to be faithful to its calling and to the mission of the Church.

These advertisements and articles are only representative.

(b) *Mennonite Mirror*

This Winnipeg-based periodical which first appeared in September, 1971, published by the Mennonite Literary Society, Inc., is probably Canada's best expression of the Mennonite faith-culture combination, even to the point of carrying extensive Mennonite Low German material. In a September, 1983 editorial, Al Reimer spelled out the periodical's guiding philosophy. *The Mirror* wants to,

> present clear, challenging, comprehensive reflections of Mennonite life, faith, and culture. The time may come when the Mennonites in this area will be virtually indistinguishable in a cultural and ethnic sense from the rest of the community. If and when that happens we may declare ourselves redundant and quit.[22]

Given the tremendous and high quality reinforcement the *Mennonite Mirror* has given Mennonite ethnicity in Manitoba and beyond, the disappearance of such Mennonite ethnicity is surely remote, especially in Manitoba. It also carries full-page Multiculturalism Canada ads.[23]

(c) Of all North American Mennonite periodicals I find the glossy and highly readable *Festival Quarterly*, launched in the spring of 1974, easily the most effective vehicle for Mennonite faith-ethnicity fusion and Mennonite culture in particular. Itself part of the renaissance of Mennonite culture and ethnic self-awareness, the *FQ*'s bold and constant self-introduction lets readers know its emphasis: "Exploring the art, faith and culture of Mennonite Peoples." The fascinating articles, which very rarely deal with evangelism or mission even broadly defined, deal with topics such as, "Mennonites Carve Soapstone,"[24] "Buggy Builders Head for Paraguay,"[25] and "The Artist as a Social Critic."[26]

A few days spent reading the *FQ* numbers for the past several years gives one the distinct experience that Mennonite art, culture, and ethnicity, in their variegated coloration, are not only alive but healthy and thriving.

Both the *Mennonite Mirror* and the *Festival Quarterly*, very fine periodicals which I recommend whole-heartedly, reflect what Isajiw has termed, the "rediscovery" of ethnicity. Persons "from consecutive ethnic generations" develop a strong "relation to the culture of their ancestors."[27]

(d) *Mennonite Reporter*

Established in 1972 as the successor to Frank Epp's ground-breaking, *Canadian Mennonite*, the *Mennonite Reporter* has become the most important Mennonite periodical in Canada. Put out by the Mennonite Publishing Service, this wide-ranging independent bi-weekly pretty well covers the Mennonite scene in Canada. While its masthead states a biblical imperative, "all that is true, all that is just and pure — fill all your thoughts with these things,"[28] its content is much more than merely religion related. In particular, the ethnic emphasis, while not dominant, is unmistakably present. If Mennonite means anabaptist, then how can one exlain a full-page article entitled, "Confesions of a Mennonite Catholic?"[29] Also, if, as the editors regularly insist, Mennonite (in Canada) does not denote or connote a particular ethnicity,[30] then why would the *Mennonite Reporter* carry Multiculturalism Canada display advertising promoting "ethnocultural" and "ethnic" well-being?[31] I have never seen the Hon. Otto Jellinek run his "Multiculturalism Canada" ads in *The Canadian Baptist, The Alliance Witness, The United Church Observer, Penticostal Testimony, Faith Today,* or any other truly and specifically church-related publications.

The *Mennonite Reporter* carries many articles which report, or analyze, or reflect Mennonite ethnicity. Many are covered in the regular, usually two-page, feature section, "The Arts."

If anything characterizes the *Mennonite Reporter* it is use, I dare say overuse, of the word "Mennonite." On the average the paper uses the word aout 300 to 350 times, not including some 200 or more abbreviations (MCC, MB, MDS, CMBC), in each 20-page issue. I find nothing like it in any other supposedly religious periodical. But maybe that is simply part of being a wide-ranging, inter-conference, ethno-religious newspaper. About 50% of the time it is used in a religious context ("Mennonite Church," "Mennonite Mission Board"), about 10% in an ethnic context ("Mennonite names," "Mennonite museum," "of Mennonite extraction," "Mennonite Catholic"), and about 40% of the time it probably refers to both (*Mennonite Reporter,* "Mennonite school," "Mennonite people," "Mennonite your way").

Perhaps, in the *Mennonite Reporter,* as in the other Mennonite periodicals, the usage may be mainly religious but it is certainly both. The reader quickly picks up the double meaning. Like ink in clear water, it only takes a little to create an entirely different coloration. And the *Mennonite Reporter,* covering the country, uses a lot of ink!

(e) *The Mennonite Brethren Herald*

This bi-weekly, with a circulation of over 13,000, is the official English-language publication of the Canadian Conference of Mennonite Brethren Churches and the second most important Mennonite periodical in Canada. Although it reflects less of an ethnic emphasis than does the *Mennonite Reporter,* the ethnic flavour is still very pronounced, despite the periodic insistence by the editors that Mennonite does not refer to ethnic.

Not surprisingly, shortly after Prime Minister Trudeau announced the establishment of official Canadian multiculturalism on October 8, 1971, the *Mennonite Brethren Herald* began carrying "Multiculturalism" ads. The issue of April 6, 1973 carried 8 full pages of federal government multicultural advertisements. In these pages one reads phrases such as, "freedom of choice... for ethnic groups in our country," "deepen the involvement of all ethno-cultural groups in the mainstream of Canadian life," "Vibrant ethnic groups give Canadians of second, third and subsequent generations a feeling that they are connected...," "Ethnic loyalties need not...detract from wider loyalties," "Every ethnic group has the right to preserve and develop its own culture," "folk arts and music of various ethnic communities," "the ethnic press," "multicultural grants," "will commission approximately 20 histories of ethnic groups in Canada," (see later reference to Frank Epp's histories of Mennonites in Canada), "ethnic studies," "Greek Folk Dance Instruction," "Music, Songs and Dances of Italy," "The Croatian Peasant Society," "Korean Cultural Festival," "Doukhobor Cultural Research," and much more. As will be described later, Canadian Mennonites applied for and received numerous, often very large, grants from the various governmental multicultural and ethnic programs. The multicultural ads continued to appear in the *Herald.*[32]

Many news accounts covering such disparate phenomena as the several Mennonite museums, Mennonite cookbooks, Mennonite names, Mennonite culture, Mennonite entertainment, Mennonite foods, and a host of other cultural/ethnic aspects appear regularly in the *Mennonite Brethren Herald.*

The topic of Mennonite Brethren identity is addressed periodically. In 1985 two major articles appeared by editors and one by a regular columnist. In January editor Herold Jantz insisted that the Mennonite Brethren are a "church," "a denomination...respected across the country...." He did not distinguish between respect and perceived accessibility by non-Mennonites.[33]

In May, associate editor James Coggins, in developing an excellent analysis of Anabaptism, spelled out his views. Mennonites, and particularly Mennonite Brethren, were described as one of the "four main traditions of Christianity in the Western world."[34] There is not the slightest hint that Mennonite Brethren are ethnic.

A particularly intriguing piece by columnist James Pankratz appeared in October. Acknowledging that perhaps "about half of our Canadian Mennonite Brethren congregations presently use the name Mennonite Brethren on the signs outside their churches," Pankratz raises several issues. His observations include the following. "The association of ethnicity with the name 'Mennonite' does occur occasionally today...but I do not encounter it very often."[35] In general he does not see Mennonites, including Mennonite Brethren, as particularly ethnic. One of his key points, namely, that "Having an ethnic immigrant history is neither a badge of distinction to be flaunted nor a disability to be concealed," is, of course, correct.[36] But that's really not the issue in the ethnicity debate which he addresses. Nor can any informed person disagree with his assessment that part of the problem concerns the ethical issues of aloofness, arrogance, and the rejection of non-Mennonites within the church. Such attitudes certainly constitute a significant part of the problem as mentioned in chapter 2. I must say, though, that I am puzzled by Pankratz' assertion that, "Our name is a statement of humility...."[37]

Pankratz's statements on ethics should be headed; his comments on ethnicity reflect interesting impressions and opinions but are inadequate. The evidence and data as presented in chapters 3 and 5, for example, are probably more instructive.

One of the most provocative articles in the *Herald* dealing with this topic appeared in May, 1986. Under the title, "Since you are Mennonite...," associate editor Jim Coggins describes the diversity and extent of ethnic material that comes to the *Herald* office. He lists "Mennonite writers"; novels having a "Mennonite theme" and funded by the "Multicultural Program of the Government of Canada"; "A 'Mennonite' drama company"; " 'Mennonite' choirs and orchestras, schools and cultural groups"; "press releases" from "The federal Ministry of Multiculturalism"; etc.

Amidst this barrage and frustration Coggins suggests that "Perhaps it is time to state clearly (again) that the *Mennonite Brethren Herald* is a publication of the Mennonite Brethren CHURCH. The qualification for membership in this church is not a common ethnic background but a common faith in the Lord Jesus Christ." Then, undermining both the logic and the effectiveness of his own argument that Mennonite does not mean ethnic, he adds, "Many of our members do not have an ethnic Mennonite background, and many people with an ethnic background do not qualify for membership." [38]

Coggins understands much of the problem. He laments the fact that an MB "provincial conference board recently sought government funding for a Mennonite Brethren school on the grounds that it teaches the German language and 'the Mennonite culture'." He criticizes the presentation of "a 'Mennonite' quilt to a representative of the federal government" and says that Toronto's Harbourfront Mennonite Festival, with its 'ethnic cooking and handcrafts' "send all the wrong signals about who we really are." [39]

Correctly he notes that "The problem we encounter is that the word 'Mennonite' has various definitions." And, again, "The problem we have with the Menno Van and other bicentennial programs, therefore is that they portray the ambiguous definition of the word 'Mennonite'.... As a result, it is not always easy to distinguish between the two aspects of our past." "That dilemma daily confronts the editors of the *Mennonite Brethren Herald*." [40]

The problem with Coggins' fine analysis is that he is trying to have it both ways. All the observations about "Mennonite themes" and "Multicultural grants," etc., describe reality. They are authentic. So if Mennonites present a drama, do crafts, apply for and get Multicultural-ethnic government grants, then why should we be either surprised or perplexed? After all, Coggins properly acknowledges that there is such a thing as Mennonite ethnicity. Therefore, if we call ourselves Mennonite, and if our periodical is called Mennonite, then why shouldn't others, including governments, assume that we are Mennonite? If it looks like a duck, walks like a duck, quacks like a duck, eats like a duck, lives with other ducks, and even calls itself a duck, then why shouldn't Multiculturalism Canada, the CBC, The City of Winnipeg, and the general public, assume that it is a duck?

Coggins writes that we should insist "on the spiritual definition of Mennonitism." [41] If only the situation were that simple — but, it isn't. Correctly he notes that,

As a Canadian of English descent, I cannot share the cultural heritage of speaking German, eating "Rollkuchen", suffering in Russia and homesteading on the prairies. If I were required to do so, I would have to leave the Mennonite Brethren Church. [42]

Coggins' analysis and logic should lead him to a certain kind of conclusion but it is not the one that he draws. He states that "those who assume we are an ethnic group are outsiders," which is largely incorrect, and adds, "It is usually others who are confused about our identity rather than ourselves," which is also largely incorrect. Somehow he thinks that for MBs the main issue is "a public relations problem." I suggest that the problem has very little to do with communications and public relations, rather, it has much more to do with substance and with official names.

Coggins continues. "This does not mean that we have to drop the Mennonite Brethren name. Merely changing the name does not seem to have solved the problem for the Brethren in Christ." [43] There are a few problems with this comment. First, the Brethren in Christ are a "peace" church, not a Mennonite church. They have never been called Mennonite and have never changed their name from Mennonite. Second, they do not have the same ethnic identity problem that Mennonites have. Third, to the extent that they have, in some respects, remained "apart" and separate, it is because they have consciously chosen to do so, not because their name sent ethnic signals to the government, to the media, or to the general public.

In general the Mennonite press, including the many other fine periodicals not mentioned here, in both Canada and the US, can aptly be described as increasingly sophisticated, primarily in-house, ethnoreligious media. Clearly all of them incorporate a major ethnic component.

5. *Mennonite Culture; a major component of Mennonite ethnicity.*
Before we look at specific aspects of Mennonite culture, some general comments seem to be appropriate. Let us begin with a press report of 1970. John L. Ruth, a Pennsylvania Mennonite clergyman and probably the most knowledgeable expert on Mennonite culture, lectured at Waterloo's Conrad Grebel College on November 7.

Dr. Ruth said Mennonites have not produced great artists but they have produced significant folk art. This was expressed in their cooking, baking, needlework, farming and handicrafts....

He contended artists today must take up the task of articulating the Mennonite heritage with artistic integrity. He felt Mennonites had a story to tell — a quiet unreported story — and that this story must be part of the formation of the future culture of society....

The essence of Mennonite culture, said Dr. Ruth, is a kind of medieval community with coherence, mutual aid and human warmth. [49]

This knowledgeable Mennonite preacher is right on two counts but not on a third. He has correctly described what happens when ethnicity and church are fused and his description of current trends and cultural developments is accurate. But he is wrong in assuming that contributing to "future culture" should be a top priority of Mennonites if — and that's the big if — he defines Mennonites as Bible-believing anabaptists. The explanation, I suggest, is that despite verbal protestations to the contrary, he and his supportive audience in fact assumed Mennonite to mean ethnic. Unless the Biblical Great Commission no longer means anything, there can be no other explanation.

In this connection we should note that the dominant and truly first class Mennonite publishing firm, Herald Press, in its 1985-86 Canadian Catalog, devotes about 10% of its space to Mennonite culture, Mennonite cookbooks and related Mennonite ethnic items.

Frequently Mennonite ethnicity expresses itself in large scale social functions. Throughout the past 30 years, in particular, Canada has witnessed scores of noteworthy Mennonite cultural events. Let us review some of them.

In April, 1980, the Rockway Mennonite School Association in Waterloo Region organized a "Mennonite Festival of the Arts." The official brochure highlighted "quilting and fine needlework," "printing and literature," "music and drama," a lecture on Rembrandt "who was associated with Mennonites in Holland during some of the productive years of his life," a "heritage display" featuring "candles and lamps as well as a visual survey of the life and work of D.B. Detweiler, one of the fathers of Ontario Hydro." The inclusion of some religious activity rounded out this fully ethnic, and very interesting, festival.

One of the highlights of Mennonite ethnic celebration has been the Mennonite involvement in Winnipeg's renowned Folklorama, a major tourist attraction. In fact, this ethnic extravaganza is rated as "one of the Top 100 Events in North America by the American Bus Association." Sponsored by the Folk Arts Council of Winnipeg, Inc., "a non-profit organization representing the city's ethnocultural performing groups," this huge celebration has provided Manitoba Mennonites with an excellent opportunity to demonstrate and explain Mennonite ethnicity.[45]

The ethnic capital of Canada annually puts on a great show. Mennonite participation in the early 1980s was reported widely, in both the secular and the Mennonite press. Writing in the *Mennonite Mirror* Al Reimer stated the following.

Last year I did not get to see the Mennonite pavilion at Folklorama....

This year, I am happy to say, I was in the thick of things at the Mennonite pavilion.... If I had any lingering doubts about the need for or purpose of a Mennonite pavilion in this ethnic folk festival I have none now....

This year the organizing committee tried to give a more rounded picture of Mennonite history, culture and faith. The Mennonite soul food of "verenike," "ploome mous" and "rollkuchen," of course, required no change. The popular entertainment was better coordinated, more restrained and more relevant. It's centerpiece was a splendid, trilingual skit which in song and verse evoked a vivid, moving picture of the Mennonite way of life, in both its secular and sacred spheres....

But our ethnic "amalgam" is distinctively our own. The Dutch-German-Russian ethos is immediately recognizable no matter what country such Mennonites live in.[46]

How right Reimer is. If, while travelling in Europe, you happened to meet an unknown couple, John and Tena Jantz (her maiden name was Wiebe), what would you think of? There is a distinctive Mennonite ethnicity, recognizable anywhere. Now if only he and others would recognize the confusion and the bad theology which results when some people keep on insisting there is no Mennonite ethnicity and that Canadian amd American Mennonites are Mennonites in the same way that Zairian or Nigerian Mennonites are Mennonites. Reimer continues.

We are fighting for ethnic survival, and anything that helps to delay our ethnic demise is to be welcomed, including a Mennonite pavilion at Folklorama. To those Mennonite snobs who thought there was too much Low German in the popular entertainment at the pavilion I say "mestsheffel." Low German is making its swan song in our Canadian Mennonite culture, and a beautiful swan song it is as sung and spoken by the brave lads and lasses of the Landmark and In House groups. With their honest, unpretentious humor and shrewd satire they are proving that "Plautdietsch" can be a fine, entertaining artistic vehicle....

So it went for an exciting week, even though I did gain a few pounds from eating "Vereniki," "ploome mous," and "rollkuchen" every night.

Incidentally, there was no crokinole this year, but there was, I believe, some Christian witness.[47]

The same issue of *Mennonite Mirror* carried extensive news coverage, including some interviews. The "mayor" of the Mennonite pavilion, Rudy Regehr, said, "I feel that the displays you see are the cultural fabric, the ethnic basket if you like. Our religion would be a part of what goes into that basket."

The hostess, Gayle Wiebe, stated, "I believe it is necessary to present both the religious and cultural aspects of being Mennonite although the religious aspect is more difficult to present visually...."

Jake Rempel commented, "Locusts and Honey or 'Heischraitje en Willa Honich' is the most popular group.... I've noticed more MBs showing up this year. The criticisms raised last year in the *MB Herald* seemed to be more of an advertisement than a detraction."[48]

What were those criticisms? In an editorial entitled, "What business do we have in Folklorama?" editor Harold Jantz tried to develop a proper Mennonite Brethren response. Having described Folklorama, with its emphasis on "song, dance and drink" he asked, "What business does a 'Mennonite pavilion' have in this setting?... For a Christian church community to put itself forward as an ethnic community is altogether wrong. It confuses our witness."[49]

But Jantz' assumptions are dubious. Yes, the witness is indeed confused but not because ethnic Mennonites call themselves ethnic and act like ethnics but because anabaptist churches call themselves Mennonite. Many of us have no race or ethnicity other than Mennonite. Does Jantz want us to deny our ethnicity and thus, ethnically, to be nobodies? Why should I deny who I am? I am a Christian, a Canadian citizen, of Mennonite ethnicity — not German, or Dutch, or Russian.

Jantz' criticism lacks both accuracy and credibility. If I'm not Mennonite than what am I ethnically? One does not simply decide Mennonite means church by saying so. On this issue the *MB Herald* incriminates itself as do other Canadian Mennonite periodicals. It extensively reports on Mennonite ethnicity and reflects Mennonite ethnicity. Partly for that reason the authorities know that Mennonite means ethnic, and the *MB Herald* agrees when it carries page after page of government multicultural advertising directed specifically to ethnic groups.

If one admits that the word Mennonite presently has a double meaning, that Mennonites in Canada are as much an ethnic as a religious group, then having the pavilion makes sense. Let an ethnic group present itself as such. On this question Al Reimer's view, I suggest, is much more in line with reality than is Harold Jantz's. Now there may be good reasons why Mennonites should not have even a "teetotalling" pavilion at Folklorama but, I suggest, it is far-fetched to cite Mennonite non-ethnicity as that reason.

Jantz rests his argument not on Canadian evidence but on the "more than forty nationalities" represented at a Mennonite World Conference assembly. In chapter 9 I shall spell out the fallacy of that argument.

The logical contradiction in Jantz's approach, which, however, probably represents the view of most Canadian Mennonites, is reflected in a later letter to the *Mennonite Mirror*. "I have no difficulty in conceding that the Mennonites of Manitoba have many of the characteristics of an ethnic group." Quite correctly, he thus sees Mennonite as meaning ethnic. Later on he says, "But we have said that anyone can be a Mennonite who joins us in a common confession of Christ." This last assertion is the one that needs much more careful analysis. Thus one is a Mennonite because one's parents were, and one becomes a Mennonite by believing in Christ. These statements cannot both be true. By insisting on calling two different things Mennonite, the picture becomes confusing and contradictory.[50] We need a new term. Maybe we should simply refer to non-Christian Mennonites as secular Mennonites, for that is what they are.

A less consequential Mennonite cultural event, the 13th Annual Manitoba Mennonite Festival of Art and Music, was held in Winnipeg on April 15, 1984. It was advertised thus. "A walkthrough display of art, antiques, crafts, books, and other interesting artifacts representing Mennonite life and culture. Entertainment by Choirs and Musical Groups. Mennonite Cuisine at its best. Adults $4; Children $.50."[51]

Another significant Mennonite cultural event took place at the classy Centennial Concert Hall in Winnipeg on November 29, 1984. Sponsored by the Mennonite Media Society it attracted 1500 people who paid $10 each to hear and see "An evening of Mennonite music and entertainment." Here are excerpts from the report, taken from 15 column-inches in the *Mennonite Reporter*: "cornball humour of a Low-German singing group," "black tie music by a string quartet," "coffee and 'tweeback'," "Low German antics," "prayer for the offering," " 'Heischratje 'n Willa Honig' (grasshoppers and wild honey)," "Koop en Bua enn Dietschlaund," "the first time that Low-German drama has been captured on film," "Kernlieder," "The 'Mennonite Singers'," "Mennonite Piano Concerto," "In the words of one observer, it was a variety show that 'truly hit the highs and lows' of Mennonite culture."[52] Yet this esteemed paper insists that there is no uniquely Mennonite ethnicity.

The impressive, 24-page tabloid, "A Guide to the Mennonite Bicentennial," published by the *Mennonite Reporter* on March 31, 1986, was itself a memorable cultural production. It captured beautifully the diversity and colouration of a major national, even international, ethnoreligious celebration. It both described and reflected. Page after page, in word and picture, exudes laudable ethnicity as well as the major anabaptist emphasis. It promoted many items and events, including a 6 1/2-hour tour which "will feature a nostalgic and contemporary look at the Mennonite culture in Waterloo county through crafts and art, music, films and folklore. Traditional foods will be cooked outdoors for a picnic lunch."[53] "A Low German film, 'Koop and Buhr Travel to Chicago' will add a lighthearted touch,"[54] "Vineland celebrates Mennonite heritage on Canada Day,"[55] "Rockway Collegiate to host Arts Festival May 10-11,"[56] and dozens more.

Two other aspects of this publication must be mentioned. The Mennonite Bicentennial *Guide* informed its readers that the "Mennonite Bicentennial Commission acknowledges financial assistance from the Ontario Ministry of Citizenship and Culture" and "The Secretary of State and Multiculturalism Canada."[57] Constituent groups and persons as well as "the governments of Manitoba, Saskatchewan and Alberta" also donated funds.[58]

The final Mennonite cultural event I shall mention is the Harbourfront Mennonite Festival, a Mennonite extravaganza presented in Toronto, August 2-4, 1986. It also was associated with the Bicentennial celebrations. *A Guide to the Mennonite Bicentennial* had the following comments on this production. "This popular tourist attraction…," will allow Mennonites "to share some of their traditions as well as current values with the many other cultural and ethnic groups of Canada," it is "focussed more directly on the general public." It is very interesting that many who generally insist that Mennonites are not ethnic, at certain times have absolutely no hesitation in promoting the very ethnicity they deny and have no hesitancy in applying for government Multicultural/ethnic grants to do so. Various "Mennonite" writers, including Patrick Friesen, are featured. The long list of Mennonite entertainers includes church choirs and, again, the rising Low German stars, "Locust and Wild Honey." "Ethnic" meals to be served will feature "Pennsylvania Dutch" cuisine, "Russian Mennonite" cooking, etc. Reference to Vietnamese or other "Mennonites" does not alter the basic message.[59]

Reporting on the major public event, witnessed by many thousands, the *Mennonite Reporter* gave full-page coverage to this ethnic indulgence; about "500-600 volunteers made the event a success." Patrick Friesen and other Mennonite writers "gave readings, some controversial, all entertaining." The "Russian Mennonite supper sold out earlier than expected." On Sunday morning Ontario's Lieutenant-Governor Lincoln Alexander "attended the service and was presented with a quilt symbolic of the history of Mennonites in Ontario."[60] The article, in summing up the affair, stated that, "Our religious commitment which runs deeper than our ethnicity helps us to make a singular contribution to this land and to its culture."[61] How can one refer to such ethnicity if one insists that it does not exist?

Now let us briefly review some elements of Mennonite ethnicity, the ethnic part of Canadian Mennonite ethnoreligious identity. Our list of twelve components is more than representative but certainly not exhaustive.

(a) Mennonite Names

In 1948 the prominent "outside" sociologist specializing in Mennonite studies, E.K. Francis, wrote, "Only about two hundred and seventy family names are found among the Russian Mennonites, and at one time forty names alone accounted for 60 per cent of the whole group."[62]

In 1972 Alan Peters, an accomplished expert on Mennonite genealogy and Mennonite names, wrote, "This history of the Mennonites has been surprisingly characterized by a continually increasing number of so-called 'Mennonite' family names.[63]

In 1975 the widely-read rural periodical, *The Western Producer*, carried an almost full-page feature entitled, "The meaning of Mennonite names." The article, a summary of "Chapter V of "Das neiderlaendische Erbe der preussischrusslaendischen Mennoniten in Europa, Asien und Amerika," the published doctoral dissertation of Johan Sjouke Postma (University of Marburg, published in 1959 by Drukkerji, A. Jongbloed C.V. in Leeuwarden, the Netherlands), lists 117 Mennonite family names plus about 25 variations, with the known or the most likely derivation of each. "A Dutch researcher's findings on the ethnic derivation of Mennonite family names", says the bold sub-title.[65]

A locally available information sheet, undated, "Mennonites Welcome You To The Regional Municipality of Waterloo," lists "Leading Names by Ethnicity," 5 for the Old Order, etc., 5 for the Amish, etc., and 5 for the Mennonite Brethren, United Mennonite, etc.[64]

For several years the *Mennonite Mirror* has carried a listing of all Manitoba Mennonite college and university graduate with "the selection... based largely on whether the last name was Mennonite and our knowledge of graduates having non-Mennonite names."[66]

In 1985, reporting on the Menno Van trip, Kathy Good states that in a Winnipeg church she and her husband witnessed a baptismal service. "As each person was introduced there were, of course, traditional Mennonite-sounding names. But one stood out. It was not an ethnic Mennonite name."[67]

In November, 1986, Katie Funk Wiebe wrote, "We can no longer speak of 'Mennonite Brethren names' and 'non-Mennonite Brethren names," because so many "new members are from non-Mennonite background."[68] Interestingly, Wiebe then bases much of her article on the analysis of the very thing she says "we can no longer speak of." At length she discusses Mennonite names and provides three appendices of name calculations, all of which refer to "non-traditional (non-ethnic Mennonite) names."[69] In order to analyze the contemporary Canadian Mennonite Brethren conference, Wiebe quite properly does what she nevertheless says cannot be done and should not be done. Such an inconsistent approach by many Mennonite writers, editors, educators, ministers, and other leaders never ceases to amaze me.

In December 1986, the *Mennonite Reporter* carried another "name" story, this one interestingly, date-lined, "Reinfeld, Argentina." The report by Martin and Kathe Durksen noted that, "A number of people with Mennonite names are scattered throughout the country."[70]

(b) Mennonite Clothing

While most Canadian Mennonites probably do not think of attire as a significant aspect of Mennonite ethnicity, the distinctive garb of the various Old Order and very conservative groups constitutes one of the mainstays in the standard Canadian Mennonite stereotype. Sociologists frequently cite it,[71] and reporters and columnists rather frequently refer to "Mennonite hats" or clothing that "Mennonites wear."[72]

Some Mennonite conferences take attire very seriously. One of them, between 1865 and 1950, passed no less than 230 resolutions on the matter, more than on any other subject.[73] The most significant analysis of Mennonite ethnic clothing is Melvin Gingerich's *Through Four Centuries*, which deals with Mennonite attire from the 16th century to the late 1960s.[74]

(c) Mennonite Quilts

Distinctive quilts and quilt making loom large in the Mennonite tradition of practical needle work and sewing related crafts. Numerous books and scores of articles have been written about it. Sociologists and anthropologists discuss Mennonite quilts at length. Some recent titles include *Mennonite Quilts and Pieces* by Judy Schroeder Tomlonson, *Amish Crib Quilts* by Rachel and Kenneth Pellman, and *Small Amish Quilt Patterns* by Rachel J. Pellman, all published by Good Books in Intercourse, Pennsylvania. These glossy, illustrated volumes have been reviewed widely, even in such prominent periodicals as *Library Journal, Country Magazine, Philadelphia Inquirer*, and the *New York Times*.[75]

Mennonite quilts were also the main attraction at a three-month exhibit of "large-scale, museum-quality," "Mennonite works" and crafts at the Kitchener-Waterloo Art Gallery. The director of the show, Nancy-Lou Patterson, University of Waterloo fine arts professor, explained that the exhibition included "the two streams of Mennonite culture," "the Swiss-German group" and "the Dutch-German group."[76]

Mennonite quilts are highly prized in the Ontario tourist trade. The better gift shops often carry them — at steep prices. For example, while on a holiday in the Muskoka region I noticed that the regional paper carried a large ad which described: "One of the most interesting antique, craft and collectibles shops in Ontario." It featured "Hand Made Wooden Toys, Carved Flying Birds, Imported Dolls, and Mennonite Quilts" as well as other "investments in Nostalgia."[77]

Not surprisingly, Margaret Loewen Reimer's "A Concise Reference Guide to Mennonite Groups in Canada" has as its main title, *One Quilt, Many Pieces*.[78]

(d) Mennonite Painting

Mennonite painting has been flourishing ever since Mennonites established their own folk identity. As I review my thick files on Mennonite paintings, and look at my own small collection of originals and prints, I note that none deal with native Indians, orientals, Hispanics, or blacks, all of whom can be found in Canadian Mennonite congregations. I also notice that all of the paintings obviously deal with Mennonites of Swiss-German or Dutch-German background. The artists, the dealers, and the purchasing public all know who is a Mennonite. The third aspect that strikes me is the fact that some of the key Mennonite artists, such as Peter Etril Snyder and Woldemar Neufeld, have no connection with any Mennonite church and seemingly not with any other church either. Yet they are always known as Mennonite artists, by Mennonites and others, and their paintings grace walls in Mennonite colleges, churches, countless homes, etc. And well they should!

Upon the publication of *A Painter's Harvest — The Works of Peter Etril Snyder*, by CBC Enterprises in 1986, Snyder commented that, "aesthetics have almost taken the place of religion for me. My inner self is massaged by visual messages." The $40-book "celebrates 200 years of Mennonites in Canada."[79] Already a renowned Canadian painter, Snyder established himself as one of Canada's best-known "Mennonites" when his painting, "The Homesteaders," was purchased by the Prime Minister's Office and presented to Prince Philip on August 20, 1986, "at a dinner hosted by External Affairs Minister Joe Clark."[80]

Mennonite paintings, many by secular Mennonites, are widely promoted and distributed in Ontario and beyond by art shops, by book stores, by chambers of commerce, by department stores, and by Mennonite establishments such as Toronto's "The Mennonite Centre" on St. Clair Avenue and The Meetingplace in St. Jacobs. In the entertainment section of a major paper one reporter wrote, "The selection of contemporary Mennonite art at the Meetingplace is the largest exhibition of its kind organized in Canada. The multi-media show, featuring work by 25 Canadian artists living in Ontario, Manitoba, Saskatchewan, British Columbia and the United States, makes for fascinating viewing for a variety of reasons."[81]

For an excellent introduction to Mennonite ethnic painting see the glossy 28-page, *Peter Etril Snyder 1987 catalogue* or, better yet, visit the Peter Etril Snyder Art Gallery in Waterloo.

Across Canada, Mennonite painting, from framed oil canvas to postcards, and from fascinating coffee table books to tourist promotion, has become a booming business. It has virtually nothing to do with the New Testament church and virtually everything to do with Mennonite ethnicity.

(e) Mennonite Music

Mennonite music, in all its diversity, has become well established in Canadian society. "Kernlieder," Low German humourous pieces, the Mennonite Piano Concerto, and an array of hymns and songs have become associated with the Mennonite people. Mennonite singers and Mennonite performers abound: Mennonite Community Orchestra, Menno Singers, Mennonite Children's Choirs, and even, some suggest, Fred Penner on CBC TV. When the Mennonite Community Orchestra presents "Peter and the Wolf,"[82] how shall the public deduce that Mennonite means Christian? And when the same orchestra plays Janacek's "Soko Fanfare" or Bizet's "Symphony in C," even if in the Portage Avenue Mennonite Brethren Church, how shall listeners infer that Mennonite means Christian?[83]

More importantly, what should prevent them from deducing that it has a different meaning? The literature on Mennonite music and music-makers is now growing rapidly, as is the phenomenon of Mennonite music itself. Two noteworthy volumes are Wesley Berg's, *From Russia With Music*,[84] and the forthcoming 500-page study by Doreen Klassen,

"Mennonite Music-making in Canada." Not surprisingly, the latter is "Funded by the Secretary of State for Canada — Multiculturalism." [85]

(f) Mennonite Drama and Film

Until a few decades ago Mennonite drama was basically restricted to church and parochial school productions. That genre continues but the ethnic stage has blossomed incredibly. We now have such impressive entities as the Winnipeg Mennonite Theatre which in 1983 presented several operas: Gian-Carlo Menotti's "The Telephone" and Haydn's "Die Apotheker." In 1984 this Mennonite theatre company presented Shakespeare's "Hamlet" and in 1985, *Die Emigranten* by Walter Schlichting, which included "standard vignettes of Russian Mennonite experience" as well as "some contemporary aspects of Mennonite life." We also have the Winnipeg-based Mennonite Media Society Inc. which on November 29, 1984 premiered the Low German Mennonite production, "Koop en Bua enn Dietschlaund," in Winnipeg's magnificent Centennial Concern Hall.

The Mennonite Media Society Inc. has already established an enviable reputation with its films. Some of its completed projects include "Menno's Reins" (1975), "Heimat fuer Heimatlose" (1980), "And When They Shall Ask" (1983), as well as "Koop en Bua enn Dietschlaund" (1985). Several other ambitious ventures are underway and more are being planned. The Society has come a long way in achieving its two-fold aim: "to help further greater self-awareness among Mennonites" and "to help Mennonites share their faith and culture with others." [87] In this connection we should also note "Winnipeg filmmaker Allan Kroeker, whose television dramas and dramatic features have won international distinctions at film festivals around the world...." [88]

Numerous regional and provincial Mennonite drama and film groups have become impressively active. For example, the Mennonite Historical Society of Ontario has produced the drama, "Trail of the Conestoga" and participated in the production of three Mennonite films, "Beyond this Land," "And When Their Time Had Come," and "Trail of the Conestoga." It has received substantial assistance from the Ontario Ministry of Culture.

In passing one should at least note Merle Good's classic and very successful major film, "Happy as the Grass was Green." [89] Then, too, one must not overlook the movie "Witness."

Many other illustrations could be cited but let me complete this section with some comments on playwright Patrick Friesen's drama, "The Shunning." It premiered October 10, 1985, "to a full house" in Altona, MB. [90] The significant aspect of this achievement is not only that Friesen has "managed to catch the Mennonite sense of humour," or even that he has produced "a new experience for Mennonites," namely, "to hear Bible verses quoted in a Mennonite accent and to hear favourite hymns sung on a stage as pure entertainment," [91] rather, what's especially significant for our purposes is that Patrick Friesen says, that "As an artist I happen to be Mennonite," but he also told Peter Gzowski on CBC's "Morningside" on October 9, 1985, that he was a Mennonite but "not a Cristian." I heard him say it. Here we have, as I understand it, an excellent example of a prominent and fascinating secular Mennonite. Significantly, "The Shunning" was described by Robert Enright, a CBC art critic and cultural reporter, thus: "it may well be the best play coming out of Canada."[92]

(g) Mennonite literature

Mennonite ethnic literature in Low German, German, and English is so vast, and is growing so extensively, that, given space constraints, I can do little more than underline some noteworthy examples. We are talking about more than 50 significant Mennonite writers, all of whom write about Mennonite people and themes. Perhaps the founding, in Winnipeg, of "The Mennonite Book Club" and the recent awarding of an honourary doctorate by the University of Winnipeg to Mennonite novelist Rudy Wiebe for, "writing about the ethnic survival and spiritual quests of his Mennonite people…" or about Indians and Metis,[93] best highlight that fact. Also noteworthy is the fact that Hildegard Tiessen teaches a course in Mennonite literature, "Mennonite Authors and Artists," at Conrad Grebel College.

The following must be cited. The twenty or so major Low German Mennonite classics by Arnold Dyck are in the process of being published in four volumes, *Collected Works of Arnold Dyck,* in Low German, by the Manitoba Mennonite Historical Society. Apparently Dyck remains "The Most Widely Read Mennonite Writer."[94] For an excellent survey of Russian Mennonite literature see Harry Loewen, ed. *Mennonite Images,* especially the third section.[95] Significantly, the secular Mennonite, Patrick Friesen, gets extensive treatment, pp. 249-255. Also highly informative is "The Poetry and Distemper of Patrick Friesen and David Waltner-Toews."[96] John L. Ruth's *Mennonite Identity and Literary Art*[97] remains a standard work on Mennonite literature and ethnicity. Jim Doelman's, "Mennonite Literature: An Outsider's View," provides an additional prospective.[98] Referring to the works of Armin Wiebe, *The Salvation of Yasch Siemens,* of Patrick Friesen, of Al Reimer, of Rudy Wiebe, and other prominent Mennonite writers, Doelman, who is not a Mennonite ("I've never eaten borscht, I can't understand Plautdietsche," etc.), and, who, having noted the Mennonite content, writes: "however, like all good ethnically based literature (and it can be argued ALL literature is ethnically based) these works are universal in spite of their particularity…." Later on he says, "There are a few things I've noticed about Mennonite literature in general which may or may not have been noticed by Mennonite readers. The first of these is a strong sense of a well-defined community, one which is both ethnic and religious."[99]

(h) Mennonite language

Although most "ethnic" Mennonites in Canada have become fluent in English, the German and Low German are still very much alive as second and third languages. Summarizing the impressions of professors and preachers I would estimate that in 1986 70% of all members of Mennonite churches in Canada understand German and 60% Low German. For Mennonite Brethren I would adjust those figures upward to 75% and 65% respectively. Partly because of the "return" of Mexican Mennonites, partly because of the burgeoning of ethnic Mennonite publications, and partly because of a renewed interest in ethnic roots, these percentages are remaining amazingly high in Mennonite communities.

Low German, often called "the Mennonite language," remains surprisingly resilient. (Interestingly, in connection with some language problems in Belgium, The *Wall Street Journal* discussed "Plattdeutsch" on its front page, October 10, 1986.) For a clear description of the nature and role of Mennonite Low German one should read, "Low German: The Language of the True Believer." [100]

The major works by Arnold Dyck, *Dee Fria* (1948), *Koop enn Bua op Reise* (1954), and *Koop enn Bua en Dietschlaund* (vol. I, 1960; vol. II, 1961), established some standard spellings and composition. Armin Wiebe's, *"The Salvation of Yasch Siemens*, is full of "folk expressions such as 'heista kop' and 'drankahma', 'fuschel' and 'fruemensch' and nicknames like Penzel Panna, Laups Leeven," etc. [101] Perhaps the most significant general collection is, *A Sackful of Plautdietsch*. [102]

Several dictionaries have appeared. In 1977 John Thiessen produced his *Mennonite Low-German Dictionary*. [103] A more substantial work appeared later when, in 1984, Herman Rempel produced, *Kjenn Jie Noch Plautdietsch?* which contains about 12,000 Low German words. [104] The 12,000 Low German words are presented with English equivalents and about 12,000 English words are presented with Low German equivalents.

Perhaps the most noteworthy Low German development is the fact that Wycliffe Bible Society working with John J. Neufeld, Winnipeg, Viola Reimer, Steinbach, and Peter Fast, Calgary, set itself the task of translating the New Testament into Low German by late 1986 or early 1987.

I should make two additional observations. "Platt Deutsch," which is "more gutteral, more earthy, more humorous" and Pennsylvania German, which is "more soft, more rhythmic, more musical," [105] play similar roles in the two main ethnic Mennonite sub-branches. Second, Mennonite Brethren have generally been very supportive of German language instruction in homes, churches, high schools, Saturday German schools, and even in Bible schools. In fact, as recently as 1950 the Canadian MB Conference established a "committee for the Nurture of the German Language," voted it a $1,000 initial budget with additions as needed, and heard its annual reports until 1963.

(i) Mennonite food

As with literature, so also with food. The evidence for Mennonite ethnicity is so overwhelming one hardly knows where to begin. Herald Press, in its 1985-86 catalog, lists 12 different Mennonite cookbooks, from *Peppernuts: Plain and Fancy* to the best-selling *More-with-Less Cookbook*. The mainstay, the *Mennonite Community Cookbook*, has been around since 1950. A very popular book across Canada is Edna Staebler's *Food That Really Schmecks: Mennonite Country Cooking*, distributed in at least 13 countries by McGraw-Hill since 1968. A big seller in Manitoba is *The Mennonite Treasury of Recipes*, which has gone into many printings at Derksen Printers, Steinbach, since 1961.

Numerous Mennonite Brethren church groups have also produced cookbooks. Many printings and editions of *Pantry Patterns*, put out by a ladies group in the Central Mennonite Brethren Church, Saskatoon, have appeared since 1960. In recent years *Homespun Flavours*, published by the Steinbach Mennonite Brethren Church Ladies, has gained substantial appeal. In Clearbrook, BC, *Grandma's Cooking*, published by the Golden Age Society in 1985, includes many "Mennonite" recipes. Good Books, in Intercourse, Pennsylvania, has also published cookbooks including, *Cooking and Memories: Favorite Recipes of 20 Mennonite and Amish Cooks*, in 1983. Add to these the numerous other congregational and regional Mennonite cookbooks, many of which now combine Dutch-Russian-German with Swiss-German cuisine, and collectively all of these excellent ventures send a powerful signal concerning Mennonite ethnicity. These books tell everyone that there is a Mennonite people, quite apart from the Anabaptist people of God, who, over the centuries, have become an ethnic group in their own right.

If the expanding cookbook component of Mennonite ethnicity catches everyone's attention, then one must also note the more recent development of Mennonite restaurants. A few decades ago there were none. Now there are many that advertise "Mennonite" dishes. For example, Opa and Omi's Cafe, in Surrey, BC offers a variety of "Mennonite dishes." In both Elmira and St. Jacobs, Ontario, the Stonecrock restaurants promote their "Mennonite" food. Significantly, the St. Jacobs restaurant manager told a reporter, "We do not pass ourselves off as being a religious organization. We are Mennonites." [106]

Perhaps the most impressive and most Russian-Mennonite restaurant in Canada is "d'8 Schtove," in Winnipeg, which prints "Mennonite Food Specialties" on all its menus. In addition to its combined Low German-English name, this restaurant uses Low German in much of its menu. You can order "Rhepspaih," "Glomms Kuuk," "Kommst Kopp," "Wrenikji," "Schinke Fleesh," "Fesch fonn B.C." and much more. And who can forget the Livery Barn Restaurant in Steinbach's Mennonite Village Museum, with its nationally promoted "traditional Mennonite food." It is all thoroughly and authentically Mennonite. I have dined in all of these restaurants, as well as in numerous other Mennonite eateries across Canada and in the US, especially in rural Manitoba, south-western Ontario, Kansas, and Pennsylvania. I can confirm that they serve excellent Mennonite food. I can also assert that they are known far and wide as Mennonite restaurants. Mexican, Italian, German, and other tpes of restaurants, even when operated by Mennonites, are not thus known and none present tortillas, lasagna, or Black Forest cake as being Mennonite.

Increasingly stores across Canada are selling Mennonite foods. For example, a 1985 advertisement informed the consumers in greater Vancouver, that the Prairie Market on Fraser Street was selling "Polish Salami," "Berlin Ham," and, in even bolder type, "Manitoba Mennonite Farmer Sausage (from Winkler Manitoba)."

Some Mennonite Brethren have recognized Mennonite cuisine for the ethnic phenomenon that it is. In "A Theology of Zwieback," [107] Louise Siemens states the case bluntly. "The French carry long, crusty loaves.... The Swedish have given us limpa. Thanks to the Russians, we have rye bread. The Mexicans enjoy their tortillas. As Mennonites we have our bread — Zwieback." [108] Here, as elsewhere, one need not agree with all of the views of those who write about Mennonite ethnicity in order to concur with their basic orientation.

Some Mennonite Brethren readers did not agree with such an ethnic analysis. They saw the incongruity and inconsistency of calling an increasingly multi-ethnic church Mennonite and also recognizing the main North American Mennonite community and its folkways as ethnic. But instead of suggesting that the church should be renamed to conform to reality, they tried to deny the existence of the all too evident Mennonite ethnic cuisine. One reader wrote, "I believe this Mennonite-ethnic association is something we have been trying to get away from. When we go to sessions of the General Conference of Mennonite Brethren Churches, we emphasize that our brotherhood includes people from all ethnic and/or racial groups.... If this is so, then it does *not* make sense to call *Zweiback* a Mennonite food.... I believe the tortillas were just as Mennonite as the Zweiback." [109] For better or worse, all the cookbooks and all the culinary experts, Mennonite and non-Mennonite, do not agree with the reader. The problem which has been clearly identified, will have to be worked at from the other end of the equation.

In reviewing past issues of *The Christian Leader* I noted that in one issue Edmund Janzen, reporting on the Mennonite World Conference, emphasized that "It is an exhilirating experience...to realize that Mennonite identity is not ethnic but theological." [110] Interestingly, the same issue carried an article explaining that the *Mennonite Community Cookbook* was published "to help preserve a particular cuisine and culture common to some groups of Swiss and German Mennonites." [111] The evidence, including the list of Mennonite foods found by Miriam Warner in the San Jose Mennonite Brethren Church, in the heartland of urban California, supports the cookbook, not Janzen. [112]

As the Canadian public spends more and more of its food dollar "eating out," as Mennonite eateries become more numerous and better known, as Mennonite foods in shops become known more widely, and as Mennonite colleges, churches, MCC sales, etc. serve Mennonite foods to hundreds of thousands, the more powerful and reinforcing will be the culinary message that Mennonite means ethnic.

(j) Mennonite religion

We must be clear about the fact that ethnicity may quite properly, and often does, include authentic religion. The fusion is natural and creates few problems as long as the ethnic group is geographically or linguistically isolated, or the group, for example like most Jewish groups, does not desire nor undertake active proselytizing or evangelism. For Mennonite Brethren, Biblical anabaptism is the religion and Mennonite, in Canada, the US, and some other countries, is the primary ethnic group. If we call both Mennonite, and the church begins to become multi-ethnic, then we obviously encounter a logical and very practical and immediate problem. My personal conclusion, after 25 years of observing and studying the matter, is that most Mennonite Brethren do not fully recognize the problem and that some simply do not want to deal with it because they find the present arrangement personally satisfying and pleasant, even though they know that theologically and logically it is indefensible. Of course, there are also many MBs who understand the basic issues and who believe that the present arrangement should be retained. They believe that the ethnic emphasis reinforces the theological emphasis. I respect them and their views.

(k) Mennonite museums

It has been said that "Religious groups build memorials, ethnic groups build museums." Mennonites in Canada do both, which is not surprising given their ethno-religious identity.

The best known and most impressive Mennonite museum in Canada is located near Steinbach, Manitoba. The Manitoba Mennonite Historical Society began planning for it in 1950. On April 25, 1958 a museum committee, including Mennonite Brethren leader Rev. John A. Toews, was elected and it set to work. On September 3, 1967, Manitobans came out by the thousands to attend the official opening celebration of this major Mennonite Centennial project, the new Mennonite Village Museum. With the stated objective, "to preserve our Mennonite heritage," the 40-acre spread has been strikingly successful.

As I spent hours viewing the Mennonite buildings; studying the Mennonite artifacts; inspecting the Mennonite furniture; photographing the hollyhocks in the traditional Mennonite garden; meditating in the white clapboard Mennonite church, one of 27 major attractions; sauntering through the Mennonite House-Barn (that's the designation on the official map); sitting in the Mennonite school; and eating delicious Mennonite food in the Mennonite Livery Barn Restaurant, I rediscovered more of my ethnic roots. Unfortunately I missed the "Hog-Butchering, Mennonite Style." The colourful restaurant placemat with its 13 "Low German Sayings", also translated into English, completed my journey into my past. Having finished my borscht and verenikji, I was in a mood to visit the Mennonite bookstore to fill my briefcase with Mennonite ethnic literature. I did. Anyone who visits this Mennonite museum and still insists that in North America tortillas are as Mennonite as "tweeback," can surely not do so with a straight face.

Over the years this Mennonite museum has received extensive publicity, regionally as well as nationally. Even before it opened, the *Winnipeg Free Press* gave it almost full-page coverage. The account contains neither the word "Christian," nor "anabaptist," nor even "religion," but as part of the ethnic description mention is made of "a combination church-school house." [113] Years later the *Kitchener-Waterloo Record* carried a major Canadian Press 4-column news story and CP Laserphoto on "a peaceful village where centuries of history come into focus." The account drew attention to the Mennonite house and barn, the "traditional Mennonite dishes" served in the restaurant, the handicrafts, the clothing, the religion, etc. The Canada-wide perception of Mennonites as ethnic was thus powerfully reinforced. The same effect was achieved with much greater, though regional, thoroughness when the Manitoba Telephone Company a few years ago put a full-colour photograph of the Mennonite Museum on the cover of its hundreds of thousands of directories.

This major mirror of Mennonite ethnicity has hit the big time. It's now listed in the prestigious *Michelin Guide of Canada* as a unique attraction: the Mennonite Village Museum, "an excellent example of Manitoba's ethnic, living heritage." Perhaps that is why a current study for the future development of the museum is funded about 75% by the federal government with the provincial government adding another $2,000 grant and private groups providing the rest. The hundreds of thousands of tourists and school children who have visited this fascinating establishment during the past two decades have taken the ethnic message far and wide.

There are other, lesser, Mennonite museums in Canada. Kitchener regularly promotes its "Mennonite Joseph Schneider Haus," an 1856 Mennonite homestead, and the *Waterloo Region Tourist Guide*, Fall, 1981 invites tourists to tour the large Mennonite Brubacher House, a museum located on the University of Waterloo campus. It "features early Mennonite furnishings and utensils." "To arrange meetings and other visits call Conrad Grebel College 885-0220."

Nor will BC's Mennonites be left out. An April, 1986 report stated that "The Mennonite Historical Society of B.C." was planning to build a Mennonite farm museum near Chilliwack.[115] A December, 1986 news story reported that the Society had accepted an offer of an eight-acre site of free land, made by the Municipality of Chilliwack, for that purpose.[116] Obviously the municipal fathers see great tourist potential.

In some respects Mennonite ethnicity may slowly be declining but one gets the impression that, at least via the message from Mennonite museums, the public awareness of Mennonite ethnicity is still increasing markedly.

(1) Mennonite Central Committee Relief Sales

MCC relief sales, which during the past 15 years have proliferated across Canada and the US, constitute one of the best expressions of Christian charity and humanitarian relief. But they also serve other important purposes, most notably, they express and reinforce Mennonite ethnicity in powerful ways. Mennonite quilts, Mennonite foods, and Mennonite crafts and artifacts of all sorts occupy centre stage. Any sponsoring participation by non-ethnic Mennonites, such as Vietnamese, however much appreciated, is strictly marginal and is not what draws the huge crowds by the tens of thousands. The busloads from Toronto and Detroit do not come to New Hamburg to sample tortillas, or Chinese or Vietnamese food. As the press, radio, and TV annually remind us, they come to eat Mennonite food.

Mennonite ethnicity has rarely received such a big boost. Beyond that, Mennonite relief sales, and all the related work, consolidates Mennonite ethnicity by bringing together Russian-German and Swiss-German Mennonites from wide regions and fostering extensive mingling and greater unity. That, too, is an important development in the resurgence of Mennonite ethnicity in North America.

I have all too briefly surveyed 12 elements in Mennonite culture. Much more could be said. I have ignored Mennonite furniture; one can read Lynda Musson-Nykor's, *Mennonite Furniture: The Ontario Tradition in York County*.[117] Much more should also be said about Mennonite schools,

Mennonite cultural radio, Mennonite credit unions, Mennonite producers and consumers co-ops, Mennonite family traditions and customs, Mennonite child-raising, the complex Mennonite networks of familiarity, the continental networks for socializing, Mennonite Christmases, and, most importantly, the collective Mennonite memory. This memory can energize an ethnic group for generations, especially if reinforced by central religious convictions and strong religious institutions.

Vast sections of Mennonite art have also been ignored. For example, a major ethnic milestone was achieved when Gathie Falk's work, in several modes, enjoyed an extended display at the Vancouver Art Gallery. "It was the largest retrospective ever granted a single artist at the gallery."[118] Gathie Falk's work in ceramics, on canvas, and using other mediums, received a major and very positive review in Toronto's *Globe and Mail*, October 14, 1985. A published introduction to this Christian Mennonite and her work is available.[119] Readers should at least know of works such as Nancy-Lou Patterson's, *Mennonite Traditional Arts*[120] and her more specialized, *Mennonite Folk Art of Waterloo County.*[121] Hopefully Hildegard Froese Tiessen's very useful survey, "The Role of Art and Literature in Mennonite Self-Understanding," which, almost unintentionally, makes an irrefutable case for Mennonitism as ethnic, will be published soon.[122] And if you wish to know about developments in Mennonite art in Southern Ontario read about "The most ambitious exhibition of Ontario Mennonite folk art ever staged." It "opened at the London Regional Art Gallery on September 14, 1985."[123]

We must also take note of the very important Chair in Mennonite Studies established in 1978, at the University of Winnipeg, "to give students an opportunity to study the cultural, religious and literary heritage of the Anabaptist-Mennonites...."[124] The "vision and material means of Mennonite leaders, of Dr. David Friesen and of his family, and of the Federal Government of Canada through its multicultural department made the establishment of the Mennonite Studies program possible." We should note that using its "University Endowment Assistance Program," the Canadian government has made possible the establishment of ethnic university chairs not only for Mennonites ($300,000 federal government money), but also for Hungarians, Ukrainians, and Acadians.

As holder of the Mennonite Chair at the University of Winnipeg, Harry Loewen has succeeded admirably in making Mennonites, and Canadians generally, much more aware of the Mennonite heritage. As founder and editor of the *Journal of Mennonite Studies* he has helped to make the study of ethno-religious Mennonites academically respectable. Volume I (1983) of this new journal contains the scholarly papers read at the international "Symposium on Mennonite Studies in North America," held at the University of Toronto, June 10-13, 1982. That watershed symposium, incidentally, was jointly funded by the Multicultural History Society of Ontario, the Mennonite Historical Society of Canada, and the Ethnic and Immigration Studies Program of the University of Toronto. Volume II (1984) deals largely with the Russian Mennonite experience and literature. Whoever thinks that in North America Mennonite does not and need not mean ethnic, should read these two fine volumes.

Lest I be misunderstood, let me emphasize that although I believe firmly that the Christian mandate requires anabaptists to stress religion, not culture, literature or history, and to indicate that priority in church and denominational names, I have no quarrel with academics who combine the various aspects. After all, in the past and even in the present, ethnic and religious were, and still are largely, combined. If the Chair in Mennonite Studies sends the message that for many Mennonites religion and ethnicity are fused, it is sending an accurate message.

Similarly, I have no negative reaction to Winnipeg's new Mennonite Studies Centre (Menno Simons College),[125] the new Mennonite Centre in Toronto,[126] the new Russian-Mennonite Studies emphasis at Conrad Grebel College,[127] or the innovative Menno Simons Centre in Vancouver.[128] All of these ventures demonstrate that there is much Mennonite culture and ethnicity to be studied, that religion plays a major role in Mennonite identity, and that Mennonites are a viable and culturally vigorous people. These recent academic ventures show clearly how at least some elements of anabaptism have continued as an authentic aspect of a noble ethnic tradition, they help us to understand the present, and may even provide enlightenment for future redirection.

When I survey the vast array of Mennonite culture in Canada and study the trends, I must agree whole-heartedly with Al Reimer: The "cultural explosion among Mennonites in this generation, especially in the urban environment of Winnipeg, has been so spectacular that it has actually outdistanced itself."[129] It has, indeed, left many Mennonites behind. Maybe this ethnocultural exuberance and assertiveness is, in part, a small part of a compensation technique. Maybe it is the expression and the fate of "a people without a homeland."[130]

6. *Views of "New" Mennonites*

One way of assessing whether or not Mennonite means ethnic, a particular kind of ethnic, in North America involves enquiring of those, coming from other cultures, who join Mennonite churches.

Upon leaving for a Mennonite Brethren pastorate in California, Louis Paul Lehman wrote in 1976: " 'I didn't know you liked buggies...and black hats...Is Edna going to wear a bonnet?' Such were the responses when I said I was going to California to assume a pastorate...Mennonite Brethren....I was constantly explaining Mennonite Brethren."[131] Although Lehman was very grateful for the reception the MBs accorded him, he never escaped from the ethnic question.

Commenting on the ethnic banter which often follows services at many MB churches, Nelda Burdett writes, "It illustrates the tensions that exist as a result of barriers unintentionally erected within the church because of ethnic and cultural tradition."[132] Gwen, a non-Mennonite who attended an MB church for 5 years and then left, said, "When we first attended,...fellowship was great." But things changed and became "different. I was lonely and got tired of always initiating friendships with little response."

Barry, "proud to have been reared Mennonite Brethren," husband of Gwen, adds, "I feel sorry for non-Mennonites coming in. There's a token response, but when it comes down to it — 'Hey, baby, you ain't in.' "

Dale, "from a non-Mennonite background, puts it a little differently: 'We were not a member of the club. It isn't a spoken thing and it's difficult to put your finger on, but it's strong. I mean it's STRONG! We felt the ethnic bond often took the place of oneness in the body of Christ. This was one reason we left.'"

Karen, "reared in a Mennonite Brethren home," soon "became disillusioned by what she observed. 'I experienced various disappointments and frustrations.... For one thing, non-Mennonite Brethren people were told they didn't belong.'"

Jim, reared MB but who left later, said, "I taught a high school Sunday school class and was dismayed to see non-Mennonite Brethren kids being shut out. Ethnic pride can and often does come before being one with all believers in Christ.'"

Dick and his wife left after attending an MB church for seven years. At first "There was great fellowship and excitement concerning being one in Christ. Ethnic barriers didn't seem to exist." But soon "cultural barriers became evident. Jean and I continued to actively serve and work, but felt less and less a part." Then they left.

Camile and her husband, Trevor, coming from non-Mennonite Brethren backgrounds, have decided to stay. Their experiences were more positive. Importantly, their experience shows that a predominantly Mennonite congregation can handle the ethnic question wisely and satisfactorily.

Sam and Julie have also decided to stay "but feel strongly about cultural exclusiveness." Sam says,

When we first visited the church people were friendly right off. But after a time we felt we were visiting someone else's family. There were few people that weren't related or knew each other from way back when. Conversations revolved around relatives, acquaintances or activities within the MB structure. And unexplained inside jokes spoken in German left me feeling like a knot on a log.

Matt and Carla, also from a non-MB background, have decided to stay, but Matt has some observations to make: "however, there are some staunch Mennonite Brethren who seem to consider it of greater importance to be MB than Christian. But they are just human.... I'm not saying they should do away with their ethnic ways but just rearrange some priorities."

Some take a sanguine attitude. Rita, of non-MB background, observes, "These people do have a strong ethnic background, and I'm not part of that. But that's no problem. I do not go there because of ethnic culture."[133]

In sum, this survey makes it very clear that MBs are strongly perceived as being ethnic and that ethnic emphases in the church can cause serious problems. It also reinforces the point that a rearrangement of priorities, a change of emphasis in the church, is just as important as any shift to a non-ethnic name.

The May 1, 1984 issue of *The Christian Leader* carried several articles on "The New Mennonites." Some "new" Mennonites report positive experiences. However, the reports of negative experiences are disquieting. Charlene Schmidt, who married a Mennonite, writes, "I've found that cultural tradition has become a bondage to some Mennonites. I often praise God that this isn't part of my life."[134] Catharine Peters, a non-Mennonite who married a Mennonite in Winnipeg, writes: "...Lord, give me strength to deal with those people who insist I'm not a 'real' Mennonite because I'm from a different background."[135]

John Cosens describes the experiences he and his wife, Brenda, had in Manitoba.

As we neared the church building I read the sign that stood on the grass in front: 'Braeside Evangelical Mennonite Church'. One word on that sign stood out from the others, so much that it stopped me in my tracks. It was not the word Braeside, or the word evangelical. You guessed it — it was the word *Mennonite....*

We soon joined the church because we saw these people as our brothers and sisters in the Lord. However, even though we joined the church, we did not consider ourselves Mennonites. The word Mennonite identified, to us, an ethnic group. Although we could go along with the doctrines of the church and could join in the fellowship and worship, we could never change our cultural heritage.

It wasn't long, however, until we discovered that the word Mennonite was being used in two different ways... cultural...spiritual....[136]

When Ken and Bev Sewell, in Burnaby, BC, "began talking about going back to church," they considered various options. Willingdon Mennonite Brethren Church was only six blocks from their home but "The idea of attending a church with 'Mennonite' in its name had not occurred to them." They finally tried it because "a neighbour nudged them." They eventually decided to attend.[137]

Almost all of the evidence seems to point in one direction. The name "Mennonite" is perceived as ethnic and constitutes an ethnic obstacle. Of course, behaviour which is ethnically exclusive and arrogant also constitutes a major obstacle. These are two distinct problems and they require two different solutions.

Hubert Brown, the black pastor of the Calvary Mennonite Church in Inglewood, California, notes candidly: "Unfortunately, the Mennonite church is held captive by its history and culture.... Average Mennonites are nice people but tribalistic.... The Mennonite church is not multicultural, nor multi-ethnic. But it can be. If Mennonites could be brought up out of their captivity to their history and culture.... Too often Mennonites tend to be closed to others, though appearing open."[138]

The ethnic element can persist among Mennonite Brethren in the US and Canada, long after the German language has disappeared from the worship services and the homes.

He was a new Mennonite with an "English" name. He had come to a Mennonite conference to learn more about his new people. Someone grilled him: "Why are you here? You do not have a Mennonite name."

After more than a dozen years as a Mennonite pastor, a man of Irish descent was told at a conference, "Oh, you're Irish. So you're not really one of us."

These actual incidents surface the problem of identifying Mennonitism with a particular culture.[139]

In this fine article Wally Kroeker nicely identifies the problems — and yet in the end he fails, for he seems not to understand the problem fully. Despite the massive evidence, he asserts, to some extent quoting others: "Remember that to be a Mennonite is to believe a certain way." "Anyone who belongs to a Mennonite church has a Mennonite name." "Enchiladas, curry, tortierre and luku are all 'Mennonite' foods." "Some will even go so far as to say one is a Mennonite by birth.... In other words, they might say, one can be a Mennonite without even being a Christian." "Some will contend that to be a Mennonite is to be 'ethno-religious'...."

The basic problem with Kroeker's responses is that they ignore the fundamental difference between the meaning of Mennonite in North America and a few other countries, and the meaning of Mennonite in the rest of the world. Until that basic difference is recognized and clearly understood — and I shall address it in chapter 9 — Mennonites in Canada and the US cannot solve their ethnic problem.

Speaking at an MCC Canada meeting at Mennonite Brethren Bible College in Winnipeg, on August 30, 1985, David Chieu, a Chinese Mennonite pastor from Saskatoon, reflected this understanding when he said that the emphasis on peace and evangelism "is important not only for you as ethnic Mennonites." And everyone present knew exactly whom he had in mind.

Non-ethnics invariably recognize the difference. Thus Dan Kelly, with years of experience in the Mennonite Brethren church, writes in the *Mennonite Brethren Herald*, "I am not an ethnic Mennonite." He, and all readers, knew exactly what he meant.[140]

7. *Mennonites as tourist attractions*

If you're a tourist, you may have heard about the Mennonites on the CBC — on both radio and TV. On February 12, 1986 Roy Bonisteel, on "Man Alive," which is telecast nationally, called Mennonites, "The number one tourist attraction of the region" around Kitchener-Waterloo. Bonisteel focused almost entirely on the quaintly-dressed Old Order. The half-hour program has a large audience.

Perhaps you read about Mennonites while flying. Air Canada's *en Route* magazine, September, 1984, featured Mennonites and "Buggy Business" on the cover and on pages 19 and 20; "They're the devout people of Ontario's Mennonite country...."[141] If you drove from the West you might already have encountered glossy Mennonite promotion in Manitoba, if not sooner. The *1986 Eastern Manitoba Travel Guide*, published by Tourism Manitoba, mentions or describes Mennonites on pages 53, 54, 55, 90, 92, 100, 103, and 105, with several instances involving full-page spreads. Aside from the numerous references to the Mennonite Village Museum, the booklet refers to "traditional Mennonite dress," "Mennonite artists," and " 'faspa', a Mennonite tradition not unlike the British tea time."

If you came to Kitchener-Waterloo, and you tuned in to the major FM station you may have heard, "FM 96 takes you on a trip through

Mennonite country."[142] Or you may have heard the ad for the Waterloo Inn, "The gateway to Mennonite country."

If you had come on November 7, 1985, you could have picked up a copy of Wilfrid Laurier University's *The Cord Weekly*, which had a 2-page spread on "The Mennonites: their history, culture and community."

A back issue of the *Kitchener-Waterloo Record*, with (another) article on the Mennonites, would have told you that, "The history of St. Jacobs is bound up with that of the Mennonites and many visitors express curiousity about the sect."[143]

Had you picked up a copy of *Sparetime*, southern Ontario's "leisure and recreation" magazine, you would almost certainly have read about the fascinating Mennonites in any issue. The October, 1986 issue carried the first of four full-page articles on the Mennonites (page 28). Predictably, the top third had a picture of a score of Old Order women and a buggy.

Waterloo Region, the local glossy tourist handbook, always features the Mennonites — the *Spring, 1986* number up to three times on one page. The folder for Kitchener's Chamber of Commerce says, "see it!"... "Mennonite Countryside"; "taste it!", "Mennonite dishes." The folder for Kitchener's famous Farmers' Market says, "Area Mennonites add rural charm to the friendly atmosphere... apple butter and shoofly pie are among the many Mennonite traditional recipes you and your family will discover...." Province-wide, *Ontario Living*, in its September, 1986, issue carried 3 1/2 pages of Mennonite ethnic content. " 'The prime appeal of the community is definitely the Mennonites,' says Brenda Kempel, manager of the Elmira and Woolwich Chamber of Commerce."[144] Small wonder that Ray Brubacher, a "progressive" Mennonite pastor in the area, "admits there is a lot of confusion about his religion."[145] The *Canadian Geographic Magazine*, in early 1987, will do a feature on Mennonites.

My files are bulging and the flood of material promoting Mennonites as a quaint, ethnic, tourist attraction continues. The biggest increase seems to be at the provincial level. The Ontario government's major tourist production, *Ontario, Yours To Discover*, constantly emphasizes Mennonitism, e.g., "Doon Pioneer Village...an excellent collection of Indian, Mennonite and Scottish artifacts."[146]

It is, thus, not surprising to read that, "The two picturesque Mennonite communities, known for their horses and buggies and good restaurants, are drawing more tourists this summer..."[147], or to see the four-column headline, "Mennonites, a boon to tourism"[148], or to be told that "To tourists, a Mennonite is a person who rides in a horse-drawn buggy and dresses as his grandparents did 100 years ago." And "the first question most tourists ask," in Elmira is, "Where can I see a Mennonite?"

The Mennonite tourist business is booming. It is certainly not yet as big as Lancaster County's where five million tourists per spend $250 million to see the Amish and the Mennonites, but it's growing very fast.[150]

We need to make four points very clear at this juncture. First, if Mennonite truly means religious, it seems very strange and odd that the whole tourist business focuses only on one religion. Baptists, Anglicans, and

Catholics should complain. Second, with modern communication reinforcing the growing tourism trade, what was once mainly a regional image, associated mainly with a few localities, has become, for most Canadians, a national image of Mennonites as fascinating ethnics. Third, even if there were no Amish and Old Order tourist boom, Mennonite Brethren would still have an ethnic problem — the tourist aspect, including the Russian-Mennonite museums, simply complicates and strongly reinforces it — across North America. Fourth, I have no problem with Mennonites being and looking ethnic, even quaint. But I am very concerned about what this does to evangelical Anabaptist churches which call themselves Mennonite!

8. *Mennonites in the media*

In southern Ontario, Mennonites get extensive press coverage. *The Kitchener-Waterloo Record* carries about 8 major Mennonite stories a year, often on the front page, with pictures, and almost always about the Old Order. About 80% of the coverage involves Mennonite school and rural scenes as well as the following type: "Dried-Apple Artistry Used to Create Mennonite Dolls," "In the Mennonite ethnic community...."(Nov. 28, 1984), "Monday was Mennonite Heritage Day at the (Joseph Schneider) Haus with demonstrations of cookery, folklore and crafts." The other 20% deal with such items as barn-raising, Mennonite Disaster Service, Conrad Grebel College, and church affairs. The big Toronto dailies periodically feature Mennonites, almost always focusing mainly on the Old Order. For example, on March 23, 1986, *The Toronto Star*, Canada's biggest daily, carried almost 2 1/2 pages on the Mennonites. All eight pictures, with a 2-column coloured one on the front page, were of the Old Order. The Winnipeg-based dailies tend to give more representative coverage but even they usually deal with Mennonites in terms of culture, business, or education. The slant is heavily ethnic. Such coverage as occurs in other big city dailies also tends to carry a clear ethnic emphasis.

Radio and television coverage, while scanty in comparison to daily press, magazine, and specialty publication descriptions, almost always emphasizes the Old Order and ethnicity. But at times a very clear ethnic description applies specifically to Russian-Mennonites. For example, a Canadian Press story out of Winnipeg, on March 2, 1982, described the father of Manitoba's Roland Penner, a prominent politician, as "Jacob Penner, a Mennonite who fled Czarist Russia,...a founder of the Communist party of Canada," Thus in Manitoba, at least, the assumption is that one can be a Communist Mennonite. The story was carried nationwide. In BC the situation is similar. On November 14, 1979, the front page of the *Abbotsford, Sumas and Matsqui News* featured a "Dutch vs. Mennonite" political contest. That same paper, on October 31, 1979, carried the following on page A5, about the town of Clearbrook.

> With no ethnic slur intended it must be remembered that the name of Abbotford's western neighbor has an ethnic connotation. As Castlegar brings to mind Doukhobors and Inuvik means Eskimos, nearly anyone who recognizes either Yarrow or Clearbrook as placenames will immediately picture a smallish Mennonite community.

As Kathy Shantz Good, of Menno Van fame, discovered, such notions of what Mennonitism means exist throughout Canada. She states, "For instance, a reporter from the Halifax newspaper fully expected to be interviewing two people dressed in black, conservative clothing.... Even a CBC producer for a Toronto talk show couldn't believe we were travelling in a modern motor home.... Even after we would patiently explain that only a small minority of Mennonites drove horses and buggies they would still treat Reg and me as the exception rather than the rule."[151] We can either recognize the situation for what it is, both the pro-Old Order bias and the more general ethnic perception and reality, or we can keep on trying to empty the ocean with a bucket and spend much, mainly wasted, time telling people that Mennonite does not mean ethnic and telling ourselves that we do not have a complex ethnic problem. We might even delude ourselves into believing such statements.

That Mennonites wear black hats and ride buggies is a media stereotype. That Mennonites in Canada and the US are an ethnic group is substance and not a mere media stereotype. It is truth. Only when we acknowledge this fact can we deal with the pressing question.

9. *Statements by Mennonites about Mennonites*

One important way of ascertaining whether Mennonite means ethnic is to investigate what Mennonites in Canada say about themselves. How do we present ourselves? That in many contexts Mennonite means religious is, of course, true. No one disputes that fact. But is there an important second meaning, another reality? Let the evidence speak for itself.

In 1965 the Mennonites of Canada, apparently as an ethnic group of "152,452 Mennonites," presented a brief to Canada's Royal Commission on Bilingualism and Biculturalism. It said: "Two contrasting characteristics of the Mennonite people — internationalism on the one hand and ethnocentrism on the other hand — provide the base for, and background to, this brief."[152] The initiative for the brief came from the inter-Mennonite group which published *The Canadian Mennonite*. Discussing the need for multiculturalism rather than biculturalism the 3-man delegation referred to "Our first-hand experience of Mennonite ethnocentrism...."[153]

In our church settings we have an amazing ability to convince ourselves that primarily Mennonite means religion. But when we speak to governments and other groups, we have an equally amazing ability to say that Mennonite also means ethnic. Let me present some representative illustrations from my thick files.

1978: Mennonite Central Committee (Canada), speaking for a national Mennonite and Brethren In Christ membership of "approximately 88,000," submitted a brief to The Canadian Consultation Council on Multiculturalism.

April, 1979: Rockway Mennonite School in Kitchener staged a Mennonite Arts Festival in a local mall. Thousands of people came to see the pottery, drawings, photography, quilts and "every craft imaginable." The large, six-column picture in the daily paper showed someone weaving.[154]

April, 1980: Another Mennonite arts festival. "The Mennonites have to be one of this area's greatest natural resources. People come from far afield to observe them in their natural habitat, and I do not know whether that's flattering to Mennonites, but the spinoff benefits to this area are uncountable...."

"The Mennonite Festival of the Arts, which gives you a different perspective of their culture, is another example. The seventh annual festival...."

"It's an event at which artists and artisans representing a number of Mennonite groups in Ontario exhibit, perform and demonstrate their arts and crafts. The traditional and always popular crafts such as quilting and fine needlework will be featured along with painting and literature, music and drama."[155]

September 1980: MCC (BC) placed a Relief Sale advertisement in local papers: "...9,000 lbs. Mennonite Farmer Sausage....Prepared Mennonite Foods...."

1980: Publication of an excellent book, *Mennonite Images: Historical, Cultural, and Literary Essays Dealing with Mennonite Issues*, edited by Harry Loewen. "We are grateful to the Multicultural Program, Government of Canada...[and others] for grants which assisted in the publication of this anthology."(p.iv.)

December, 1981: Conrad Grebel College holds a conference on "separation and integration" of the Mennonites as an ethnic group. A significant part of the cost was paid by the government. "Why have a conference on ethnicity when there are all these concerns about nuclear war and global starvation?" the co-convener says in an interview. "Ethnicity is very relevant...."

"All of us need the kind of tradition that an ethnic identity can yield.... A social group like the Mennonites has been an excellent case study of this principle...." *(Kitchener-Waterloo Record*, December 30, 1981, p.8.)

1982: The Alberta Cultural Heritage Council issues its *10th Anniversary Report, 1972-1982*. On page 4 the Minister, the Hon. Mary J. LeMessurier, affirms all "the ethno-cultural communities of the province." More than 50 "ethno-cultural peoples" are represented. Who are these people? The Arab, the Metis, the Chinese, the Lithuanian, the Russian, the Serbian, the Filipino, etc. and the Mennonite, represented between 1973-1981 by the following: "Peter Dyck-Mennonite," "Don Kauffman-Mennonite," "David Lefever-Mennonite," "John Toews-Mennonite". "The members of Council in 1982" includes the Mennonite representative — "David Hubert-Mennonite."

April, 1985: *The Mennonite Reporter*, April 29, page 13, carries a news story, head-lined, "Writers explore Mennonite culture at Winnipeg cabaret." Allan J. Siebert writes, "The winding road of 'Mennonite culture' took another curious turn in mid-April as Mennonite writers attracted sold-out audiences to hear their poems read in a cabaret setting...."

"Jack Thiessen regaled the crowd with a Low German parody of the sermons he heard while growing up...."

"The Just Plumb Hollow Group [a satire of Plum Coulee] singing group had the crowd whooping it up with their renditions of gospel songs...."

"Patrick Friesen took the lead in organizing the 'Missing Mennonite Cabaret'...." [Patrick Friesen is the poet who announced on national radio that he was not a Christian.]

October, 1985: The German-Canadian Congress and the Manitoba Parents for German Education hold a celebration in Winnipeg. "Frank Isaac of the Springfield Heights Mennonite Church represented the Mennonites."[156]

October, 1985: "A succession of arts events at the Mennonite Centre in Toronto continues...."[157]

April, 1986: *The Mennonite Reporter* headlines a news story thus: "Are British Columbia Mennonites really Mennonite?" Trotting out all the credentials, Bruce Hiebert adds, "Nor is our ethnicity in question...."(page 7)

April, 1986: *The Mennonite Reporter* states that: "Residents of Mennonite colonies in four Latin American countries — Mexico, Paraguay, Bolivia and Belize — number some 93,020.... The census is of total residents of European ethnic background, not only baptized church members." (page 3.)

1986: Reports from Multiculturalism Canada are issued. Multiculturalism grants have gone to:

*Rosthern Junior College: for publication of "History of Rosthern Junior College."

*The Mennonite Historical Society of Canada: for publishing *Harvest*, "Anthology of Mennonite Writing in Canada 1874-1974."

*Mennonite German Society of Winnipeg for "Anthology of German-Mennonite Writing in Canada."

*Reinland Centennial Committee, Winkler, Manitoba, for "Reinland: An Experience in Community."

*Mennonite Publishing Service, Waterloo, for "Russian Mennonite Centennial Publication."

*Royden Loewen, Blumenort, Manitoba for "Blumenort. A Mennonite Community in Transition."

*John D. Rempel and Paul Tiessen, Kitchener and Waterloo, for "Forever Summer, Forever Sunday." "Peter Gerhard Rempel's photographs of Mennonites 1980-1917."

*Frank H. Epp, Waterloo, for "Mennonites in Canada, 1920-1940."

*Patrick Friesen, Winnipeg, for "The Shunning." "Poems expressing the author's feelings about his Mennonite past." [Obviously Multiculturalism Canada considers Friesen to be a Mennonite. So does Friesen.]

*George K. Epp and Heinrich Wiebe, The Mennonite German Society of Canada, Canadian Mennonite Bible College Book Store, Winnipeg, for "Unter dem Nordlicht: Anthology of German-Mennonite Writing in Canada."

And many more!

Despite the above, some editors wonder why they get multicultural and ethnic mailings from the governments. And some editors and some others wonder why some people think Mennonite also means ethnic.

Let three informed observers have the last comments in this section.

In 1966 a younger Rudy Wiebe wrote:

The word "Mennonite" does not primarily call up, even to ourselves, a new understanding of Christian discipleship, a body of committed and practicing Christians, an ethic of love in all human relations.

That is the kernel of our Anabaptist spiritual heritage, but it remains obscured behind "Mennonite" folk festivals in Kansas and Pennsylvania, behind "Mennonite" names like Reimer and Yoder, behind borscht and shoofly pie.

The very idea of Mennonite is so ethnic and culture-centred that even a usually enlightened inter-Mennonite paper can decide [to present] a brief... to the Canadian government's Commission on Biculturalism. Blood and culture, not belief, make the Mennonite....

When will we repent of this and ask God's help to cut the spiritual life within our Mennonite churches free from this cultural hangman's noose?

There is not much time left to pray such prayers....

For the Anabaptist vision to survive at all, it must be reinterpreted by men who will not fear to leave behind those things that deserve to be left there; the "Mennonitism" of culture is one of those things.[158]

In 1972 Walter Klaassen, professor of history at Conrad Grebel College, wrote that his "personal experience is that it is difficult for a Mennonite to shed his ethnicity for another but that it's virtually impossible for an 'outsider' to become a Mennonite. There is a tension here that Mennonites will have to face sooner or later."[159]

In 1983 Beth Graybill wrote: "I have a sneaking suspicion that, like a Jew who remains Jewish regardless of religious practices, my Mennonite heritage is an inescapable pain and gift."[160]

10. *The Views of Mennonites who have left the Mennonite church*

Of all the evidence at hand I shall cite only a few items. Already in 1948 the very perceptive and widely recognized expert on Mennonites, E.K, Francis, wrote: "A number of individual Mennonites have joined other churches and sects but are still referred to as 'Mennonites' by other group members. Most of the dissidents remain loyal to the Mennonite group as well as to certain elements of the Mennonite culture."[161]

Presenting a full-page statement of how he switched his allegiances in 1968, Ivan J. Kauffman, former executive secretary of the Mennonite Central Committee Peace Section, stated, "Over the years I've decided I'm a Mennonite Catholic." He explains how he tries to combine the Mennonite and the Roman Catholic tradition.[162]

Speaking to the annual meeeting of the Mennonite Publishing Service which publishes the *Mennonite Reporter*, Eric Friesen of Minneapolis stated: "I am a symbol of a whole lot of Mennonites whom I would describe as non-official Mennonites.... We are cultural Mennonites, fringe Mennonites, occasional Mennonites, or hyphenated Mennonites."[163] I think I know what Eric Friesen means for I sense a kinship with such people. When I see them on TV, hear them on radio, read about them in the papers, watch them on sports teams, read or otherwise enjoy their art, or simply meet them, I experience a sense of kinship, to a considerable degree, even if they are not Christians, let alone anabaptist Christians. I feel as if I am encountering someone who somehow is part of us or at least should be. I experience some common Mennonitism. They are my people. We share at least a human, ethnic peoplehood.

A particularly forthright statement comes from Peter Lorenz Neufeld, for many years very active in Mennonite communities and Mennonite affairs in Manitoba.

Some of my Mennonite relatives and friends claim that when my wife (of same ethnic background) and I left the Mennonite church in late 1950s and joined the United Church, we ceased being Mennonites. Presumably, overnight we reverted to being simply a mixture of ethnic Dutch, Swiss, etc.

To many, it seems, ethnicity (at least where this particular group is concerned) somehow revolves around holding membership in an active Mennonite denomination. Yet, if that silly criteria is applied, then even the children and young people aren't truly Mennonite either until they are baptized and actually join a congregation. Also, is there a cut-off date: 18 years, 25, 30, 40, 50, 60 by when someone must join to become a Mennonite? If not, then someone of similar ethnic background who never joins that Church, or one who leaves it, is every bit as ethnically Mennonite as the most ardent church members....

About nine years ago, a comprehensive study in Manitoba dealt with Changes in Rural Manitoba's 'Ethnic Mosaic' 1921 to 1961. Population figures were divided into four broad groups: British, French, other whites, non-whites. From the 'other whites' category, two ethnic groups were chosen for concentrated study. One was Mennonite because, "Not only does this group most clearly meet the qualifications of 'ethnicity', but numerically it represents one of the more important ethnic groups in the province...."

Even if there's no country Menno, the term 'Mennonite' as commonly used now revolves around ethno-nationality factors — relates to terms like Anglo-Saxon, Swede, Ukrainian, rather than (to) narrow church affiliation... like Anglican, Lutheran and Catholic. It may have started out like that four centuries ago, but it's obviously not like that today....

I...consider myself an ethnic Mennonite and am proud of it.... But I do see red whenever someone suggests that changing to another denomination somehow changes my ethnicity. No way! That revolves around conceiving babies, not a pen stroke. Nothing on earth can change the fact that an ethnic Mennonite I was born and an ethnic Mennonite I will die.[164]

In a more restrained manner the Hon. Jake Epp, who grew up as a Mennonite Brethren and was active for decades in the MB church, still says, "I perceive myself to be a Mennonite.... If I told the secular press that I wasn't Mennonite, they would ask, 'What do you mean?' " Jake Epp several years ago ceased being a member in a Mennonite church.[165]

11. *Description of Mennonites in scholarly literature*

Again one encounters massive evidence. Let the reader consider this representative documentation or research the literature himself.

At the end of World War II the Manitoba government, together with a regional historical society, funded research into ethnic groups. In 1945 the sociologist, E.K. Francis, began his path-breaking research among Manitoba Mennonites. Almost a decade later his major research publication began with this sentence, "The Mennonites of Manitoba are a small but distinctive group within the ethnic mosaic of the oldest of Canada's Prairie Provinces."[166] At the end of his volume he wrote, "When we look for the factors responsible for the striking revival of Mennonite group solidarity in Manitoba we are thinking first of the three basic elements of their social fabric: the region, the church and the family."[167] "History, more than anything else, provides the Mennonites with an intelligible explanation of the fact that they have remained distinct from their neighbors. It gives them a feeling of being something better than all the others."[168] And in his closing paragraph he writes that, "They have changed and still are changing from a religious group to an ethnic group."[169]

After Francis' pioneering work on Mennonites in Manitoba a veritable floodtide of ethnic evidence ensued. Mennonites are a distinct ethnic group and "Kultur Mennonitism" now exists in tension and conflict with Biblical Christianity, said George Thielman.[170] Winfield Fretz wrote that, "American Mennonite communities today are still characterized by their ethnically homogeneous character...."[171] Leo Driedger came to similar conclusions. "Compared to other ethnic groups in Winnipeg, Mennonite cultural identity was as strong as any, including that of the Jews."[172] Non-Mennonite scholars agreed. Chapter 20 in a history of ethnic groups in British Columbia describes Mennonites as one of 44 major groups. The analysis is sandwiched between chapters on "Baltic Peoples" and "The Doukhobors." G.G. Baerg, the major consultant to the writer, also served as a member of the 35-person "Ethnic Organizations Sub-Committee of the British Columbia Centennial '71 Committee."[173] The situation was the same in Alberta.

Land of the Second Chance: A History of Ethnic Groups in Southern Alberta, by Howard Palmer (Lethbridge: *The Lethbridge Herald*, 1972), has a chapter on Mennonites. Explaining the relationship between religion and ethnicity Leo Driedger noted that, "The Jews, like Mennonites, have depended a great deal upon their religious community for the socialization of their offspring into the ethnic enclave."[174] At the same time Frank Epp said that, the "religious meaning of 'Mennonite' was supplemented, and sometimes overshadowed, by a new cultural and ethnic meaning." Mennonites, "were at the same time Dutch, German, and Russian, yet not really any one of these. They were marked by both ethnic and religious characteristics, but their superficial definitions of both their own ethnicity and their own religiosity tended to invalidate each other and to be mutually exclusive."[175]

Frequently Mennonites are put in a category with Hutterites and Doukhobors. Dealing with what Canadians think of ethnic groups,

Gardner and Kalin note that a large-scale study revealed "a fourth very distinctive cluster represented" by "Doukhobors, Hutterites, and Mennonites."[176] In similar vein *Canadian Families Ethnic Variations*, edited by K. Ishwaran (McGraw-Hill Ryerson, 1980), has a chapter on Mennonites, Hutterites, Doukhobors, etc.

In Ontario the perception of Mennonites as being ethnic is now well established. *The 1981-1982 Ethnocultural Directory of Ontario* discusses Mennonites as one of the regular ethnic groups in Ontario (Pages 27, 62, 105, etc.) In June, 1982, about 50 academics from Canada and the US met at the University of Toronto in a conference entitled, "Mennonite Studies in North America: The State of the Art." If the establishment of the chair in Mennonite Studies in 1978 marked the formalization of Mennonite Studies as an independent academic pursuit, the 1982 Toronto conference marked its formal recognition and acceptance on the campus of the country's biggest and most highly regarded university as well as in the academic community generally. The 1982 catalogue of *Mennonite Source Material Held by the Multicultural History Society of Ontario* lists taped interviews with 196 individual Mennonites, many Mennonite Brethren names are listed. The society also has 17 reels of microfilm material describing 79 Mennonite churches. In its "Ethnocultural Voices Series" the Society has a 1982 hardcover book, *The Gordon C. Eby Diaries, 1911-13: Chronicle of a Mennonite Farmer*, edited by James M. Nyce.

James Urry, the currently popular non-Mennonite expert and guru in Mennonite Studies, writes that "For a hundred years 'Russian' Mennonites have been searching for an identity acceptable both to themselves and to the wider world."[177] "The Russians had always considered Mennonites a distinct group of colonists. Though mainly from West Prussia and using a low-German dialect the Mennonites were not considered 'German' colonists."[178] "Most Mennonites felt little or no allegiance to Germany."[179] The "term 'ethnic group' was increasingly accepted as a term to describe their own communities" in Canada.[180] Since the beginning of Multiculturalism, "Mennonites have been active in the multicultural programs, receiving grants and income from government advertisements in Mennonite newspapers promoting multiculturalism.... Low-German has been revived, particularly in plays.... Kulturfests have been arranged, with men dressed in dark costumes and women in nineteenth-century crinolines.... There has even been a Mennonite beauty queen."[181]

Again and again scholars arrive at the same conclusions. "Jews, Hutterites, and Mennonites are especially noted as ethno-religious groups who set themselves apart from the larger society, and these communities are also seen as being traditional."[182] Some Mennonite scholars have begun writing about themselves, for example, Laura H. Weaver's, "A Child's Own Vision of Mennonite Plainness" in the *Journal of Ethnic Studies* (Fall, 1984), pp. 51-59. An excellent scholarly analysis of Mennonite life in Canada, combining historical and sociological perspectives, is Hans Mohl's *Faith and Fragility: Religion and Identity in Canada*

(Trinity Press, 1985), pp. 354. Many scholars have provided useful explanations. John W. Friesen states that "...Mennonites certainly fall into the category of a separate and distinctive culture." And, quoting Winfield Fretz, he adds, "What began as a strictly religious group has in the course of history also become a distinctive cultural group."[183] Al Dueck writes that, "Historically and psychologically the ethnic group predates modernity.... Entry is by birth and continuing membership comes by conformity.... The Mennonite community is part of the ethnic tradition...."[184]

Donald Kraybill's research deserves special attention because of his keen insight. He states that, "This analysis takes for granted the fact that the Mennonite experience is an ethnic experience...." An ethnic identity "is rooted in some distinctive sense of its history."[185] He continues. "While there has been a consistent historical consciousness in traditional Mennonite ethnicity, the primary time orientation was fixed on the immediate present. Relatively speaking, beliefs and definitions of ethnicity were quite homogeneous". "In spite of the much acclaimed virtues of 'voluntarism' and 'believer's church', ethnic group membership was intrinsically assumed and taken for granted as the 'way things were or would be'."[186] "Modernization transformed the local and immediate ethnicity of the past into a more generalized, abstract and universal ethnicity.... Mennonite literature, novels, dramas, films, other artistic expressions such as the *Festival Quarterly*" express "a high degree of ethnic self-consciousness.... The outburst of abstract expressions of ethnicity, bottled up for several generations, pouring forth now in the form of novels, plays, films, music and dissertations, are in many ways functional equivalents of the older concrete symbols.... The hallmark of Mennonite identity today is first and foremost historical...."[187]

Kraybill offers a fascinating and critically important comment on history, one which helps us understand the growing emphasis placed on, and budgets assigned to, Mennonite Brethren historical centers, archives, historical associations (to which I also belong), and historical writing. Significantly, such historical emphases are found in all MB post-secondary schools and the most important one of all is associated with the theological training center, the Mennonite Brethren Biblical Seminary in Fresno, California. Mark his perceptive comment well: "...one might argue that a group's attention to or preoccupation with its own history is an operational measure of its degree of ethnicity."[188] It follows, then, that when Russian-Mennonites and Swiss-Mennonites go back to the Mennonite shrines of Europe, in tours or through literature or other media, they are drawn closer together. History becomes a major Mennonite common denominator. "And perhaps most importantly, history is a palatable and polite form of ethnic identity in a multicultural modern society...."[189]

"As the modern Mennonite navigates back and forth between numerous social worlds in the course of a day, Mennonite identity can be conveniently disguised or displayed in accordance with the situational requirements. Mennonites can 'pass' as a typical citizen or raise the Mennonite flag...the modern Mennonite professional likely has several resumes, each reflecting the 'appropriate' degree of ethnicity for the particular situation."[190] Kraybill hit the nail right on the head. I have three different resumes, just as he assumes.

Today, in North America, says Kraybill, we find "At least a hundred Mennonite periodicals and magazines of all sorts which are part of the portable networks.... The proliferation of ethnic organizations provides a relatively high degree of institutional completeness, a functional equivalent of the older agrarian community."[191] Thus the ethnic reinforcements remain strong. In fact, "In areas with a large Mennonite population, it is possible to go from the cradle to the grave in a Mennonite institution. With the exception of going to prison, a Mennonite can live in an institutionally complete ethnic world consisting of school, work, leisure, travel, insurance, credit union, therapist, physician, lawyer, camp, retirement community, and professional organizations, to name just a few of the ethnic institutional worlds."[192] Many other vocations could be added. For example, in numerous communities there are also Mennonite funeral directors and even specifically Mennonite cemeteries. For Kraybill, "The epitome of the portability and completeness of the social structure undergirding Mennonite ethnicity is 'Mennonite Your Way Hospitality' where one can travel coast to coast and around the world in a Mennonite world!"[193]

Kraybill notes that "Some scholars...have worried that this transformation of ethnicity is an identity crisis which signals the demise of Mennonitedom...." But, "The proliferation of both formal and informal Mennonite institutions garners well for the future of Mennonite ethnicity, since such institutions not only provide the plausibility structure to maintain and transmit a world view, but as institutions they are by their very nature imperialist."[194] Clearly the proclaimers and prophets of the death of Mennonite ethnicity are as far removed from the truth as were those misinformed and misguided souls who, a few decades ago, arrogantly assured the world of "the death of God."

12. *Field research dealing with Mennonite ethnicity*

Since there are more than twice as many Mennonites in Canada as there are Icelandic people in Iceland, it is not surprising that during the last two decades various quantitative field research projects have been undertaken. We shall review some of the important studies.

In 1971 the journal, *Canadian Ethnic Studies*, carried an article by John W. Friesen describing a survey of Mennonite and non-Mennonite views about Mennonite identity.[195] This southern Alberta survey involving lengthy interviews with ninety Mennonites and thirty non-Mennonites, but only non-Mennonites "who had some knowledge of Mennonite ways,"[196] revealed that "no significant differences (statistical) existed between Mennonite and non-Mennonite responses for any of the questions."[197] In other words, both groups held virtually identical views concerning Mennonites. For example, "87 of 90 Mennonites and 29 of 30 non-Mennonites agreed that there exists such an entity as a Mennonite subculture in Canada.... It is clearly indicated... that the ways, manners and customs of Mennonites differ significantly from those of other Canadians, so that they are easily distinguished by non-Mennonites as well."[198] Friesen concludes, "The perpetuation of Mennonite culture is assured if the opinions of persons interviewed in this study is any indication."[199]

The 1971 Friesen survey revealed one major difference between Mennonite and non-Mennonite responses. For readers who take seriously "The Basic Questions" spelled out in an earlier section of this monograph, the Mennonite response is disconcerting while the non-Mennonite response underlines the very great urgency of the re-direction task at hand. Concerning "Mennonite Parents' Goals for Their Children," 33% of the Mennonite respondents opted for "Being Mennonite," 22% for "Being Christian," with 36% identifying "Function in Both Worlds." However, only 1 non-Mennonite checked the option which said that Mennonite parents had "Being Christian" as the highest goal for their children while an incredible 50% of the non-Mennonite responses identified "Being Mennonite" as the highest goal of Mennonite parents. What an indictment even this limited survey reveals — only 2.6% of non-Mennonite responses credit Mennonite parents with ranking "Being Christian" at the top while 50%, 19 responses, were checked for "Being Mennonite." The respondents were allowed more than one responses — the 30 non-Mennonites provided 38 responses.[200] A final noteworthy finding in this survey was that half of the respondents doubted whether Mennonites would "ever" be assimilated into the dominant culture.[201]

Field studies have repeatedly come to similar conclusions. A 1973 survey by Leo Driedger and Jacob Peters revealed that considering endogomy (marrying your own kind), choice of friends, participation in ethnic organizations, and several other factors, "Mennonites possessed a higher identity supported by a greater institutional completeness than that of other Germans."[202]

In 1975, after completing a major study of Mennonites in rural and urban settings, Leo Driedger reported his findings. As part of the research Driedger compared 820 ethnic students in Winnipeg and found that "the Mennonites, Jews and French score much higher than other ethnic groups with respect to six cultural identity factors (language use, endogamy, choice of friends, and participation in religion, parochial schools and voluntary organizations.) Comparison of sample of students indicated that the Mennonite composite behavioural identity score was the highest...followed by the French and Jews."[203] Significantly, "A majority of the Mennonite sample were urban students, which indicates that Mennonite cultural identity in Winnipeg is high."[204]

For the 8 groups the composite score was:

Mennonites	59.0	Polish	31.5
French	55.0	British	29.3
Jewish	44.2	German	28.9
Ukrainian	36.8	Scandinavian	16.4

Of all these groups the Mennonites were the most ethnic. Thus, if we are honest with ourselves and with one another, we must not only acknowledge that Mennonite ethnicity is vigorous and strong, but also accept the fact that among the 8 groups assessed it was easily the strongest.

Surveying his evidence Driedger concludes, not surprisingly, that "The establishment and maintenance of an ethnic community may be a good Old Testament Jewish model, but it hardly seems adequate as a New Testament model." [205] Driedger finally says that which responsible church and conference leaders should have said long ago. Instead they rejected or ignored the message when it was raised by a few lonely voices. [206]

In 1984 John W. Friesen undertook another major survey, a national study of "Concepts of Mennonites in School Curricula." [207] Friesen surveyed 22 Mennonite educational institutions, from elementary schools to colleges. In only two schools were Mennonite values studied in the context of "ethnic groups." [208] Much emphasis was placed on Mennonite history while the study of anabaptist theology also ranked high. Interestingly, in the matter of "Course aims/objectives," the option "To instruct in appreciation for Mennonite and Anabaptist heritage and history" received 18 notations, while, "To teach an appreciation for the Anabaptist position (theologically)" received only 17. "To teach biblical appreciation" received only 2. "To teach Anabaptist/Mennonite values, faith, beliefs" received 13. [209]

"The results of this survey," writes Friesen, "lend support to the idea of schooling as maintaining culture." [210] That assessment is made despite the fact that concerning certain questions many schools insisted that they were emphasizing religion rather than ethnicity. The data deems to point in the other direction.

As part of his research Friesen also contacted 200 school districts in the five Western provinces. His response rate varied from 39.6% in Saskatchewan to 72% in Manitoba and 73.2% in Ontario. Of the 114 districts which responded, 59, or 52%, indicated that they had Mennonite content in their curriculum. [211] The reasons for including Mennonite content warrant close attention. Thirty-nine districts checked, "To teach tolerance and appreciation for other lifestyles," 14 checked "Historical significance," and 12 "To note contribution to past and present." [212]

Friesen's concluding recommendations include the following:

"1. The Mennonite community will have to struggle with and hopefully, settle the matter of identity, i.e., are they a cultural, religious, ethnic group, or an admixture of these traits....

2. Since this survey attracted many requests for relevant and pertinent information about Mennonites, this is a challenge that should probably be taken up, and even considered an open door." [213]

13. *Statements by governmental and other officials concerning Mennonite identity*

As part of my research I wrote about 12 government agencies and organizations to ascertain their views. Since the recipients all were somehow related to ethnic groups, I phrased my main sentences as follows: "Specifically I would like to know whether your agency considers Mennonites to be part of a larger German ethnic group, whether you consider Mennonites to be a separate ethnic group, or whether you do not consider Mennonites to be an ethnic group. I am not looking necessarily for any official policy statement but only for an indication of general perception and practice." I also enquired about grant applications. the letters went out during 1985 and early 1986.

I sent letters to the governments of the five western provinces, as well as the government of Canada, and to several ethnic organizations. The relevant government agencies in B.C. and Ontario promised to send an answer but never did. The nine letters which follow constitute the total of all answers which I received to my questions.

Note that all 9 respondents consider Mennonites to be an ethnic group. In particular, note that in Manitoba, Mennonites have registered with the Manitoba Intercultural Council. All of the letters reflect keen perception but the analysis by Professor Harney is exceptionally instructive. Surely these responses should tell us something very important. Or do we simply dismiss them?

The letters are appended in chronological order.

The
Multicultural History Society
of Ontario

17 April 1985

Professor John H. Redekop
Co-ordinator of Canadian Studies
Wilfrid Laurier University
Waterloo, Ontario
N2L 3C5

Dear Professor Redekop,

Your letter of March 18th was forwarded to me by Mrs. Wally
Mraz.

Mennonites are considered to be an ethnic group in their
own right in the day-to-day operations of the Society.
For example, primary and secondary source materials on
the group are catalogued under the "Mennonite" heading
in our archives collection.

Yours sincerely,

Lillian Petroff, PhD
Postdoctoral Fellow

Saskatchewan
Culture and
Recreation

Saskatchewan

3rd Floor, Ratner Building
1942 Hamilton Street
Regina, Saskatchewan
S4P 3V7

December 2, 1985

Mr. John H. Redekop, Ph.D.
Professor of Political Science and
Coordinator of Canadian Studies
Wilfrid Laurier University
Waterloo, Ontario
N2L 3C5

Dear Mr. Redekop:

Thank you for your letter concerning your current research
project on the ethnic designations of cultural groups.

One of the functions of the Department of Culture and Recreation
is to serve as a consultative body to cultural organizations,
both provincial and local. Through the department, the provincial
government provides financial assistance to an extremely
wide range of organizations for projects with an event greater
range of diversity.

This year, the department provides funding for the MennoVan,
a travelling exhibit across Canada explaining the history
of the Mennonite community in Canada from 1786-1986. From
the perspective of the department, then, cultural groups
have already defined their ethnic identity in real terms
of purpose, goals and objectives, prior to their approach
to the department. In this sense, the department's role
is one of acceptance rather than interpretation.

The Saskatchewan German Council is an umbrella organization
which represents all German speaking people throughout the
province, including the Mennonite community. Generally speaking,
however, the Mennonites are regarded as a separate ethnic
group based primarily on their religion and their cultural
history.

. . . 2

Saskatchewan
HERITAGE
1985
Commemorating our Past, Building our Future

Because of my background in cultural anthropology, I find
the questions of ethnic identity a fascinating one. It is
a subject that I would be delighted to discuss with you.

Please call me at 787-5728 if I can be of any further assistance.

Sincerely,

Chuck Sutyla
Director
Arts and Multicultural Branch

CS/cn

CULTURE
Cultural Heritage Division

2nd Floor, 12431 Stony Plain Road, Edmonton, Alberta, Canada T5N 3N3   403/427-2927

December 10, 1985

Professor John H. Redekop
Wilfrid Laurier University
WATERLOO, Ontario
N2L 3C5

Dear Professor Redekop:

I enclose a copy of the definition of "culture" and ethnicity" we use
here at Cultural Heritage. You may recognize the latter as having
originated in the <u>Harvard Encyclopaedia of American Ethnic Groups</u>.(1981)

Our practise is to allow community groups to decide for themselves whether
they are an ethnic group. The Mennonites of Alberta have chosen to accept
this self-definition and to participate on our advisory body – The Alberta
Cultural Heritage Council – where they have played an active role.

Regarding your second question, I have no record of any grant applications
being made by Mennonite organizations.

Sincerely,

W.R. Petryshyn
Director
Cultural Heritage Division

Enclosure

WRP/ol

Manitoba

**Minister of
Culture, Heritage
and Recreation**

Winnipeg, Manitoba, CANADA
R3C 0V8

December 17, 1985

John H. Redekop, Ph. D.
Professor of Political Science and
Co-ordinator of Canadian Studies
Wilfred Laurier University
Waterloo, Ontario
N2L 3C5

Dear Professor Redekop:

This is to acknowledge receipt of your letter dated November 29, 1985
inquiring about the Mennonite community in our province.

We in this province have accepted the principle that ethnocultural
communities have the right to determine how they wish to be identified. The
Mennonite Community has chosen to be identified as a separate ethnocultural
group from the German community and participates as such in various
intercultural endeavours.

Funding from my Department of Culture, Heritage and Recreation is
available to ethnocultural organizations for the purpose of preserving and
sharing culture. Those ethnocultural organizations who comply with this
criteria are eligible to apply for grants for operations, special projects and
linguistic support. The Mennonite community has for the most part availed
itself of the Linguistic Support program and have received in 1983-84
$7,640.00; 1984-85 $14,060.00; 1985-86 $25,000.00 for a special grant for
Mennovan, however, final figures for the disbursement of grants in this fiscal
year are not yet available.

Should you require any further information or clarification, please
contact Nadya Bailey of my staff, at 8th Floor - 177 Lombard Avenue, Winnipeg,
Manitoba, R3B OW5 or telephone (204) 945-4509.

Please accept my best wishes for the Holiday Season.

Yours truly,

Eugéne Kostyra
Minister

**Manitoba Youth
Moving Ahead
International
Youth Year 1985**

**THE
UNIVERSITY
OF CALGARY**

THE RESEARCH CENTRE FOR
CANADIAN ETHNIC STUDIES

2500 University Drive N.W., Calgary, Alberta, Canada T2N 1N4

Telephone (403) 220-7257

December 23, 1985

Dr. John H. Redekop
Department of Political Science
Wilfrid Laurier University
Waterloo, ON   N2L 3C5

Dear Dr. Redekop,

In acknowledgment of your letter regarding the ethnic designation
of Mennonites, the editors of Canadian Ethnic Studies consider
the Mennonites to be a separate ethnic group.

We hope this is helpful in your research and wish you good luck.

Sincerely,

Myrna Neyland

for   A.W. Rasporich
Co-Editor
CANADIAN ETHNIC STUDIES

AWR/mh

Olympic Village and Speedskating - 1988

December 27, 1985

Dr. John H. Redekop, Ph.D.,
Professor of Political Science,
Wilfrid Laurier University,
Waterloo, Ontario,
N2L 3C5

Dear Dr. Redekop:

In response to your letter of November 29, 1985, I wish to advise
you that Mennonites are registered with the Manitoba Intercultural
Council as a separate ethnocultural community. I wish to explain
this by noting that under our By-laws, copy of which is attached,
every ethnocultural community has the right to be represented,
and the basis for determining representation is a community's
<u>self-identification</u>. Therefore, it is up to the community orga-
nization itself to determine its own ethnicity. In practice,
every Mennonite-based organization has indicated its identification
with Mennonite rather than as German. It is my understanding
however, that Mennonites do also consider themselves to be a germanic
as distinct from a German people.

I trust this will be useful to you. Please accept my apologies
for the delay in responding to your request. If you have any
questions I would be pleased to discuss this with you.

Sincerely,

Michael Goeres,
Executive Secretary.

mm

Enclosure

MG-12352(a)

Manitoba

105

The
Multicultural History Society
of Ontario

January 10, 1986

Professor John H. Redekop
Coordinator of Canadian Studies
Wilfrid Laurier University
Waterloo, Ontario
N2L 3C5

Dear Professor Redekop:

In response to your letter about Mennonite identity, I write more as academic director of the Multicultural History Society and the University of Toronto Ethnic and Immigration Studies Program, I guess, than as past president of the Canadian Ethnic Studies Association.

I believe that the Mennonites of Canada are best understood as an ethnic group. When we use the ethnonym Mennonite here, we mean the evolving ethnoculture and sense of peoplehood which has grown up over time among early Mennonite immigrants of Germanic descent as well as the infusion of Russlander Mennonite culture in the last ninety years or so.

I must admit that when the Multicultural History Society organized the Mennonite conference a few years ago, I was taken aback by a call or two from historians complaining that we should run Anglican or Presbyterian conferences, and that Mennonites were only a religion, not a people. My response was that we mount conferences on Jews, not on Judaism, and were making a similar distinction between ethnos and religion in this case; or at least that we were concentrating on profane history in North America, not sacred history, theology or Old-World history.

My certainties were further shaken by several young Mennonite journalists at the conference who pointed out to me that there

...2

were more Mennonites in Zaire or Taiwan than in Ontario. Ethnic
groups don't proselytize, but I persist in my view that there is
by ethnogenesis a North American ethnic group called Mennonite,
no matter how religiously inspired the original peoplehood was,
or what divisions exist between Russlander and earlier people.

I should also add that I find it absurd, or at least a
confusion of language and racialisms with nationality, when
"scholars" of the larger German group decide to incorporate the
Mennonite experience. They are often the same chaps who put
Einstein on the covers of books about German immigration, but
don't bother to mention Jews as Germans inside the covers.

I hope this helps and is not too idiosyncratic.

Yours sincerely,

Professor Robert F. Harney
Academic Director

Department of the Secretary
of State of Canada

Multiculturalism

Secrétariat d'État
du Canada

Multiculturalisme

Ottawa, Ontario
K1A OM5

February 3, 1986

Professor John H. Redekop
Coordinator of Canadian Studies
Wilfrid Laurier University
Waterloo, Ontario
N2L 3C5

Dear Professor Redekop:

     In response to your request concerning Mennonites,
I am enclosing listings of projects funded under
Multiculturalism's Canadian Ethnic Studies Program, Writing
and Publications Program and Canadian Ethnic Histories
Program. As you will note, Mennonite projects are funded
and listed as Mennonite projects and not as German projects
or as a sub-group under the heading of German projects.
Mennonites are definitely considered to be an ethnic group.

Yours sincerely,

Adrian Papanek
Program Officer
Canadian Ethnic Studies

Enc.

Canada

UNIVERSITY OF SASKATCHEWAN

DEPARTMENT OF SOCIOLOGY

SASKATOON, CANADA
S7N OWO

John H. Redekop   March 21, 1986
Coordinator of Canadian Studies,
Department of Political Science,
Wilfred Laurier University,
Waterloo, Ontario
N2L 3C5

Dear Dr. Redekop:

As part of a national interdisciplinary research project dealing with
ethnic designations, you have inquired whether my "agency" considers
Mennonites to be part of a larger German ethnic group, or to be a separate
ethnic group, or not an ethnic group.

In reply, first I must explain that I am no longer editor of the Canadian
Ethnic Studies Assoc. Bulletin, nor has a new editor been officially appointed
yet (though it will likely be Dr. Cornelius Jaenen, History Dept., University
of Ottawa). Nor do I represent that association in any capacity. On the
other hand, as a regular researcher and writer on Mennonites, and as past
editor of the Bulletin, I can comment that Mennonites are usually considered
a unique ethnic group in social science publications, better yet as an "ethno-
religious" group. Most Mennonites view themselves this way, ie. quite distinct
from the German Canadians as a whole, with their own Mennonite historical
tradition, customs, religious affiliation, and at least dialect (if not
language). My own research, and others', has revealed exceptions, however:
people who strongly claim Mennonite ethnicity but not religious affiliation,
also people (such as many "liberal" General Conference Mennonites) who claim
to be Mennonite churchgoers but not ethnic Mennonites, ie, who deny that
Mennonites are an ethnic group.

I suppose the inevitable "safe" conclusion is that Mennonites are not easy
to classify!

Sincerely,

A.B. Anderson
Assoc. Professor

ABA:srs

This was one person's "official" response.

"Hey, man, where'd ya get the groovy outfit?"

While the Government of Ontario did not officially answer my letter, I did receive various materials. The listing on page 23 in *Multicultural Information* speaks for itself.

MULTICULTURAL
INFORMATION
A SELECTED BIBLIOGRAPHY
OF MATERIALS
AVAILABLE IN THE MINISTRY
NOVEMBER, 1985

The Ontario Ministry of Citizenship and Culture

ETHNOCULTURAL GROUPS
GENERAL

A.   Americans, Amish, Anglo-Saxons, Arabs, Asians

B.   Balts, Blacks, Byelorussians

C.   Chileans, Chinese, Croatians and Slovenes, Czechs

D.   Doukhobors, Dutch

F.   Finns

G.   Germans, Greeks, Gypsies

H.   Haitians, Hispanics, Hungarians

I.   Indians, Italians

J.   Japanese, Jews

L.   Lithuanians

M.   Macedonians, Maltese, Mennonites

N.   Norwegians

P.   Pakistanis, Poles, Portuguese, Punjabi

S.   Scots, Slavs, Slovaks, Sudetans

U.   Ukrainians

V.   Vietnamese

W.   West Indians

Y.   Yugoslavs

In concluding this section I wish to draw attention to the official stance of the Canadian government. On November 18, 1982, the Canadian Press carried a news story about Perrin Beatty, Progressive Conservative MP, revealing in the House of Commons that the government had a "confidential list of 130 ethnic groups." The Mennonite Central Committee was on the list and that information was carried across the country. In a bold, five-column headline on page one, the *Kitchener-Waterloo Record*, November 18, 1982, read, " 'Ethnic list' includes Mennonites." Most of the House of Commons debate centered on the fact that some groups, but not the Mennonites, were described as "neo-Nazi, racist, extremely anti-Semitic, communist, radical," etc.

What I found more intriguing than the inclusion of Mennonites in the official list, which did not surprise me at all, was the reaction of Jacob Letkeman, director of MCC Manitoba, who was quoted as being "annoyed," and of Ray Schlegel, director of MCC Ontario, who apparently was surprised. Why should Mennonites be surprised if, after having applied successfully for many ethnic grants, they are then included in an ethnic list?

A few days later the Ottawa director of MCC Canada, responded. "The director of the Ottawa office of the Mennonite Central Committee (MCC) will recommend that the agency seek neither an apology nor an explanation from the federal government for including it in its 'ethnic list'."[214] William Janzen was entirely correct. Having paraded ourselves as ethnic for generations, why should we even consider requesting an apology or explanation, as many Mennonites wanted done?

14. *Conclusion: Mennonites are ethnic*

Reviewing all of the evidence presented in this lengthy chapter as well as in previous sections, I believe that I have substantiated my hypothesis that in North America, and in a few other countries, there is a strong ethnic group called "Mennonite." I have clearly demonstrated that Mennonites in contemporary Canada constitute an ethnic group. Are we now agreed that it is an indisputable fact that in addition to its religious meaning, "Mennonite" also refers to a specific ethnicity?

Of course, in some respects Mennonite ethnicity is declining, some acculturation has occurred, but in some other important respects, it is still growing. But even if there is a net decline, which is questionable, the public perception and stereotypes, largely based on reality, will not change for generations. Mennonite will continue to mean ethnic in Canada for a long time. Not only is reality still being reinforced, but also, in these matters, reputation outlasts reality by at least a generation.

How should we, Christian Mennonites, react to demonstrated Mennonite ethnicity? Some people can see no problem. Katie Funk Wiebe writes: " 'If you're a Mennonite, why do not you wear black stockings and an apron?' A third grader questioned my young daughter a number of years ago.... We chuckled when a perplexed daughter reported the conversation at the dinner table."[215] I have in mind a different response; for me the issue is not particularly a laughing matter.

I consider Mennonite ethnicity to be deeply rooted and vigorous. I believe that Mennonite ethnicity, in itself, is positive and praiseworthy.

I consider some present attitudes, practices, and some name usages as unwise, unnecessary and confusing. And I shall shortly present a three-part proposed solution to the Mennonite "ethnic problem."

Chapter 4 — FOOTNOTES

1. Donald B. Kraybill, "Modernity and Identity: The Transformation of Mennonite Ethnicity," in a paper read at Conrad Grebel College, Waterloo, ON, May 30, 1986, p. 8. See also Alan Anderson and James Frideres, *Ethnicity in Canada: Theoretical Perspectives* (Toronto: Butterworths, 1981), pp. 38-45.
2. Kraybill, *ibid.*, p. 9.
3. Jack Bavington *et al.*, *Culture in Canada* (Toronto: 1976), p. 27.
4. Stephanie Bernarda, *The Ethnic Almanac* (New York: Doubleday & Co., 1981), pp. 31, 99-100, 251, 252, 292, 535.
5. Paul Wasserman and Jean Morgan, (eds.), *Ethnic Information Sources of the United States* (Detroit: Gale Research Company, 1976), p. 190, 743.
6. For example, Alfred Hecht, R. G. Sharpe, and A. C. Y. Wong, *Ethnicity and Well-Being in Canada* (Marburg: Selbstverlag des Geographischen Instituts der Universitaet Marburg, 1983), p. 10.
7. *A Day in the Life of Canada* (Toronto: Collins, 1984).
8. *Ibid.*, pp. 66-67.
9. *Mennonite Reporter*, July 7, 1986, p. 6.
10. Stephen Thernstrom, (ed.), *Harvard Encyclopedia of American Ethnic Groups* (Cambridge: Harvard University Press, 1980), pp. 1076.
11. *Ibid.*, p. 697.
12. See, for example, Anderson and Frideres, *ibid.* pp. 38, 43, 184, etc.; Hecht, *ibid.*, p. 10.
13. Charlotte Sloan Cooper, *The Mennonite People* (Saskatoon: Western Extension College Educational Publishers, 1978), p. 66.
14. *Ibid.*, p. iii.
15. *Mennonite Reporter*, April 15, 1985, p. 12.
16. *Ibid.*, p. 12.
17. *Abbotsford, Sumas & Matsqui News*, March 7, 1979, p. 13A.
18. *Mennonitische Rundschau*, November 27, 1985, p. 15.
19. *Mennonitische Rundschau*, December 25, 1985, p. 31.
20. *Mennonitische Rundschau*, March 19, 1986, p. 22.
21. *Mennonitische Rundschau*, October 1, 1986, p. 12.
22. "The *Mirror's* Faith in the Future", September 20, 1983, p. 30.
23. *Mennonite Mirror*, April, 1985, p. 4.
24. *Festival Quarterly*, February-March, 1983, p. 19.
25. *Festival Quarterly*, May, June, July, 1983, p. 11.
26. May, June, July, 1982, p. 10.
27. W. Isajiw, "Definitions of Ethnicity", *Ethnicity*, I, 1974, p. 121. This rediscovery may be symbolic or substantive. For Canadian Mennonites, to the extent that there is a rediscovery rather than a continuity, the rediscovery is clearly substantive rather than symbolic.
28. Philippians 4: 8.
29. *Mennonite Reporter*, November 11, 1985, p. 5.
30. Ron Rempel, "Play the Mennonite game, but play it right", *Mennonite Reporter*, July 7, 1986, p. 6.
31. *Mennonite Reporter*, December 9, 1985, p. 12.
32. See, for example, December 13, 1974, p. 32.
33. Harold Jantz, "On being who we are," *Mennonite Brethren Herald*, January 11, 1985, p. 11.
34. James Coggins, "Where do Mennonite Brethren fit in?" *Mennonite Brethren Herald*, May 17, 1985, pp. 3-4.
35. James Pankratz, "Mennonite Identity," *Mennonite Brethren Herald*, October 18, 1985, p. 21.
36. *Ibid.*, p. 21.
37. *Ibid.*

38. Jim Coggins, "Since you are Mennonite...," *Mennonite Brethren Herald*, May 16, 1986, p. 2.

39. *Ibid.*, p. 3.

40. *Ibid.*

41. *Ibid.*

42. *Ibid.*

43. *Ibid.*, p. 2.

44. *Kitchener-Waterloo Record*, November 9, 1970.

45. Quotations are taken from glossy promotional literature distributed across North America. One brochure is entitled, "Your passport to North America's largest multicultural event."

46. *Mennonite Mirror*, September 1981, p. 22.

47. *Ibid.*, p. 22.

48. *Ibid.*, pp. 11-12.

49. Harold Jantz, "What business do we have in Folklorama?" *Mennonite Brethren Herald*, August 29, 1980, p. 13.

50. Harold Jantz, "Mennonites in Folklorama," *Mennonite Mirror*, November, 1980, p. 27.

51. *Mennonite Mirror*, April, 1984, p. 24.

52. *Mennonite Reporter*, December 24, 1984, p. 4.

53. "A Guide to the Mennonite Bicentennial," Waterloo: Mennonite Bicentennial Commission and Mennonite Publishing Service, March 31, 1986, p. 17.

54. *Ibid.*, p. 17.

55. *Ibid.*, p. 5.

56. *Ibid.*, p. 15.

57. *Ibid.*, p. 2.

58. *Ibid.*

59. *Ibid.*, pp. 16-17.

60. *Mennonite Reporter*, August 18, 1986.

61. *Ibid.*, p. 9.

62. E. K. Francis, "The Russian Mennonites: From Religious to Ethnic Group," *The American Journal of Sociology*, LIV, 2, September, 1948, pp. 101-107. The quotation comes from footnote 7, p. 105.

63. Alan Peters, "The Impact of the Family in Mennonite History," *Direction*, July, 1972, pp. 74-81. The quotation is found on page 78.

64. The 5 in the last category are "Dick-Dyck-Dueck, Reimer, Klassen, Rempel, Neufeld."

65. Edward Brandt, "The Meaning of Mennonite Names," *The Western Producer*, July 3, 1975, p. C2.

66. *Mennonite Mirror*, June, 1985, pp. 12-13.

67. *Mennonite Reporter*, July 8, 1985, p. 14.

68. Katie Funk Wiebe, "The New Mennonite Brethren: In But Still Out?" in a paper read at Mennonite Brethren Bible College, Winnipeg, November 15, 1986, p. 2.

69. *Ibid.*, pp. 13 and 14.

70. *Mennonite Reporter*, December 8, 1986, p. 2.

71. For example, Anderson and Frideres, *ibid.*, p. 42 f. 7.

72. See, for example, "Mennonite like me" by columnist Tom York, *The Cord Weekly*, January 23, 1986, p. 7.

73. Elmer S. Miller, "Marking Mennonite Identity," *The Conrad Grebel Review*, Fall, 1985, pp. 251-263. See especially page 260.

74. Melvin Gingerich, *Through Four Centuries* (Breinegsville, PA: The Pennsylvania German Society, 1970), pp. 192.

75. See eight review excerpts in *Mennonite Reporter*, April 15, 1985, p. 11.

76. "Treasures from the Mennonites' past," *Kitchener-Waterloo Record*, June 8, 1974, p. 21.

77. *The Muskoka Sun*, August 15, 1985, p. 9.

78. Margaret Loewen Reimer, *One Quilt, Many Pieces: a Concise Reference Guide to Mennonite Groups in Canada* (Waterloo, ON: Mennonite Publishing Service, 1984), pp. 60.

79. *Mennonite Reporter*, July 28, 1986, p. 10.

80. *Mennonite Reporter*, September 2, 1985, p. 8.

81. *Kitchener-Waterloo Record*, July 4, 1986, p. C2.

82. *Mennonite Reporter*, November 10, 1986, p. 13.

83. *Mennonite Reporter*, November 11, 1985, p. 8.

84. Wesley Berg, *From Russia With Music* (Winnipeg: Hyperion Press, 1985).

85. *Mennonite Brethren Historical Society Newsletter*, vol. VIII, No. 1, May, 1986, p. 3.

86. *Mennonite Reporter*, April 15, 1985, p. 13.

87. "Mennonite Media Society Inc.; Understanding Ourselves, Sharing Ourselves," A brochure, Winnipeg, n.d.

88. Hildegard Froese Tiessen, "The Role of Art and Literature in Mennonite Self-Understanding." A paper read at Conrad Grebel College, May 19, 1986, p. 6.

89. For a useful discussion with Good see, Sanford Pinsker, "Interview Mennonite as Ethnic Writer: A Conversation with Merle Good," *Journal of Ethnic Studies*, Vol. 3, No. 2 (Summer, 1975), pp. 57-64.

90. *Mennonite Reporter*, October 28, 1985, p. 8. On the same page the date is also given as October 7.

91. *Ibid.*

92. *Ibid.*

93. *Mennonite Reporter*, November 10, 1986, p. 13.

94. Roy Vogt, "The Most Widely Read Mennonite Writer," *Mennonite Mirror*, 3, No. 5, 1974, p. 6.

95. Harry Loewen, (ed.), *Mennonite Images: Historical, Cultural, and Literary Essays Dealing with Mennonite Issues* (Winnipeg: Hyperion Press, 1980).

96. Margaret Loewen Reimer and Paul Tiessen, "The Poetry and Distemper of Patrick Friesen and David Waltner-Toews" in Harry Loewen, and Al Reimer, (eds.), *Visions and Realities* (Winnipeg: Hyperion Press, 1985), pp. 243-253.

97. John L. Ruth, *Mennonite Identity and Literary Art* (Scottdale, PA: Herald Press, 1978), pp. 72.

98. Jim Doelman, "Mennonite Literature: An Outsider's View," *Mennonite Mirror*, November, 1986, pp. 11-12.

99. *Ibid.*, p. 11.

100. Katie Funk Wiebe, "Low German: The Language of the True Believer," *Festival Quarterly* August, September, October, 1983, pp. 12-14.

101. Hildegard Tiessen, *op.cit.*, p. 25.

102. Al Reimer, Anne Reimer, and Jack Thiessen, (eds). *A Sackful of Plautdietsch*, (Winnipeg: Hyperion Press, 1983), pp. 190.

103. John Thiessen, *Mennonite Low-German Dictionary; Mennonitisches Woerterbuch* (Marburg: N. G. Elwert Verlag, 1977), pp. xii, 70.

104. Herman Rempel, *Low German Dictionary, Kjenn Jie Noch Plautdietsch?* (Altona, MB: Friesen Printers, 2nd ed. 1984), pp. 295. Published by the Mennonite Literary Society.

105. James C. Juhnke, "Mennonite History and Self Understanding; North American Mennonitism as a Bipolar Mosaic." A paper read at Conrad Grebel College, May 30, 1986, p. 20.

106. *Kitchener-Waterloo Record*, October 11, 1980.

107. Louise Siemens, "A Theology of Zwieback," *The Christian Leader*, May 11, 1976, pp. 5-6.

108. *Ibid.*, p. 5.

109. *The Christian Leader*, July 6, 1976, p. 20.

110. *The Christian Leader*, September 8, 1981, p. 13.

111. *Ibid.*, p. 18.

112. Miriam E. Warner, "Mennonite Brethren: The Maintenance of Continuity in a Religious Ethnic Group," University of California, Berkeley, 1985, p. 89.

113. *Winnipeg Free Press*, February 25, 1967, p. 8.

114. *Mennonite Reporter*, August 18, 1986, p. 13.

115. *Mennonite Reporter*, April 14, 1986, p. 3.

116. *Mennonite Reporter*, December 22, 1986, p. 10.

117. Lynda Musson-Nykor, *Mennonite Furniture: the Ontario Tradition in York County* (Toronto: James Lorimer, 1977), pp. 95.

118. *Mennonite Reporter*, November 11, 1985, p. 8.

119. *Gathie Falk Perspective* (Vancouver: Vancouver Art Gallery, 1985), pp. 78.

120. Nancy-Lou Patterson, *Mennonite Traditional Arts* (Toronto: Canadian Antiques Collector, 1971).

121. Nancy-Lou Patterson, *Mennonite Folk Art of Waterloo County* (Toronto: Ontario Historical Society, 1969).

122. Hildegard Froese Tiessen, "The Role of Art and Literature in Mennonite Self-Understanding." A paper read at Conrad Grebel College, May 29, 1986.

123. *Mennonite Reporter*, September 30, 1985, p. 8.
124. "Mennonite Studies," *University of Winnipeg Journal* February, 1984, p. 9.
125. See the *Mennonite Reporter*, April 29, 1985, p. 4.
126. *Mennonite Reporter*, February 4, 1985, p. 10.
127. *Mennonite Reporter*, December 9, 1985.
128. *Mennonite Reporter*, September 15, 1986, p. 3.
129. Al Reimer, "Two Solitudes: Mennonite Version," *Mennonite Mirror*, June, 1, p. 30.
130. Hans-Juergen Goertz, "The Confessional Heritage in its New Mold: What is Mennonite Self-Understanding Today?" A paper read at Conrad Grebel College, May 28, 1986, p. 6.
131. *The Christian Leader*, May 25, 1976, p. 7.
132. Nelda Burdett, "Shut out? Do ethnic barriers still make people feel excluded from our churches? Yes, say some who left." *The Christian Leader*, November 4, 1980, pp. 6-7. The quote is from page 6.
133. *Ibid.*, p. 7.
134. *The Christian Leader*, May 1, 1984, p. 4.
135. *Ibid.*, p. 5.
136. *Ibid.*, p. 7.
137. *Ibid.*, p. 9.
138. Hubert Brown, "Becoming a Salad Bowl?" *Festival Quarterly*, Summer, 1984, pp. 12-13.
139. Wally Kroeker, "So you're not really one of us: One view of Mennonite ethnicity," *The Christian Leader*, July 23, 1985, p. 2.
140. *Mennonite Brethren Herald*, October 18, 1985, p. 27.
141. Max Wickens, "Buggy Business," *en Route*, September, 1984, p. 19.
142. November 25, 1986 and many other times.
143. *Kitchener-Waterloo Record*, September 18, 1980, p. 15.
144. *Ontario Living*, September, 1986, p. 21.
145. *Ibid.*, p. 20.
146. *Ontario, Yours to Discover*, May, 1984, p. 10.
147. *Kitchener-Waterloo Record*, August 21, 1986, p. B3.
148. *Kitchener-Waterloo Record*, May 22, 1980, p. 7.
149. *Ibid.*, p. 7.
150. *Kitchener-Waterloo Record*, July 7, 1986, p. D1.
151. *Mennonite Reporter*, September 15, 1986, p. 11.
152. *The Canadian Mennonite*, December 28, 1965, p. 6. The initiative for the brief came from the inter-Mennonite group which published *The Canadian Mennonite*.
153. *Ibid.*, p. 7.
154. *Kitchener-Waterloo Record*, April 30, 1979, p. 21.
155. *Kitchener-Waterloo Record*, April 22, 1980.
156. *Mennonite Reporter*, October 28, 1985, p. 16.
157. *Mennonite Reporter*, October 28, 1985, p. 9.
158. Rudy Wiebe, "Last Chance for Mennonites," *The Canadian Mennonite*, January 18, 1966, p. 7.
159. *Mennonite Reporter*, June 26, 1972, p. 8.
160. Beth Graybill, "Thinking About Being Mennonite," *Festival Quarterly*, August, September, October, 1983, p. 7.
161. E. K. Francis, "The Russian Mennonites: From Religious to Ethnic Group," *The American Journal of Sociology*, LIV, 2, September, 1948, pp. 101-107. The quotation appears on page 106.
162. Ivan J. Kauffman, "Confessions of a Mennonite Catholic," *Mennonite Reporter*, November 11, 1985, p. 5.
163. *Mennonite Reporter*, March 4, 1985, p. 5.
164. Peter Lorenz Neufeld, "On 'Being Mennonite'," *Mennonite Mirror*, January, 1985, pp. 17-18. These excerpts are taken from page 17.
165. *Mennonite Reporter*, October 13, 1986, p. 3.
166. E. K. Francis, *In Search of Utopia; the Mennonites of Manitoba*, (Altona, MB; D. W. Friesen & Sons, 1955), p. 1.
167. *Ibid.*, p. 276.
168. *Ibid.*, p. 277.
169. *Ibid.*, p. 278.

170. This is the central thesis of George G. Thielman's unpublished Ph.D. dissertation, "The Canadian Mennonites: A Study of an Ethnic Group." Western Reserve University, 1955.

171. Winfield Fretz in *Mennonite Encyclopedia*, vol. I, 1959, p. 656.

172. Leo Driedger, "The Anabaptist Identification Ladder," *Mennonite Quarterly Review*, 51, October, 1977, p. 285.

173. John Norris, *Strangers Entertained; a History of the Ethnic Groups of British Columbia*, (Vancouver, British Columbia: Centennial '71 Committee, 1971), pp. 254. See p. viii.

174. Leo Driedger, ed., *The Canadian Ethnic Mosaic* (Toronto: McClelland & Stewart, 1978), p. 278.

175. Frank H. Epp, "Problems of Mennonite Identity", in Leo Driedger, ed., *The Canadian Ethnic Mosaic* (Toronto: McClelland & Stewart, 1978), p. 283.

176. Robert C. Gardner and Rudolf Klein, *A Canadian Social Psychology of Ethnic Relations* (Toronto: Methuen, 1981), p. 46. The chapter in question was written by Francis E. Aboud. See also pages 28, 199 and 200.

177. James Urry, "Who are the Mennonites?", *Arch. europ. sociol.*, XXIV (1983), pp. 241-262.

178. *Ibid.*, p. 246.

179. *Ibid.*, p. 247.

180. *Ibid.*, p. 256.

181. *Ibid.*, p. 259.

182. Leo Driedger, Raymond Currie, Rick Linden, "Dualistic and Wholistic Views of God and the World", *Review of Religious Literature*, vol. 24, no. 3, March, 1983, p. 229.

183. John W. Friesen, *When Cultures Clash: Case Studies in Multiculturalism* (Calgary: Detselig Enterprises, 1985), p. 149. Chapter 7 is entitled, "Mennonites in Canada."

184. Al Dueck, "Psychology and Mennonite Self-Understanding." A paper presented at Conrad Grebel College, May 30, 1986, pp. 1-2.

185. Donald B. Kraybill, "Modernity and Ethnicity: The Transformation of Mennonite Ethnicity." A paper read at Conrad Grebel College, May 30, 1986, p. 7.

186. *Ibid.*, p. 19.

187. *Ibid.*, p. 20.

188. *Ibid.*, p. 21.

189. *Ibid.*, p. 22.

190. *Ibid.*, p. 24.

191. *Ibid.*, p. 27.

192. *Ibid.*, pp. 27-28.

193. *Ibid.*, p. 28.

194. *Ibid.*, p. 29.

195. John W. Friesen, "Characteristics of Mennonite Identity: A Survey of Mennonite and Non-Mennonite Views," *Canada Ethnic Studies*, III (June, 1971) pp. 25-41.

196. *Ibid.*, p. 25.

197. *Ibid.*, p. 26.

198. *Ibid.*, p. 27.

199. *Ibid.*

200. *Ibid.*, p. 37.

201. *Ibid.*, p. 38.

202. Leo Driedger and Jacob Peters, "Ethnic Identity: A Comparison of Mennonite and Other German Students," *Mennonite Quarterly Review*, vol. XLVII, July, 1973, pp. 225-244. The summary quotation is taken from Donovan E. Smucker, *The Sociology of Canadian Mennonites, Hutterites and Amish: A Bibliography with Annotations* (Waterloo, ON: Wilfrid Laurier University Press, 1977), pp. 75-76.

203. Leo Driedger, "Canadian Mennonite Urbanism: Ethnic Villagers or Metropolitan Remnant?" *Mennonite Quarterly Review*, vol. 49, July, 1975, pp. 226-241. This statement appears on page 230.

204. *Ibid.*, p. 230.

205. *Ibid.*, p. 234.

206. See, for example, John H. Redekop, "The Mennonite Brethren as a Believers' Church," *Yearbook of the Canadian Conference of Mennonite Brethren Churches* (Winnipeg: Christian Press, 1978), pp. 142-158, especially pp. 153 ff.

207. John W. Friesen, "Concepts of Mennonites in School Curricula," Calgary, 1984, undertaken for the Mennonite Bicentennial Commission of Waterloo.

208. *Ibid.*, p. 11.

209. *Ibid.*, p. 13.
210. *Ibid.*, p. 20.
211. *Ibid.*, p. 22.
212. *Ibid.*, p. 27.
213. *Ibid.*, pp. 34-35.
214. "Ethnic listing all right, Mennonite office rules." *Kitchener-Waterloo Record*, November 24, 1982.
215. Katie Funk Wiebe, *Who Are The Mennonite Brethren?* (Winnipeg: Kindred Press, 1984), p. 3.

STEINBACH • MANITOBA
CANADA

MENNONITE VILLAGE MUSEUM

Our Living Heritage

CHAPTER FIVE

ARE MENNONITE BRETHREN ETHNIC?

1. *The Present Situation*

If chapter 4 has documented the assertion that in general, Mennonites in Canada are perceived as being ethnic and tend to function as ethnics, might it still be plausible that Mennonite Brethren, as a smaller and more carefully circumscribed subgroup, are not substantially ethnic? To that question we now turn our attention.

The various brochures, articles in denominational periodicals, and most historical accounts describing the Mennonite Brethren Church generally ignore the matter of ethnicity. For example, a recent undated, 8-page, glossy brochure entitled, "Introducing the Mennonite Brethren Church," states, "The word 'Mennonite' in our name links us with Menno Simons, who, like other Reformers, emphasized faith based on Scripture. The word 'Brethren' suggests equality of members within the church irrespective of status in society or ethnic background. The word 'Church' identifies us as the 'redemptive community'." There's certainly no hint of ethnicity here.

In an otherwise perceptive, if perhaps overly sympathetic, discussion of Mennonite identity, the prominent editor and spokesman, Harold Jantz, downplays the question of ethnicity. He recognizes as a great challenge the problem of "How to make the transition to a fellowship of churches which can communicate their faith and full acceptance to people of all ethnic backgrounds...."[1] But nowhere does he acknowledge that the Mennonites rooted in Russia are themselves an ethnic group whose church vision has been encumbered by an ethnic web.

Ken Reddig, the knowledgeable Canadian MB historian and conference archivist, takes a similar stance. In his various writings he seems to recognize the reality of Mennonite Brethren ethnicity while simultaneously ignoring, almost denying, its theological significance. For example, in describing the recently formed, largely French-speaking, Mennonite Brethren conference in Quebec he writes as follows. "Only a handful of the 626 members (1985 yearbook) are of Mennonite extraction. Yet these French Canadian MBs are in every sense Anabaptist-Mennonite."[2] Now if there is such a thing as "Mennonite extraction," and Reddig correctly states that there is, and if the Quebec MBs are not of Mennonite extraction, then by what stretch of logic can they be "in every sense Anabaptist-Mennonite," as Reddig insists? The answer, of course, is that they are not Mennonite in "every sense" of the term. They are not of "Mennonite extraction," for they were not born as ethnic Mennonites.

In several later statements in the same article Reddig appears to acknowledge the reality, although he never does so explicitly. "In fact, some of them consider themselves more Anabaptist than Mennonite." He also quotes one "French Canadian Mennonite" thus, "We can relate to the problems of the early Anabaptists with the state church.... It is often difficult to identify with Russian-Mennonite historical concerns."[3]

The November, 1983 compilation *Another Look at the Mennonite Brethren Church*, edited by Canadian Conference minister Henry Brucks, contains thirty-four brief essays, none of which deals with ethnicity. In fact, ethnicity is mentioned in only one or two. Clearly, most Mennonite Brethren leaders do not see ethnicity as a noteworthy reality, let alone a problem. At least they tend not to discuss it.

In her popular introduction, *Who Are The Mennonite Brethren?* Katie Funk Wiebe expresses similar views.[4] She introduces the MBs as "a body of believers," "a church body."[5] Concerning the designation "Mennonite" she notes that, "The name question keeps coming up. Does the name represent an ethnic or a religious group? Most of our leaders would agree we are not primarily an ethnic group but a denomination with peoples of various ethnic descent among its membership,... So MB can mean almost any racial heritage today."[6] Wiebe, together with almost all other MB writers on the topic, makes the point too glibly. Granted, from a global perspective the Mennonite Brethren designation refers to numerous racial and ethnic groups but that situation does not negate the well-documented fact that in Canada, the US, and several other countries, the designation "Mennonite," does, in fact, refer overwhelmingly to one particular ethnic group. Beyond that, the general North American perception of the category "Mennonite" necessarily affects the meaning of Mennonite Brethren.

Interestingly, when Wiebe later discusses the roots of the Mennonite Brethren in Russia, she acknowledges that Mennonite does, in fact, refer to an ethnic group by referring to people of "Mennonite birth."[7] She also refers to "those who join our congregations from other ethnic backgrounds."[8] Even as she valiantly asserts that Mennonite and Mennonite Brethren are not ethnic designations, she thus repeatedly acknowledges that they are.

The matter of MB ethnicity was already addressed by a few researchers more than a generation ago, although they tended not to use the term. In 1949 John H. Lohrentz broadened the scope of analysis beyond the commonplace historical and theological emphases with his essay,

"Religious and Cultural Background of the Mennonite Brethren."[9] In his M.A. thesis at the University of Toronto in 1951, Jacob John Toews substantially extended the enquiry into social and economic aspects of Mennonite Brethren origins.[10]

More recently a younger generation of MB scholars and leaders has been drawn increasingly into discussion about the nature and role of ethnicity in MB life. While most of these commentators have acknowledged an ethnic aspect, virtually all have minimized its significance. Only a handful have recognized the existence of a problem and fewer than that have addressed it forthrightly.

As early as 1960 Leslie Stobbe, editor of the MB-produced *Mennonite Observer*, spoke of ethnic or race consciousness as an "effective barrier to the fulfillment of our God-given purpose as a church."[11] Rudy Wiebe, as conference-oriented first editor of the Canadian *Mennonite Brethren Herald*, concurred two years later: "the heavy accent is still on Mennonite and not on Brethren. With few notable exceptions our city churches tend to foster ethnic differences rather than Christian witness."[12] In 1970 he made the point again. "On the whole we have remained ethnic in the eyes of the public. And often young people leave simply to get away from old-fashioned ethnicity... rather than because the claims of Jesus Christ are presented too rigorously in our church."[13]

A particularly insightful analysis comes from John E. Toews' reflection on the 1982 "Mennonite Brethren Church Membership Profile" research project.[14] Toews comments on the 1972-1982 comparison thus. "The Profile pictures an ethno-religious group losing its historic religious identity...."[15] With keen discernment he describes how North American Mennonite Brethren are moving through the various acculturation stages of immigrant ethno-religious groups. He suggests that because of "continued waves of immigrants," and several other factors, Canadian MBs experience more "ethnic group resistance to acculturation" than do American MBs.[16] "Mennonite Brethren in Canada", he suggests, "have a critical mass in a more affirmative ecumenical and national setting that nurtures ethno-relogous pluralism generally...."[17] Surveying the larger sweep of events he asserts that, "In the new world the Mennonite Brethren became an ethnically isolated community preoccupied with boundary maintenance."[18]

John E. Toews' analysis is right but still incomplete on two counts. First, as will be explained later, the MB ethnoreligious community was already functioning energetically in Russia before it was established in North America. The second and more important shortcoming in Toews' reflection involves an incomplete assessment of how the denominational retention of an ethnic name substantially undermines efforts to prevent further erosion of Biblically-based Anabaptist distinctives. As we shall see in chapter 6 and 8, Toews has a clear understanding of the general theological issues but seems not to address the matter of practical, corrective action.

In an interesting study of Canadian Mennonite Brethren, presented at the November, 1986 Winnipeg Symposium on "Dynamics of Faith and Culture in Mennonite Brethren History," Peter M. Hamm, whose doctoral dissertation provides much useful information,[19] addresses our present question directly. "Despite obvious change in the degree of ethnicity and the increased self-criticism which it engendered, ethnicity nonetheless prevails...." And again, "Yet, intimations of ethnicity continue to characterize Canadian Mennonite Brethren."[20]

Another noteworthy presentation at the November, 1986 Winnipeg symposium was that by Paul Toews. While not clearly addressing the theological consequences of an ethno-religious fusion, he nevertheless makes numerous sound observations. "The importance of the faith/ culture issue in Mennonite life is heightened by our ethno-religious quality. The Mennonite Brethren, like virtually all other Anabaptist groups, are a religious ethnic group.... We have been a double minority — religious and ethnic.... Even after the forced enclavement was unnecessary we maintained a voluntary enclavement."[21] "Distinctive language, ethnic seclusion and traditionalism all maintained cultural barriers that bounded the Russian Mennonites during the first 6 or 7 decades of their sojourn in the new land. Mennonites had historically cultivated their social ethics in the context of a corpus culturum."[22] "The current discussion of the faith and culture question largely hinges on the issue of ethnicity.... We became an ethnic community in the classic sense of that term — a people with a distinctive sense of peoplehood."[23]

What does one make of all these assessments? Are Mennonite Brethren in North America ethnic? The eminent MB historian, John A Toews, states explicitly that "throughout the history of the M.B. church faith and culture have often been in conflict."[24] But nowhere in his extensive analysis does he acknowledge the need for contemporary Mennonite Brethren to deal in fundamental and practical ways with the complicating question of church-encumbering ethnicity.

This brief survey of most of the significant MB writers on the topic has indicated both a growing awareness of the degree to which North American Mennonite Brethren are ethnic and a realization that this continuing, denomination-related, ethnicity has important theological consequences. Unfortunately, even those students of the topic who recognize the existence of ethnicity and have even perceived it to be a problem, it seems to me, have not carried their analysis to the logical conclusion. Before we address the matter of solution or resolution, we must consider several other aspects, one of which involves public perceptions and opinion, both Mennonite Brethren and public. We therefore turn now to the results of a major field study.

2. *The San Jose Survey*

The most significant anthropological or sociological field study of Mennonite Brethren in either the United States or Canada was undertaken by Miriam E. Warner in San Jose, California between February, 1983 and October, 1984. Using the pseudonyms "Lakewood" for Lincoln Glen and "Harrison" for San Jose, Professor Warner, of (Old) Mennonite background in Virginia, undertook an extensive analysis of the 400-member Lincoln Glen MB Church.[25]

The purpose of this dissertation is to describe and analyze an urban congregation of the Mennonite Brethren, a religious ethnic group, in Harrison, California. Members of this group have been urban residents for over forty years. This study was concerned with the ethnic component of Mennonite Brethren identity and its persistence in the urban environment.[26]

Although the first MBs came to San Jose at least as early as 1927, the MB church was organized formally in 1940. Since the California MBs, and particualrly the congregation in San Jose, have been assimilated at least as much as the MBs in central and Western Canada, the findings of this thorough analysis are highly relevant and extremely instructive for us.

The author notes that "people were surprised that I should be interested in their ethnic background and social relationships instead of their religious beliefs."[27] They "seemed amazed that I should be interested in ethnic foods. First they said there were not any but then as they remembered certain foods they would tell me about them...."[28]

Professor Warner's observations and conclusions warrant summary quotation.

The Mennonite Brethen group in Harrison is both a religious and ethnic community. The church accepts non-Mennonites into its membership and such converts receive religous membership. The ethnic Mennonite Brethren, however, have a dual membership — the ethnic and the religious.... Ethnic affiliation, I discovered, is expressed in the city much the same way it is in the rural and small town environment. There is a strong emphasis on kinship ties, not only direct family ties, but the broader ties of ethnic brotherhood.... The dichotomization of the value systems is not always overt and often there is a synthesis of the ethnic and religious systems.[29]

Significantly the author concludes that "the ethnic value system is the more important because the social grouping based on this system is the more meaningful to the group."[30]

I suggest that the Mennonite Brethren, at present, are living in a voluntary cultural enclave. Within the enclave, the processes of cognitive and psychological enclavement are operative. These are largely unconscious but they are the means by which the group maintains its collective identity. Cultural assimilation is occurring in the Mennonite Brethren community but the ethnic identity of the group remains intact.[31]

Thus it happens that ethnic identity can survive even substantial cultural assimilation. In assessing the relevance of this finding, Canadian MBs should remember that transition to the English language and the onset of cultural assimilation generally occurred about a generation earlier in the US than in Canada.

Definitions are important.

In this study I am defining a religious ethnic group as a self-perceived group of people who share a common cultural and religious heritage and who, because of this heritage, is united as a group by common emotional bonds. The members of a religious ethnic group have a sense of belonging to the group and they are concerned with the cultural and religious preservation of the group. The main difference between an ethnic group and a religous ethnic group is the emphasis the latter group places on its religious heritage.[32]

In such a group, religion functions as a component of the overall ethnic uniqueness. The result may be very consequential. "A religious ethnic group often develops a sense of moral superiority. This superiority is based on their firm convictions that their cultural/religious beliefs and practices are unique and better than those of other groups."[33] The origins of such a view, for the MBs, go back a long time. "The Mennonite Brethren group developed a sense of cultural and moral superiority while still in Russia."[34] Some Mennonite ethnicity, however, was initiated already during the Polish era.[35]

Professor Warner observed various instances of ethnic reinforcement. A key one was the showing of *And When They Shall Ask* which she terms "an experience of ethnic intensification."[36] The Mennonite Piano Concerto evoked intense ethno-religious emotion and "The film credits read like a roll call of an ethnic community."[37] The film "portrayed both the ethnic and religious continuity of the group."[38] Warner notes that

the film did have a religious message, but the mood, interaction and reaction of the audience both before and after the movie was more ethnic than religious. People attending knew each other intimately. Ethnics who were no longer religious members of the group attended and were greeted warmly. The film and the reaction to it were the most powerful and emotionally laden incidents of ethnic consciousness I observed while interacting with the Lakewood church congregation.[39]

Warner's assessment of this movie experience is all the more noteworthy because the Lincoln Glen MBs have for years played down their ethnic value system and largely consider themselves to have succeeded in this de-emphasis.

The overt reaction in religious terms of the Mennonite Brethren group does not negate the presence of the more powerful ethnic feelings. It is natural, however, for the Mennonite Brethren to see this film in light of their religious heritage. Their ethnic heritage has not been articulated in an overt way. They have always been ethnics and it is quite difficult at times to separate the religous and ethnic components of identity. There is also the fact that the Mennonite Brethren in Harrison are not viewing their ethnic heritage in a positive way. They are trying to submerge it. However, in such incidences as the showing of *When They Shall Ask*, the ethnic heritage and identity cannot be overlooked, submerged or forgotten. This cannot be done because in situations such as this, ethnicity becomes more important than religion in binding the group together.[40]

And When They Shall Ask was shown widely in Mennonite communities across Canada and the US. On August 29, 1985, it was telecast, in an abridged 60-minute version, across Canada on the CBC national network. The non-Mennonite response was mixed. The Toronto *Globe and Mail* reviewer, Rick Groen, wrote, "We're introduced to the family all right, but are never granted membership, never quite made to feel its motivating energy." Groen concluded that "the inner audience will doubtless be greatly inspired, the outer only mildly edified." [41]

Warner suggests that The Mennonite Central Committee Relief Sale constitutes another major ethnic event, at least for the Mennonites involved. "There is a strong emphasis on food at the MCC sale. There are traditional Mennonite dishes...." [42] The sale "is a time for a renewal of acquaintances and distant kin.... More importantly, it is a time of renewal of the ethnic consciousness and identity among the Mennonites and the Mennonite Brethren." [43]

Underscoring a point noted also by other observers, Warner reports that, "Whether Mennonites are proud of their ethnicity or not, they still like to congregate with others of their kind." At the Fresno-regional MCC sale which she observed, the event generated "extensive and often intensive interaction." Thus "information can travel very rapidly and get to all the West Coast Mennonite Brethren communities in a matter of a few days." [44]

Ethnic ties are reinforced in various other ways.

When two or more Mennonite Brethren who are strangers meet, there is always this commonality of ethnic kinship. In such a situation, three questions of importance are asked of the 'strange' Mennonite Brethren. The first one is, 'Who is your father?'; the second question is, 'Where did you grow up?'; and the third question often is, 'Where did you go to school?' Often only the initial question is needed because the additional information will be volunteered. If they do not know each other personnally they can discuss someone they know in common. [45]

In her investigation Warner encountered various fundamental ethnic traits. "I would suggest that the markers of Mennonite Brethren ethnicity in Harrison include distinct surnames, a common Mennonite (German) cultural heritage, a common religious history and a strong kinship network." Despite the 40 years of urbanization and apparent cultural assimilation in San Jose, marriage to fellow MBs "is the preferred marriage pattern and most Mennonite Brethren choose their intimate friends from within the ethnic group." [46]

What ranks as the most widespread ethnic trait? "The possession of an ethnic surname is the most common identity marker." In keeping with the evidence marshalled by other observers Warner adds, "This must be qualified, however, for many of the ethnic names are shared with other Mennonites who once lived in Russia. They are very conscious of surname authenticity as this labels a person status-wise immediately." [47]

As corollary evidence for her own conclusions Warner quotes an article by the well-known Mennonite Brethren genealogist, Alan Peters. "It seems to be the general feeling nowadays that it is better for one's child to marry an unconverted person with a Mennonite heritage than to marry a converted non-Mennonite." [48]

How does the church fit into this ethnic configuration? "The most important voluntary association for most Mennonite Brethren is the church. The churches have a wide variety of activities for all aged [sic] individuals.

This membership in the church is the means by which to circulate news of interest to the ethnic group." [49]

Warner notes that the "common Mennonite cultural heritage," is "German in origin." Some important "features of this heritage such as language and food preferences are several centuries old. This cultural tradition was preserved in Russia by the process of forced enclavement." [50] Nowadays this common cultural heritage is reinforced by residence patterns which Warner terms "voluntary enclavement." Mennonite Brethren consciously make "a choice to live close to other Mennonite Brethren." [51] "The residence and kinship patterns of the Harrison Mennonite Brethren community are different from those of the wider society." [52] "The term 'enclavement' does not imply complete social isolation." But it "does imply the existence of boundaries." [53] "The use of enclavement by the Mennonite Brethren has fostered the development and retention of their identity system which is based on their ethnicity." [54]

Professor Warner's analysis of the interaction of religion and ethnicity in this supposedly assimilating Mennonite Brethren church deserves careful attention. "There are two types of membership in the Mennonite Brethren community in Harrison: ethnic membership and religious membership. A knowledge of this dichotomization is essential if the interplay between religious values and social action is to be understood." [55]

Warner's assessment is penetrating and straighforward:

The religious membership is achieved. No amount of religious knowledge or zeal can confer on a person the more important ethnic membership which is ascribed. Ethnic members of the Mennonite Brethren make the distinction between themselves and non-ethnic as a person who has not been born into the group and thus is not part of the ethnic brotherhood. [56]

In this, perhaps the most forceful section of her study, Warner asserts that,

The differentiation between ethnic and non-ethnic Mennonite Brethren has a profound effect on the social interaction in the community. All religious members are brothers and sisters in the church but the non-ethnics do not have the dual membership afforded to the ethnic Mennonite Brethren. The door to the ethnic group is closed and many of the Mennonite Brethren want to keep it that way. [57]

All of this reality raises a very fundamental question.

One might legitimately ask if Mennonite Brethren affiliation is ethnic, religious or both. Strictly speaking, it is an ethnic classification. Familial connections are more important than adherence to specific religious beliefs. The ethnic classification has been imbued with a meaning almost sacred. [58]

Any ethnic value system tends to be complex and the MB situation is no exception.

The ethnic value system consists of several values all of which are interwoven with the basic theme of Mennonite Brethren life. Many of the ethnic values are subjective and have to do with feelings of

126

belonging and emotional security. Members of the Mennonite Brethren group consider themselves part of a fraternal brotherhood. Their upbringing has been similar and there is an emotional warmth and intuitive understanding not present in associations with non-ethnics.[59]

In clarifying the subtle realities Warner reminds her readers that, "It could be said that the ethnic group is the family writ large." Accordingly it follows that, "To be a Mennonite Brethren ethnic is to be interested not only in one's own extended family but also in the extended families of all ethnics."[60]

The influence of ethnicity can be not only extensive but also largely unrecognized.

It is difficult at times to make a clear distinction between the religious and ethnic value system. Members of the group are not always aware that both sets of values are operative in their lives. I would suggest that the interpretation of many of the religious values of the group is ethnic and that the ethnic code is not always consistent with the religious.[61]

The discrepancy involves numerous ethical issues relating, for example, to wealth, professional success, racial and ethnic equality. Warner notes that, "many of the group are not aware of the reasons for, or the extent of, their uniqueness as a religious ethnic group."[62]

Professor Warner cites numerous ways in which Mennonite Brethren ethnicity expresses itself and thrives. "When ethnics are alone, there is an ease of communication not present when the group is mixed."[63] One ethnic Mennonite commented about a non-ethnic member, "Oh, she has been in the church or other Mennonite Brethren churches for over twenty years, but she is not one of us."[64] This member's explanation constitutes a sobering truth if not an indictment.

The average Mennonite Brethren has not been able to distance himself from his ethnic experience sufficiently to see the difference between religious values and implicit ethnic attitudes characterizing these. He is unaware that some of the reasons the church has been unable to attract large numbers of middle-class people to the church is due to the ethnic boundaries separating off the church.[65]

The views of various non-ethnic persons tell a powerful and sobering story. One Lakewood member said,

I have been in this church for a long time. I know all the members. I know all their children. I know their relatives that have visited here but when I attended a conference where most of the people were ethnic Mennonite Brethen, I felt completely out of place. All the talk was ethnic. They told ethnic jokes and everything dealt with their ethnic background. I felt I didn't really belong.[66]

Another non-ethnic put her experience thus.

I'd like to think that my family and I are at home in the church and most of the time we feel we are. But we very seldom are invited to the private dinner parties many of the ethnic members have. I try not to think about it too much but it really hurts at times. When

I think about it, it is as if the ethnics see us as second-class Mennonite Brethren.[67]

A third Lakewood member described her experience as follows.

When I first joined the church I didn't understand why there was so much kinship dialogue going on after church on Sunday, at all of the meetings and at the social events. First, I thought it was because of the church emphasis on brotherhood but I soon realized how wrong I was. That wasn't the reason — the real reason was kin folks. I have decided that is really what the Mennonite Brethren are most interested in. They act like it is part of their religion.[68]

One Lakewood member summed up the situation in these words.

We used to have a lot more non-ethnics serving in the church here. Many of them left. I think they knew they really weren't welcome here. They told me they tried hard to work in the church but they felt their ideas were not welcome. I think it was the ethnic part of the church that drove them away. They didn't feel at home. If we are going to bring more non-ethnics into the Lakewood church we are going to have to make them feel more at home.[69]

Professor Warner makes many additional comments of great importance for anyone seriously interested in this topic. Her dissertation deserves wide circulation; one can only hope that it will be published very soon. A few additional insights and assessments must suffice. "The more informal the activity," such as picnics, retreats, banquets, "the more it is apt to be marked by ethnic rather than religious membership."[70] "The religious and ethnic values in the Mennonite Brethren are closely interlocked. Thus, the functions of religion may be partly or largely ethnic at times and at other times they are primarily religious."[71] "Most of the time the Mennonite Brethren themselves are not aware of the synthesis."[72]

When non-ethnics join they, "are unaware that ethnic membership accords a constancy and consistency of belonging that as non-ethnics they will never attain."[73] The "ethnic group is a community one joins at birth and leaves at death."[74]

Warner says that the "Mennonite Brethren group does not always distinguish" between religion and ethnicity. "It is my feeling that they indeed are separate even though at times they may seem to be inextricably woven together in Mennonite Brethren life."[75] Thus they can be separated. That's a vital point for us to remember as we contemplate possible solutions. Interestingly, the ethnic identity is strong even though at Lakewood, "affirmation of their ethnicity is not present."[76]

Mennonite Brethren ethnicity rests largely on "a common place of origin, unique cultural and religious traits and a subjective sense of belonging to the group."[77]

"The majority of Mennonite Brethren in Harrison are not comfortable discussing their ethnicity.... They view the distinctiveness of their identity as religious and not ethnic."[78]

Two thought-provoking excerpts conclude this review of Professor Warner's astute investigation.

"The strength of the Mennonite Brethren group in Harrison lies in the continued presence of a collective identity system. This identity system has both religious and ethnic components. These components are prioritized — the ethnic is more important." [79]
"The Mennonite Brethren are a religious ethnic group which has a closely knit kinship network not only in Harrison but in the wider Mennonite Brethren denomination in both the United States and Canada." [80]

Chapter 5 — FOOTNOTES

1. Harold Jantz, "Who are the Mennonite Brethren?" *Christian Leader,* August, 12, 1980, p. 4.
2. Ken Reddig, "Quebec Mennonite Brethren Take Their Conference Back to Anabaptist Beginnings." *Mennonite Mirror,* May, 1986, p. 11.
3. *Ibid.,* p. 12.
4. Katie Funk Wiebe, *Who Are The Mennonite Brethren?* (Winnipeg: Kindred Press, 1984).
5. *Ibid.,* p. vii.
6. *Ibid.,* p. 5.
7. *Ibid.,* p. 71.
8. *Ibid.,* p. 102.
9. Lohrentz, "Religious and Cultural Background of the Mennonite Brethren." *Conference on Mennonite Cultural Problems,* VII, June, 1949, pp. 139-150.
10. Jacob John Toews, "The Cultural Background of the Mennonite Brethren Church." Unpublished M. A. thesis (University of Toronto, 1951).
11. *Mennonite Observer,* January 22, 1960, p. 2.
12. *Mennonite Brethren Herald,* March 16, 1962, p. 4.
13. "The Meaning of Being Mennonite Brethren," quoted in Peter Hamm, "Continuity and Change Among Canadian Mennonite Brethren, 1925-1975; a Study of Sacralization and Secularization in Sectarianism." Unpublished Ph.D. dissertation (Hamilton: McMaster University, 1975), p. 549.
14. "Theological Reflections," *Direction,* Fall, 1985, pp. 60-68.
15. *Ibid.,* p. 64.
16. *Ibid.,* p. 66.
17. *Ibid.,* p. 67.
18. *Ibid.*
19. Peter M. Hamm, "Continuity and Change Among Canadian Mennonite Brethren, 1925-1975; A Study of Sacralization and Secularization in Sectarianism." Unpublished Ph.D. dissertation (Hamilton: McMaster University, 1975).
20. *Ibid.,* p. 6.
21. Paul Toews, "Faith in Culture and Culture in Faith: Mennonite Brethren Entertaining Expansive, Separate and Assimilative Views about the Relationship," pp. 4-5.
22. *Ibid.,* p. 13.
23. *Ibid.,* pp. 17-18.
24. John A. Toews, *A History of the Mennonite Brethren Church: Pilgrims and Pioneers* (Fresno: Board of Christian Literature, General Conference of Mennonite Brethren Churches, 1975), p. 338.
25. Miriam E. Warner, *Mennonite Brethren: The Maintenance of Continuity in A Religious Ethnic Group.* Ph.D. dissertation in Anthropology (Berkeley, University of California, February, 1985), pp. 228. Copyright by Miriam E. Warner. The following selections are quoted with permission.
26. *Ibid.,* p. 1.
27. *Ibid.,* p. xiii.
28. *Ibid.,* p. xiv.
29. *Ibid.,* p. 2.
30. *Ibid.,* p. 4.
31. *Ibid.*
32. *Ibid.,* pp. 19-20.

33. *Ibid.*, p. 21.
34. *Ibid.*, p. 37.
35. *Ibid.*, pp. 44f.
36. *Ibid.*, p. 82.
37. *Ibid.*, p. 81.
38. *Ibid.*, p. 83.
39. *Ibid.*
40. *Ibid.*
41. See *Mennonite Reporter*, September 16, 1985, p. 10.
42. Warner, *op.cit.*, p. 126.
43. *Ibid.*, p. 127.
44. *Ibid.*
45. *Ibid.*, p. 85.
46. *Ibid.*, p. 87.
47. *Ibid.*, p. 87.
48. "The Impact of the Family in Mennonite History: Some Preliminary Observations," *Direction*, Vol. 1, no. 3, July, 1972, p. 79. The quotation appears on p. 88 in Warner's dissertation.
49. Warner, *Ibid.*, p. 88.
50. *Ibid.*, p. 89.
51. *Ibid.*, p. 148.
52. *Ibid.*, p. 91.
53. *Ibid.*, p. 174.
54. *Ibid.*, p. 179.
55. *Ibid.*, p. 102.
56. *Ibid.*, p. 103.
57. *Ibid.*
58. *Ibid.*
59. *Ibid.*, pp. 104-105.
60. *Ibid.*, p. 105.
61. *Ibid.*, p. 106.
62. *Ibid.*, p. 107.
63. *Ibid.*, p. 108.
64. *Ibid.*, p. 109.
65. *Ibid.*, p. 108.
66. *Ibid.*, p. 109.
67. *Ibid.*
68. *Ibid.*, p. 154.
69. *Ibid.*, p. 108.
70. *Ibid.*, p. 128.
71. *Ibid.*, p. 130.
72. *Ibid.*, p. 131.
73. *Ibid.*, pp. 131-132.
74. *Ibid.*, p. 132.
75. *Ibid.*, p. 135.
76. *Ibid.*, p. 151.
77. *Ibid.*, p. 173.
78. *Ibid.*, p. 201.
79. *Ibid.*, p. 203.
80. *Ibid.*, p. 204.

CHAPTER SIX

MENNONITES AND ETHNICITY; SOME RELIGIOUS AND HISTORICAL CONSIDERATIONS

1. *Ethnicity as a Problem in Church Ministries*

The ethnic question confronts us in several respects, most notably when we commit ourselves to true home missions. As long as we stuck mainly to foreign missions, or arms' length missions in Canada, presumably because we spoke German in an English milieu, we could avoid it. But having become integrated linguistically, vocationally, and largely geographically in urban neighborhoods, we can avoid it no longer. We can only avoid it in our present surroundings if, simultaneously, we are prepared to deny the Great Commission.

A call to Christian renewal is required, as many respondents to my questionaire emphasized, but, in itself, it is not sufficient. We need to redefine what is to be renewed. We need to be clear about what we are calling people to do? Which community are we inviting them to join?

Do we have an ethnic problem in church ministries? James Nikkel notes the potential for a problem. "Churches with an ethnic or cultural history are particularly vulnerable to growth barriers. If our roots and heritage do not help us to be faithful to the Scripture, they will become a barrier to fulfilling the great commission."[1] Writing out of much experience, Floyd Born observes, "Mennonite evangelism at home has many elements of cross-cultural evangelism which we generally associate with foreign missions. The cultural identity of (Dutch or Russian) and Swiss Mennonites is so strong as to make reaching out to others feel like foreign missions...."[2]

John E. Toews speaks candidly about establishing the correct perspective.

> Our missionary efforts have often been less than effective because we have not been clear about our christological and ecclesial identity. It has been easy for us to confuse our ethnic or our national identity with our Christian identity, and to offend our pagan friends, our converts, and other Christians. Our text (I Peter 2: 4-10) calls us to a Jesus-centeredness and to an ethno-national inclusiveness....[3]

Non-ethnic Mennonites, at times, seem to perceive what many traditional Mennonites miss. Speaking as a "non-Mennonite" Mennonite, David Chiu challenged a large gathering of Canadian Mennonite leaders to take seriously the desire of his Chinese Mennonite Church, "We just want to be a church with Anabaptist essentials."[4] Chiu recounted an experience. "I went to a bookstore in downtown Winnipeg to get a few books about the Mennonite faith. The salesperson was shocked when she knew that I was a Chinese Mennonite. Her question was how I could be a person of two races!"[5] At the same convention James Nikkel, evangelism secretary for the Canadian Mennonite Brethren Conference, stated that "The ethnic-cultural distinctives which have woven themselves into the theological fabric have weakened the churches' position with reference to evangelism."[6]

In assessing problems associated with ethnicity, we must be careful to maintain a balanced perspective. "Ethnic consciousness will not halt church growth if a group sees itself as part of the larger body of Christians...."[7] But that's precisely the problem. Mennonite Brethren want to be ethnically inclusive, yet hold to a name which in North America has a particular ethnic meaning!

> Finally, to be Anabaptist we will have to let Jan. 21, 1525, stand in judgment over Aug. 16, 1874. That is, present Mennonite ethnicity, including Mennonite Brethren ethnicity, must not be identified with Anabaptism, or viewed as the faithful expression of it in the 20th century....
>
> To be Anabaptist necessitates the rejection of ethnicity as in any way determining Christian faith and Christian faithfulness. Our 16th century forefathers recognized the basic contradiction between the emphasis on ethnicity and the missionary nature of the church.[8]

So far, so good. Now, if we really took that excellent, Biblical exhortation to heart, we would not keep on sending out exclusivist signals by designating our denomination or our seminary by a uniquely ethnic name. A call for such a change, involving changed ethnic attitudes, changed ethnic actions, and changing ethnic denominational labelling, would follow logically if we carried Toews' incisive exegesis right through, all the way, to its proper and practical conclusion.

2. *What Does the Bible Say About Ethnicity?*

The Bible addresses the matter of ethnicity in numerous passages. We cannot investigate all of them, and we will not repeat the earlier exegesis of the pivotal passage in I Peter 2: 4-10, but we will review some salient teachings and note some insightful comments.

In Isaiah 56: 3-7 we encounter an early divine denunciation of ethnic/nationalistic egoism and pride.

And blessings are for gentiles, too, do not let them think that I will make them second-class citizens....

As for the gentiles, the outsiders who join the people of the Lord and serve him and love his name....I will bring them also to my holy mountain of Jerusalem, and make them full of joy within my House of Prayer. (Living Bible)

As we know, the early church struggled over ethnic problems, as recorded in the sixth chapter of Acts. Selwyn Hughes comments thus.

The church at Jerusalem never quite got over being Jewish. While Jewish history was clearly an essential prelude to New Testament Christianity, some of the Jewish Christians in Jerusalem failed to sense what God was doing in forming a single new humanity in Christ and for a while hindered rather than helped the growth of the church.[9]

It's a failure which existed in the anti-semitic churches in Nazi Germany, in the forcefully segregated churches in the US south, and still exists in the apartheid churches in South Africa, as well as in all churches throughout the world which build barriers instead of bridges. Hughes adds that, significantly, the launching base for missions into Europe was Antioch, not Jerusalem, even though the Holy Spirit had been given first in Jerusalem. We can learn from that account.

In studying Biblical guidelines in these matters we need to be very careful how we exegete certain Biblical terms. Consider the following comments found in an editorial by Ron Rempel, the editor of the *Mennonite Reporter.* "Perhaps 'ethnicity' is not the villain that some have made it out to be. In fact, the term is based in one of the New Testament descriptions of the church. A chosen race (genos), a holy nation (ethnos) — these are the apostle Peter's words (I Peter 2: 9-10). They do not draw artificial lines between common beliefs."[10] Yes, indeed, the church is a new "ethnos," but it is specifically "new," it is not an ethnos based on birth, on names, on all of the items described in chapter 4. God's "ethnos" does not apply to the government for ethnic grants; it does not seek ethnic recognition with race-based ethnicities at Folklorama; it does not sponsor irreverent entertainment in a cabaret; it does not build a museum to commemorate foods, folklore, farming pioneers, and folkways; and it neither claims nor presents as fellow heirs in the "ethnos" those who publicly disclaim any faith in God —, as the *Mennonite Reporter* regularly does with "gifted Mennonites," like Patrick Friesen, who claims no faith. The *Mennonite Reporter* is inconsistent when it suggests that in North America, Mennonite is equivalent to the ethnos in I Peter 2, yet simultaneously and happily accepts as Mennonites people who are not Christians. We cannot have it both ways. The affirmation and celebration of Mennonite ethnicity in Canada is a far cry from the celebration of "ethnos" as described in I Peter 2.

A more convincing discussion of some Biblical guidelines comes from the pen of Wally Kroeker. He reminds us that the Apostle Paul, in Ephesians 3, makes exhortations about Christian unity "in the context of the Jew-Gentile rift, which is an extreme first-century example of the ethnocentrism that can be found among many Mennonites."[10] Citing also Ephesians 2 he presses the point that "all natural social, racial and economic barriers are bridged.... Followers of Jesus Christ become part of a new reality that transcends all earthly loyalties."[12]

He continues "For Paul, the church was above ethnicity; those for whom racial heritage continues to separate and divide have not, according to Paul, apprehended the gospel....In short," he states, "the Christians totally lost their old identities in the life of the church."[13] That's exactly what we need to hear — and heed — particularly heed! Or have we forgotten the truth that words without deeds won't get us anywhere, except to the point of self-deception!

"If Paul were addressing his letters to Mennonites today, we might hear him say that Christ's lordship is above everything, including our cherished ethnic culture. All of life, including ethnicity, is to be lodged in its rightful place — beneath the Lordship of Christ."[14] But if we name the church Mennonite, then how can Mennonite ethnicity be seen as secondary? Beneath Christ's lordship? That is precisely my point. As I see it, the Mennonite Brethren "group defines itself primarily in terms of blood heritage, cultural traditions..."[15] when it waves the ethnic flag above all else. Wally writes his words as warning but they are already fact. Moreover, the Mennonite Brethren Conference doesn't have to "define itself" overtly. By taking on an ethnic designation it already does so.

We should let Wally's warnings take us considerably farther than they took him in his excellent analysis.

Mennonites who take seriously Paul's message in Ephesians will ensure that all newcomers are welcome as full-fledged participants in the believing community. They will be careful not to exclude people on the basis of name. They will strive to remove feelings of alienation rather than build walls of division....[16]

All of this advice is fine, but insufficient and, therefore, ultimately frustrating for all involved, for it addresses only part of a problem, the attitudinal and behavioral part. But important as that part obviously is, it cannot be solved by itself, in isolation. That's why decades of dilligent effort on the part of many Mennonite Brethren has produced only meagre results.

As Paul points out in Colossians 3 verse 11, "there is neither Greek nor Jew,...Barbarian, or Scythian..." in Christ's church. That surely means that a church (assuming that it is not language-bound) which seeks to include these races dare not call itself "The Greek Church," or "The Barbarian Church," or "The Scythian Church," or "The Slave Church." Only where a particular church, for very specific language reasons, ministers to one ethnic group, can it justify, usually only for a transitional period, a narrowly ethnic designation.

Such a non-ethnic perspective lines up perfectly with Paul's insistence that "for the sake of Christ," he "now considers [as] loss," as rubbish, his entire excellent ethnic heritage. (Philippians 3: 7-11.)

Jesus, himself, knowing how prone his followers would be to mistake the love of sect, or race, or nation, or party for the true zeal for the church, prayed fervently that in their secondary and functional diversity, his followers would "be one," even as he and his father were one. (John 17: 21-23.)

Some years ago the venerable John A. Toews, in his little booklet, *Christians Between East and West*, wrote that "All identifications of Christianity with Western culture or the 'American way of life' must be completely eliminated." (page 22) He was right. But, in order to be fully consistent, and Biblical, we must extend that requirement to include any specifically and restricting ethnic identification as well, for if ethnic identification is exclusive and misleading, it is also wrong. Unfortunately, for all of his great insight, Toews never managed to carry his analysis that far.

Let me stress two truths in concluding this cursory survey. First, the opposite of love is not hate, but self-love. That fact applies also to the community of ethnic Mennonites in North America. Second, Jesus once was asked, "Where are your brothers?" He countered by asking, "Who are my brothers?" Then he answered his own question. "Whoever does the will of my Father in heaven is my brother and sister and mother." (Matthew 12: 48-50.) Concerning brothers and sisters in the faith, as contrasted with brothers and sisters in the ethnic clan, we should have the same questions and the same answers as Jesus had.

3. What Did the Early Anabaptists Say About Ethnicity?

E. K. Francis, a scholar who specializes in Mennonite affairs, points out that in The Netherlands, "between 1530 and 1566 Protestantism was almost identical with Evangelical Anabaptism." One of Menno Simons' greatest accomplishments was that he "succeeded in consolidating the often rather vague beliefs of various Anabaptist congregations into a distinct system," and in doing so he provided "a common basis for a closer co-operation between originally separate sects."[17]

During those years, "the Mennonite sect, which then comprised ethnically heterogeneous elements, resembles an institutional group whose point of orientation is a distinct body of religious beliefs and practices."[18] Thus, at the outset, Mennonites were strictly a religious group and not an ethnic group.

Menno's own words on the topic remain instructive. He said that the whole evangelical Scriptures teach that Christ's church was and must be a people separated from the world in doctrine, life and worship....since the church always was and must be a separated people;...therefore we are constrained by the Spirit and word of God to...gather not to us but to the Lord, a pious, penitent assembly or church.[19]

135

In this passage, and in many others, Menno Simons emphasizes repeatedly that he is gathering a people to God, not to himself. Menno would surely be saddened and bewildered were he to discover that in the nineteenth and the twentieth centuries his followers had fused his beliefs to an ethnic perspective and named that fusion after him. I think he would have vehemently objected on both counts. The fact of Mennonite ethnicity, as we have seen, can not and should not be denied, but it really has nothing to do with Menno. And the reforms I shall set forth do not do violence to Menno but, in actual fact, reinforce what he said!

A hundred years later, Menno's followers still defined "ethnos" in strictly Biblical terms. The Dordrecht Confession of Faith in Article VII, described the church thus.

> We believe in and confess a visible church of God, consisting of those who....have truly repented, and rightly believed...[have been] incorporated into the communion of the saints on earth. And these we confess are a chosen generation, a royal priesthood, an holy nation, who have the testimony that they are the bride of Christ; yea, that they are children and heirs of eternal life....[20]

Calvin Redekop, in discussing these excerpts, notes that "The references to the 'holy people' can be multiplied...." It is clear, "that the concept of a holy nation, a chosen people, set off from others with a special relationship with God cannot be denied. It is important to note that the Anabaptists reflected the biblical language in the use of the term and considered themselves as bona fide representatives of the Kingdom of God."[21]

Given such a clear Biblical view of the church it is obvious that the numerous ethnic and cultural non-Christian Mennonites (according to their own words), who are regularly portrayed positively and supportively — like kinfolk — in the pages of the *Mennonite Reporter*, the *Mennonite Mirror*, the *Festival Quarterly*, and even in the *Mennonite Brethren Herald*, would have felt thoroughly out of place among the followers of Menno at that time. More importantly, they would not have been received into the covenant community unless they had become God's "children and heirs of eternal life." Of course, it is not the fault of the cultural Mennonite non-Christians that "Mennonite" today has come to mean what it does; that is now a given fact. Nor is it the fault of the Christian Mennonites. But the Christian Mennonites do have a Biblical responsibility to clarify the situation and to insist that the church not be equated to, or easily confused with, the ethnic group.

If we had space to review the broader European scene in the 16th and 17th centuries we would find that Anabaptist founders such as Conrad Grebel, who was Swiss, Menno Simons, who was Dutch, and others, who were German, not only constituted a multi-ethnic leadership group for a multi-ethnic people, but also insisted on maintaining such a Biblical peoplehood and such Biblical, rather than ethnic, separation.

4. *The Development of Ethnicity*

Given the widespread denial among Mennonites that in certain countries Mennonite means ethnic, one would think that the development of Mennonite ethnicity has not been adequately chronicled. In fact, however, a review of the literature suggests widespread awareness among scholars, both Mennonite and non-Mennonite. The judgements do not all agree in detail but concerning the general developments there is full agreement. A brief review of some of the literature will help us better to understand the present phenomenon.

In contrast to some scholars, Richard Kyle sees an early development of Mennonite ethnicity.

> The concept and practice of separation in Mennonite history has largely been determined by two factors: Anabaptist theology and cultural isolation. It was during the sojourn in Prussia (1540-1790) that the second factor became prominent. Here the Mennonites became an ethnic group. The Dutch colonies of the Vistula Delta eventually grew into homogeneous Mennonite communities, separate from the larger population, with a culture of their own based on a Low German-Dutch social heritage and Mennonite religious institutions.[22]

James Urry's assessment differs very little.

> Before migrating to Russia Mennonites considered they were a distinctive group because of their faith. The fact that their solidarity was as much a result of kinship ties, social structure and geographic isolation did not occur to them. In Russia Mennonites were seduced into the economic, educational and religious systems of a wider world, and thus attempted to identify with developing Russian nationalism. It was not their identity....Thus the boundaries of their own identity were weakened and when they were rejected by the Russians, instead of appealing to Mennonite identity, they appealed to concepts which were entirely alien.[23]

What were these concepts? These alien concepts included, at various times, identifying with the Dutch or claiming to be German. Thus we see that already in Russia the Mennonites had difficulty accepting their ethnicity. The Russian authorities, says Urry, never considered the Mennonites to be German.[24] The Russian authorities saw the Mennonites as having a unique identity. They correctly saw them as German-speaking but not German. That's a very important point to remember.

Rodney Sawatzky asserts that, "The Anabaptist phase of Mennonitism was short-lived, even though these dedicated Christians had a strong missionary program as they fanned out across Europe pursued by their persecutors....A literal diaspora rapidly followed as ghettoes of Mennonites migrated to various centres of Europe, to Prussia, to Russia, and to America."[25] Over time the practice of withdrawal, separation from the world, and an emphasis on "Die Stillen im Lande," (the Quiet in the Land), together with persecution "fostered an in-group in mentality and heredity. 'Mennonite' came to denominate an ethnic as well as a religious entity."[26]

One of the earliest and clearest accounts of how Mennonites became ethnic, although rarely cited in Mennonite literature, is E. K. Francis's article, "The Russian Mennonites: From Religious to Ethnic Group." [27] In Russia, writes Francis, "the separation of church and state led also to the paradoxical situation that it became possible for one to be a Mennonite and yet not a member of the Mennonite church." [28]

In his later book, *In Search of Utopia: The Mennonites in Manitoba,*[29] Francis developed some of his analysis further. He titled his first chapter, "From Religious Movement to Ethnic Group." He writes: "It seems that at the moment when the Mennonite utopia, the community of the saints and the saved, lay within reach of realization, it became secularized and void of spiritual content, a commonwealth of ordinary people....Religion was institutionalized, and religious institutions were but one factor among many other institutions...."[30]

Francis concludes his chapter with this poignant sentence. "In the period between 1790 and 1870 the Mennonite sectarians in Russia had become a people whose conspicuous secular successes were bought at the price of institutionalization of religion and secularization of the inner life of the group." [31]

Interestingly, many later North American Mennonite writers concur with Francis's assessment. For example, concerning the formation of the Mennonite Brethren church, historian John B. Toews writes: "The Brethren nevertheless wanted to be Mennonites but they did not want to include the entire ethnic community within the church." [32] Donald B. Kraybill comments that "In the codification era, ethnicity legitimated with Biblical and religious injunctions expressed itself in concrete, specific and tangible forms which were attractive to a rural people with minimal education and a practical agrarian mentality." [33]

Mennonite Brethren historian John A. Toews focuses more on language and German culture than on Mennonite ethnicity. In this emphasis he differs, but not convincingly, from the non-Mennonite experts and also from many Mennonite analysts of that era. "In Russia, two factors tended to promote the close association, if not identification, of German culture and Mennonite faith: the geographic and social isolation from the Russian people, and the aversion to identify with an inferior Slavic culture." [34] He seems to understand the problem, although not necessarily in terms of a uniquely Mennonite ethnicity, when he says that the "constant identification of true Mennonitism with German language and culture" had "created serious problems for the faith and mission of the church." [35]

Toews' valiant attempt to insist that Mennonitism still referred to the true religion in Russia and not ethnicity is not supported by the growing amount of analytical scholarship. As virtually all experts on the topic have amply documented, by the mid-19th century at the very latest, Mennonitism in Russia had become predominantly ethnic. The German language had become the vehicle of expression but the Mennonite culture itself was not German. Mennonites had developed their own ethnicity. John A. Toews' historical error on this point, or his reluctance to acknowledge this fact, or whatever the explanation may be, has been extremely consequential for Mennonite Brethren, especially in North America. His seemingly inaccurate interpretation of the Russian situation, as reflected in his official and supposedly definitive history, has doubtless influenced the thinking of many, perhaps most, current Canadian Mennonite Brethren leaders. In fact, it may be the clue to understanding why so many otherwise well-informed Mennonite Brethren still insist that Mennonite is not ethnic. If Mennonite culture in Russia is identified as German, as Toews and some others wrongly insist, then the cultural problems in North America should be related primarily to the German language and ought to disappear when the German language is replaced by English. That's precisely the erroneous view which many North American Mennonite Brethren hold. They have been conditioned to think that way. Such analysis and such conclusions are faulty.

Interestingly, Katie Funk Wiebe perceives the situation clearly. Concerning the development of the Mennonite Brethren church in 1860, she acknowledges the basic ethnic reality in her reference to birth. "At that time anyone born into a Mennonite family could become a church member and partake of the Lord's Supper. The document also spoke to the issue that baptism was being administered to anyone who was of Mennonite birth." [36]

In November, 1986, James Urry again addressed the matter of Mennonite identity in Russia. Discussing the larger Mennonite setting he writes: "In Russia the colony-communities were now linked into a broader commonwealth of congregations and settlements. The emergence of the Mennonite Commonwealth was given added impetus by changes in the attitude of the Russian government to the Mennonites as a distinct religious and cultural community." [37] He adds later, "In a sense the Mennonite Commonwealth resembled a new nation state in the industrial world just as the old colony-congregation had resembled an advanced agrarian state. At the level of the Commonwealth-community it was culturally homogeneous...." [38] The primary thrust of Urry's analysis again shows that the Mennonites in Russia had become a distinct ethnic people.

Francis Hiebert rightly echoes this view when she says the following about Mennonites in Russia in the mid-19th century. "Blind traditionalism, spiritual indifference, and ethnic pride are seen as having contributed to moral decay." [39]

Paul Toews has a similar assessment about Mennonite ethnicity in Russia. "We became an ethnic community in the classic sense of that term — a people with a distinctive sense of peoplehood." [40]

Leo Driedger again demonstrates clear insight. "During the 1870s the Biblical theology of Anabaptists," who had recently come to Canada from Russia, "was turned into a traditional religion which became so strongly linked with culture that it often took fourth place in the sacred canopy." The first three pillars were culture, community, and land. "Culture and land sustained them; religion was no longer a driving, cutting edge. Their identity had been molded into a static mausoleum which sacralized the ritual of baptism, controlled and disciplined the deviants, and buried the dead." [41]

Concerning the Mennonite Brethren specifically, Miriam Warner writes: "Ethnic membership was synonymous with religious membership in the Russian Mennonite Church. The Mennonite Brethren leaders in 1860 wanted to separate religious affiliation from the ethnic. Officially this has been the stance ever since. The practical application of this principle can be questioned." [42]

A great Christian heritage became a religious culture; a religious culture produced a new ethnic group; out of the ethnic group came several renewal movements. Now it falls to the fortunate heirs of that great Christian anabaptist heritage, which was never completely lost, to re-establish or, as needed, reinforce, the church as a separate community, clearly differentiated from the larger ethnic whole.

Chapter 6 — FOOTNOTES

1. Quoted in Katie Funk Wiebe, *Who Are The Mennonite Brethren?* (Winnipeg: Kindred Press, 1984), pp. 6-7.
2. *Mennonite Brethren Herald*, March 23, 1984, p. 3.
3. John E. Toews and Hugo Zorilla, "Who are God's People?" *Program and Information Book* (Strasburg: Mennonite World Conference, 1984), p. 96.
4. *Mennonite Reporter*, February 4, 1985, p. 1.
5. *Ibid.*, p. 6.
6. *Ibid.*
7. Wiebe, *ibid.*, p. 103.
8. John E. Toews, "Where to, Mennonite Brethren...?" *The Christian Leader*, January 6, 1976, pp. 4.
9. Selwyn Hughes, *Everyday With Jesus* (Walton-on-Thames, UK: CWR, May, 1986), p. 2.
10. *Mennonite Reporter*, July 7, 1986, p. 6.
11. Wally Kroeker, "So you're not really one of us", *The Christian Leader*, July 23, 1985, pp. 2-4. This quote appears on page 3.
12. *Ibid.*
13. *Ibid.*
14. *Ibid.*
15. *Ibid.*
16. *Ibid.*
17. E. K. Francis, "The Russian Mennonites: From Religious Group to Ethnic Group," *The American Journal of Sociology*, vol. LIV, no. 2, September, 1948, p. 103. This assessment of Menno remains valid despite the recent "polygenesis" interpretation of 16th century anabaptism by Hans-Juergen Goertz and others.
18. *Ibid.*, p. 103.
19. Harold S. Bender, *Menno Simons' Life and Writings* (Scottdale, PA: Mennonite Publishing House, 1936), p. 74.
20. John C. Wenger, *Glimpses of Mennonite History and Doctrine* (Scottdale, PA: Mennonite Publishing House, 1947), p. 209.
21. Calvin Redekop, "Anabaptism and the Ethnic Ghost," *Mennonite Quarterly Review*, vol. LVIII, no. 2, April 1984, pp. 133-146. The quotation appears on page 134.
22. Richard Kyle, "The Concept and Practice of Separation from the World in Mennonite Brethren History", *Direction*, January/April, 1984, p. 34.
23. James Urry, "Who are the Mennonites?" *Arch. europ. sociol.* XXIV, 1983, p. 260.
24. *Ibid.*, p. 246.
25. Rodney Sawatzky, "Pacifism and Mennonite Identity" in Henry Poettcker and Rudy A. Regehr, (eds.), *Call to Faithfulness: Essays in Canadian Mennonite Studies* (Winnipeg: Canadian Mennonite Bible College, 1972), p. 192.
26. *Ibid.*, p. 193.
27. E. K. Francis, "Russian Mennonites: From Religious to Ethnic Group", *The American Journal of Sociology*, vol. LIV, no. 2, September, 1948, pp. 101-107.
28. *Ibid.*, p. 104.

29. E. K. Francis, *In Search of Utopia: The Mennonites in Manitoba* (Altona: D. W. Friesen & Sons, 1955).

30. *Ibid.*, pp. 23-24.

31. *Ibid.*, p. 27.

32. John B. Toews, "The Early Mennonite Brethren", *Mennonite Quarterly Review*, vol. LVIII, no. 2, April, 1984, pp. 85-86.

33. Donald B. Kraybill, "Modernity and Identity: The Transformation of Mennonite Ethnicity." A paper read at Conrad Grebel College, Waterloo, May 30, 1986, p. 17.

34. John A. Toews, *A History of the Mennonite Brethren Church* (Hillsboro, KA: Mennonite Brethren Publishing House, 1975), p. 324.

35. *Ibid.*, p. 14.

36. Katie Funk Wiebe, *Who Are the Mennonite Brethren?* (Winnipeg: Kindred Press, 1984), p. 71.

37. James Urry, "A religious or a social elite? The Mennonite Brethren in Imperial Russia." A paper read at the Mennonite Brethren Bible College, Winnipeg, November 14, 1986, p. 35.

38. *Ibid.*

39. Frances F. Hiebert, "Apples, Oranges, Anabaptists and Mennonite Brethren", *Direction*, July, 1982, p. 9.

40. Paul Toews, "Faith in Culture and Culture in Faith." A paper read at the Mennonite Brethren Bible College, Winnipeg, November 15, 1986, p. 18.

41. Leo Driedger, "Fifty Years of Mennonite Identity in Winnipeg," in Harry Loewen, ed., *Mennonite Images: Historical, Cultural, and Literary Essays Dealing With Mennonite Issues* (Winnipeg: Hyperion Press, 1980), p. 129. The evidence supports the interpretation and conclusion of Driedger, Kyle, Urry and Francis rather than John A. Toews' interpretation of "true Mennonitism" in Russia as being anabaptist Christian.

42. Miriam Warner, "Mennonite Brethren: The Maintenance of Continuity in a Religious Ethnic Group." A Ph.D. Dissertation in Anthropology. (University of California, Berkeley, 1985), p. 144.

CHAPTER SEVEN

COMING TO TERMS WITH ETHNICITY: THE OPTIONS

If I stretch my thinking I see at least eight ways in which those Mennonites, who are Christians, can respond to the fact of Mennonite ethnicity in Canada.

1. *Fusing Mennonite ethnicity and anabaptist Christianity.* Those who advocate such a stance shall for convenience sake be called "the fusers."

This option appeals to many Mennonites because in their own lives they have experienced the fusion of religion and ethnicity. It's part of their identity.

But the situation is not that simple. What seems to be comfortable for individuals may not be proper or right for the whole group. For a congregation or a denomination to take such a stance means that if a person with a non-Mennonite ethnicity wishes to join that Mennonite church, he must try to adopt some Mennonite ethnicity, a frustrating and almost impossible task, or he can become only a partial Mennonite.[1]

Not only is this option inward-oriented, but it also leaves very little place for cross-cultural evangelism. Adopting such a stance creates more problems than it solves. I'm reminded of the reported views of some churches, a few decades ago, that the acceptance of non-Mennonites "might weaken the faith, and cause trouble for the faithful."[2] Fortunately such sentiments are now rare, but some statements raise disquieting questions. For example, according to press reports, Paul Toews, speaking in Winnipeg in November, 1986, "protested the current attempts by many Mennonite Brethren to reject any linkage between faith and a particular culture.' He called that movement a 'fad' that will one day be regretted...."[3]

However, declaring as virtually synonymous two phenomena which are not the same, creates major problems, I suggest, both logically and theologically. Having made my point I am quite prepared to agree that the ethnic factor can be a means for reinforcing anabaptism. But, on balance, the two emphases ultimately are more in tension than in agreement, given what Mennonitism means in North America today and what anabaptism stands for.

2. *Seeing the anabaptist church as a part, but only a part, of the Mennonite ethnic group.* Those who advocate such a stance shall be called "the elitists."

Perhaps this perspective is more an attitude than a reasoned stance but it certainly has influenced many Mennonites. John W. Friesen's research, as reported in chapter 4, documents the persistence of such a mindset. The strength of this stance is that it distinguishes between the ethnic group and the church. The major weaknesses are three: the relative priority of church and ethnic group gets reversed; such a church erects again the ethnic/racial barriers which New Testament writers urged Christians to set aside (I Peter 2: 4-10; Colossians 3: 11); and such a church, by its norms, undermines the universal availability of the very Gospel which, with its exclusivist stance, it ostensibly seeks to conserve. However, if a congregation or conference is content not to proselytize or evangelize outside of the one ethnic group to which it belongs, or does not undertake evangelism at all, then such a stance is feasible and acceptable. It seems that some MBs tilt that way.

3. *Seeing the Mennonite ethnic group and the anabaptist church as constituting two overlapping communities and calling both "Mennonite."* Advocates of this view shall be termed "the overlappers."

Many, perhaps most, Mennonites in North America today hold to such a view. They recognize that "anabaptist church" is not synonymous with "Mennonite ethnic group," but they are very reluctant to do anything to change a situation which has simply evolved historically. Though they differ from the "elitists" in endorsing Christian evangelism and growth, often pursuing these ends vigorously, they ignore the identity problems and the questionable theological stance which their arrangement entails.

The "overlappers" emphasize that for the church, Biblical anabaptism constitutes the uniting glue. Correctly they see this glue and the growing, faithful church as properly extending beyond the Mennonite ethnic group, and at times they work themselves to a point of frustration and exhaustion trying to make "newcomers" feel welcome. But in most cases they have no good response to non-ethnic Mennonites, attenders or members, who say, as one long-time Mennonite Brethren member and deacon told me: "I am a member of a Mennonite Brethren church but I am not a Mennonite." As Miriam Warner's survey data and the many interviews described earlier make clear, most of these "non-ethnics" soon sense that only membership in both of the overlapping communities makes people "real Mennonites" and then they either live with their frustrations or leave. Those members who belong to both communities, meanwhile, often do their utmost to make these frustrated "others" feel welcome. They get them to sample Mennonite culture and they practice much hospitality, but the ultimate ethnic transition, it if occurs at all, is still only one-way — towards Mennonite culture.

4. *Viewing the Mennonite ethnic groups and the anabaptist church as distinct entities but still calling both Mennonite.* People holding to this view shall be termed "the parallelists."

This group, to which many Mennonites belong, differs from the "over-lappers" only in degree. They adopt a two-track view of their identity and the functioning of the church. They know that, other than in immigrant and "minority" churches for linguistic reasons, and normally only for a transitional period, the faithful Christian church must not raise, let alone reinforce, ethnic barriers. Yet they do not wish to deny or reject either their Mennonite ethnicity or their "Mennonite" church. They function fully in both but they try to keep their two identities, and the two meanings of "Mennonite", separate. Their involvements proceed in parallel fashion.

The "parallelists" have the right motivation and some good ideas, but they are attempting to solve the problem the wrong way. They face at least three major, if not insurmountable, problems. In trying to operate an open church they are forcing themselves to give up their own integrated wholeness, their culture. Authentic Christianity never requires that of us. Christians should never be ashamed of their race and ethnicity and should never be required to compartmentalize their lives.

The "parallelists" second problem is that they have difficulty recognizing or ascertaining when they are functioning as anabaptist Mennonites and when as cultural Mennonites. Everything has the same name. In the end, while many keep on trying to separate, sometimes even suppressing, their Mennonite ethnicity, they rarely succeed in the separation of the two parts.

The "parallelists" third problem is that the "non-ethnics" have an even harder time than the ethnics in knowing when Mennonites function culturally and when "religiously." At various kinds of religious and social functions the whole arrangement falls apart. The "parallelist" solution turns out not to be a solution at all. That's why we're still facing and discussing the problem today!

If I call my faith "Mennonite" and I have an ethnicity that is Mennonite, as many of us now do, then what shall the person call himself who has come to share my "Mennonite" faith but has Spanish parents and culture? He says that he is Spanish. Can he join my church and be a religious "Mennonite" knowing that for me "Mennonite" has another meaning? Could I feel at home in his church if his English-language anabaptist church were called "Spanish"? Could I, and my newly-Christian Scottish neighbor, ever feel fully accepted in English-language churches if the church were called Italian, French, Hutterite, Doukhobor, Icelandic, Norwegian, Portuguese, Vietnamese, Chinese, or Punjabi? We are asking individuals, groups, and congregations to do this all the time. If we were asked to identify with such a church, would many of us not be inclined to attend elsewhere on the grounds that for these various anabaptist congregations a particular ethnicity is held in such a high esteem that people of other ethnicities are asked to take on its name? Alternatively, might we not conclude that such a church was established only for a particular immigrant or minority group?

5. *Seeing Mennonite ethnicity as the starting point and then trying to reform and revise it.* The advocates of this view shall be known as "the ethnicists."

I encounter this type occasionally—a few times a year. I have some difficulty knowing exactly what the "ethnicists" have in mind but I think that the common element can be described thus. At present not all members of the Mennonite ethnic group are Christians and some seem to have become rootless or confused about their identity. As Mennonites we must address that problem so that it can be rectified and then Mennonite will again mean Christian, specifically anabaptist Christian. Then we will have a truly praiseworthy ethnoreligious group.

Unless I misread the article, Menno Wiebe's analysis seems to identify, at least somewhat, with this view. Consider his statements.

> Before Mennonites talk about themselves as a religio-ethnic body of peoples [Can one ethnicity contain several "peoples"?] they tend first to look both ways to see who is listening....
>
> I think it could be fairly said that Mennonites are suffering from a case of ethnic shame....
>
> If teachers are the pioneers of urban Mennonitism, then it is significant that these are better equipped than some others to understand the basic Mennonite ideology.... [Since when have supposed Christians been commissioned to have an ideology?]
>
> It is a particular strong point to the advantage of wholesome ethnic reformulation that Mennonites have an abundance of teachers....[4]

Later, in an important section entitled, "Mennonite Ideology Reformulated," Wiebe writes that, "Future Mennonite cohesiveness, if it is not dependent on externals, must be sought elsewhere. Perhaps it can be found in an honest assessment of who Mennonites are sociologically and what they are supposed to be theologically. In other words, the ethnic quality of Mennonites should be regarded as a given."[5] After elaborating on his view, including the need to "inject" Christianity into an unchristian world, Wiebe adds, "But it is above [all] else a Mennonite dream that is needed for a fruitful and valid reformulation of a Mennonite peoplehood."[6]

But why begin with an ethnic Mennonite peoplehood? Why not focus, rather, on the Christian church? Granted, Christians in any ethnic group have a special responsibility to the fellow members of that group, but is it really the ethnic aspect that needs prior attention, prior "reformulation"?

6. *Denying Mennonite ethnicity.* The proponents of this view we shall call the "anti-ethnics."

I have in mind assorted Christians, including some who hold to anabaptist theology, who simply deny that there is, in North America and some other regions, a specific Mennonite ethnicity and who strive to defend and practice Mennonitism as a religion only. They have trouble with the term Mennonitism ("Mennonitentum") because it implies a specific, positive orientation towards a particular set of social-cultural values. Mennonitism, as James Juhnke reminds us, "could be an ongoing cultural establishment." [7]

I took this stance for a few years, more than three decades ago, but found it to be untenable. It was untenable because it was inaccurate and therefore ultimately untrue. It forced me to deny an important part of my heritage and identity and to ignore the social reality in Canada. I would see drunken, non-Christian, Mennonites with whom I had much in common in other respects, individuals whom all non-Mennonites in the community knew were Mennonites, yet I stubbornly insisted that they were not Mennonites at all. Integrity, and the fact that no one believed me, soon compelled me to abandon this option. I have gone the route of the "anti-ethnics" and know that it leads nowhere. This option becomes increasingly indefensible as more and more strong Mennonite communities, often with some non-Christian spokespersons, develop in cities from Ontario to the west coast.

7. *Denying both Mennonite ethnicity and rejecting anabaptist theology.* I shall call such people "the double-denyers."

Their numbers are growing. Here we encounter those Mennonites who, for various reasons, try to deny at least their own Mennonite ethnicity, try to erase all references to Mennonite, and simultaneously reject anabaptist Christianity.

They come in two main categories. One group, perhaps the minority, would like to retain anabaptist theology but as long as it is fused with Mennonite ethnicity or at least goes by the same name, they believe that they must reject both so that the task of evangelization and the healthy process of church growth will not be hindered. Numerous MB pastors belong to this group. Members of the other group, for various reasons, reject anabaptist theology because of its emphasis, as well as Mennonite ethnicity, and then attempt to discard both.

As long as Mennonite ethnicity and anabaptist theology are fused, or go by the same name, we cannot make a very strong case to these groups for the retention of Biblical anabaptism. But if we separated the two somewhat in the official orientation and emphasis of the church, and if we gave them different names, then we could make a strong, hopefully convincing, case. To the first group we would say, "Now you are free to preach Christian anabaptism apart from formal denotations pertaining to any one ethnicity. Your church no longer presents itself as the official bearer of a particular culture." To the second group we would say, "Your excuses are no longer valid. We call you to accept the full Biblical tenets of anabaptist theology. Whether and how you wish to emphasize any ethnicity or culture is up to you. Officially your church now calls you to the whole counsel of God, not to the whole counsel of God officially wrapped in specific ethnic trappings. The theology we proclaim was rediscovered in the 16th century but its rootage is in the 1st century and in the Word of God."

If people in these groups happen also to be pastors, we should also tell them that whatever reasons they might have had for eliminating denominational emphases and designations, these are now gone. Or, at least, they can now be overcome. If, perchance, their problem involves resistance to some anabaptist theological emphases, such instances become cases for counselling. If we have pastors who reject clear teachings of Scripture, teachings which at one time — when they became conference members and/or took up the ministry — they officially and publicly accepted, then we have a problem involving lack of integrity.

At one time, motivated by a desire to be faithful to the Great Commission, I toyed briefly with the idea of publicly, at least in church settings, rejecting both Mennonitism and anabaptism. I was trying to build bridges to other ethnic groups. But I soon realized that my well-motivated attempts resulted in a denial of the great anabaptist rediscoveries of the full Gospel message as well as of my ethnic identity and I therefore rejected the idea.

Sadly, from my perspective, many young Mennonite Brethren leaders and numerous Mennonite Brethren congregations are choosing this unfortunate option.

8. *Separating Mennonite ethnicity from anabaptist theology, in a formal and official sense, and then reaffirming both.*

Those of us who hold to such a view I shall call "the separators—reaffirmers."

This option describes the nature of my commitment to both Anabaptist theology and Mennonite ethnicity, in that order. I derive my identity from both and can strongly and unashamedly affirm both, but I can do so only by separating the two phenomena publicly and officially and by giving them different names. While my particular church might still have Mennonite ethnics as the largest ethnic group, and in my own life the two would still be naturally intertwined, my particular ethnic group would no longer have the only preferred place of privilege and public recognition. By simply removing the ethnic label "Mennonite" we would be eliminating one major hurdle. Where a sense of Mennonite ethnic exclusivity or superiority would still be a problem, attitudinal revision would also be required. It would, in fact, be necessary in order to enhance and maximize the ethical and strategic significance of a formal name change.

As we ponder these options and then proceed, let us always keep this basic guideline in mind. We must arrange our situation in such a way that first generation anabaptists today can become full-fledged church members. They must be able to experience Bible-based anabaptism just as much as those people who were born into homes where such precepts were the norm. That kind of anabaptism is, in the final analysis, the only kind worth retaining.

Chapter 7 — FOOTNOTES

1. Some of the material in this section will appear under the title, "More than Ethnic; Redefining Mennonite Identity," in a book edited by Harry Loewen, *Why I Am A Mennonite* (in press).
2. Reported in an article by Frank Bergman, "We Set The Light In The Window And Then We Lock The Door," *The Canadian Mennonite*, January 28, 1964, p. 5.
3. *Mennonite Brethren Herald*, December 12, 1986, p. 21.

4. Menno Wiebe, "Mennonite Adaptation and Identity" in Henry Poettcker and Rudy A. Regehr, (eds.), *Call to Faithfulness: Essays in Canadian Mennonite Studies* (Winnipeg: Canadian Mennonite Bible College, 1972), pp. 179-181.

5. *Ibid.*, p. 184.

6. *Ibid.*, p. 188.

7. James Juhnke, "Mennonite History and Self Understanding." A paper delivered at Conrad Grebel College, Waterloo, May 30, 1986, p. 16.

CHAPTER EIGHT

A MODEST PROPOSAL

The responses to my national survey, as described in chapter 3, reveal a startling fact. A majority, 55%, want to retain the Mennonite name (many said that they could not think of a suitable alternative), but 75% also say that Mennonite ethnicity is a major or minor problem in the Mennonite Brethren conference in Canada. Since, according to the same survey, 63% of Mennonite Brethren respondents believe that the term Mennonite has an ethnic connotation, we need to face and then deal with a complex problem relating to ethnicity. And as we think and plan we should remind ourselves that already in 1972 only 16% of Mennonite Brethren in Canada got "very much" satisfaction in being known as Mennonites. The data on this point are not encouraging.[1]

Given the obvious trends and all of the other pressing issues described in chapters 1 and 2, as well as in most of the other sections of this book, it seems clear to me that we need change. We need wisdom, courage, and boldness to deal with a logical, theological, and practical problem. We need to think and restate who we are and what we want to be in the future, and we need to do so before our increasing theological diversity becomes theological disarray and then educational and organizational disunity. For anabaptists, of all people, should not fear to break with traditionalism or even tradition.

Mere slogans such as, "Mennonite Brethren is beautiful" won't get us very far. We need some basic re-orientation and clarification concerning our denominational emphasis. We also need to have more clarity in presenting ourselves to others. We need to do this because of confusion in our own ranks as well as in Canadian society generally. The image of Mennonite Brethren is blurred and becoming more blurred. And it's becoming more blurred because of factors we can change or correct, to a considerable degree. Therefore we must act, for we are responsible. Opportunity, or need, plus ability creates accountability.

We must complete, or at least significantly advance, the renewal movement which launched the Mennonite Brethren in 1860. That important event in Russia brought evangelical renewal but not a separation of the renewed church from a specific ethnicity to which it had become culture-bound. Given the social setting, such a separation was perhaps not needed at the time. But times change, and now the time has come for us to initiate some more changes. The Apostle Paul writes, "David served his generation." (Acts 13: 16) Our forefathers in 1860 served their generation. The leaders in our day must serve this generation.

There comes a time when we leave the human agenda, but not the doctrines, of our fathers. There comes a time when we cease to be preoccupied with the agenda of the founders. They had an understanding of their times, they had the will to do what they knew ought to be done. We do not reject that past; we are grateful for it, build on it, and move forward and beyond it. And as we move ahead we affirm that God has not called us first and foremost to be Mennonites but to be Christians, a faithful community of believers. Accepting this priority as valid, means for us that we must be willing to accept the consequences, even if those consequences exact a cost in terms of tradition, sentiment, and personal preference.

Specifically my proposal consists of three parts. The first two, while very important, are not controversial and will not be given much attention here. However, they will need to be given a great deal of attention if my proposal gains acceptance.

Part 1: Concerning Attitude.

The Conference of Mennonite Brethren Churches in Canada [if it's possible, then we should substitute North America] shall commit itself to undertake positive steps to develop more wholesome, more Christian, attitudes towards non-ethnic Mennonites. We need to overcome what has been termed, "a cliquish attitude, intolerance of immaturity, or fear of change." [2] We commit ourselves not to think of other ethnic groups as second class. We pledge ourselves to take Jesus' attitude towards other ethnic groups as our model. (e.g. Matthew 15: 21-28; John 4)

Part 2: Concerning Actions.

The Conference of Mennonite Brethren Churches in Canada shall commit itself to take concrete steps to ensure that attenders and members are not slighted or put down by personal or official actions. We must express and practice full acceptance of people from various ethnic and racial backgrounds and treat them as equals. We must not let ethnicity or race be a determining factor in accepting people as members, treating people with respect and love, or selecting people for ministry, leadership, or other service.

Part 3: Concerning the Name.

The Conference of Mennonite Brethren Churches in Canada should, in the near future, give serious consideration to changing its name. In my view the most appropriate and suitable name would be: "Canadian Conference of Evangelical Anabaptist Churches." A second choice would be: "Canadian Conference of Evangelical Anabaptist Churches (Mennonite Brethren)." The first choice has the advantage of being clear and concise. The second has the advantages of indicating background and providing a Mennonite Brethren label for those who strongly wish to retain it. It would be analogous to "The Lutheran Church (Missouri Synod)" or, "The Church of God in Christ (Holdeman)."

In order for the ethnic problem to be resolved all three parts must be implemented. Any one alone, or even any two by themselves, will not help us very much. Many efforts in the past have failed because only some of the holes in a leaking bucket were closed, so to say. The result, all too often, has been discouragement and the acceptance of the view that the problem cannot be solved. It can be solved but only if we address all three aspects. The three corrective plans must move forward together, like horses drawing a Russian troika. All three have been implemented at various times, but singly, by local churches, and have understandably proven to be inadequate. An attitude change without concurrent changes in actions and in name will produce only isolated and often superficial progress. Changes in action not accompanied by attitudinal change and name change lack integrity. And a name change without real Christ-likeness in attitude and actions won't help us much either. If we are not prepared to act on all three fronts, then our ethnic problems will probably stay with us. Even if we act on all three questions we cannot be assured of progress; we can only be assured that then major progress will be possible. That's a very important distinction.

If we move ahead on these three issues with faith and dedication, then, in my view, on the basis of voluminous written responses on my questionnaires, real progress is more than possible, it is probable. If we do not move ahead on all three issues, then the present problems, especially weakening of denominational ties and increasing theological diversity, will worsen and will become denominational disintegration and theological disarray.

Progress in these three ethnic issues should be accompanied by a fourth major undertaking. As a conference we should officially rededicate ourselves to anabaptist theology with its Biblical emphases as described in previous parts of this monograph. We should stress primarily its Biblical and only secondarily its historical aspects. I must not be misunderstood. The historical development, especially by the 16th century radical reformers, is very important but it remains secondary. The reformers added nothing new — they are significant because they rediscovered and re-applied what Jesus taught, what the entire New Testament taught, and what the early church practiced. I'm optimistic. I believe that if we do well on the ethnic fronts, the progress in this fourth area might well be substantial.

To suggest that we re-evaluate and revise the use of "Mennonite" in order to strengthen anabaptism is unusual, perhaps even novel. But, I submit, it is fully consistent. Many people will doubtless react negatively to this double proposal because they concentrate only on the first part. They likely assume that to question an emphasis on Mennonitism in the church is another attempt to minimize Biblical anabaptism, especially our traditional, if often violated, peace position. But my stance is the opposite of what they fear. I advocate a reassessment of Mennonitism, in the Church, because I want more, not less, anabaptism. Given such a purpose, it may well be that the biggest adjustment will have to be made not by those Mennonite Brethren who are high on Mennonite ethnicity, but by those who are low on anabaptist emphases.

Now let us briefly discuss several important issues which relates to my proposal.

(1) *How serious is the erosion of anabaptist theology among Mennonite Brethren?*

Richard Kyle has documented the decline of anabaptism as Mennonite Brethren have moved from sect to denomination.[3] The data in the 1972 Kauffman-Harder study and the 1982 Mennonite Brethren Church Membership Profile Study tell the same story. While some of our educational institutions, and some of our periodicals, and some of our pastors, and some of our leaders may have become more anabaptist, the bulk of our membership and many of our pastors are becoming less so. Addressing this question specifically John E. Toews writes that, "The responses indicated a progressive weakening of Mennonite Brethren commitment to Anabaptist-Mennonite faith....Only 42 percent of Mennonite Brethren believed Jesus was normative for daily living....Only 54 percent of Mennonite Brethren in 1972 and 1982 rejected participation in war."[4] Toews observes that, "The Profile pictures an ethno-religious group losing its historic religious identity as it is assimilated into American cultural religion."[5] While the Canadian situation is somewhat different from the American, it seems clear that if we do not very soon, and with dedication, address both the three-fold ethnic issue and the theological question, we may soon lose our historic Biblical theology and Mennonitism will linger as a mainly secular ethnic residue. Our conference would then have little reason to exist.

Toews concludes that, "The Profile suggests the Mennonite Brethren Church is at a critical moment in history....The hope for the Mennonite Brethren Church is to become more Anabaptist-Mennonite Brethren."[6] I concur with him fully on the first point. Because of the evidence presented in this volume, I would delete "Mennonite" from the second, but otherwise I agree there also. Anabaptism needs to be stressed anew in our churches, to traditional as well as to first generation Mennonite Brethren, but not in Mennonite ethnic terms. New Mennonite church members will likely accept the substance of our official theology, many have done so already, provided that it comes as Biblical truth rather than as part of someone else's ethnicity.

As we re-emphasize Biblical anabaptism, especially the peace teachings, we must stress that they apply not primarily to military situations but to all Christians at all times. Many pastors have relegated the peace emphasis to the sidelines because we have often defined it much too narrowly. Jesus spelled out his teachings to Jewish audiences that were not even eligible to serve in the military. The Apostle Paul extended the teaching to those gentiles who could and did serve. We must make it relevant to neighborhood families and daily lifestyles in the 1980s and 1990s.

In sum, let us take the following to heart. "To be anabaptist necessitates the rejection of ethnicity as in any way determining Christian faith and faithfulness."[7] And, further, our rekindling and celebration of the "founding of Anabaptism judges all forms of Christian ethnicity and calls for rebirth of a radical faith and a new church that is true to Jesus and the New Testament."[8] That's where I stand and that's what I am urging us to do.

(2) *Is the Canadian Mennonite ethnic problem so serious that we need to consider decisive action now?*

Yes, the situation, as we have seen, is serious. The problems are not becoming fewer or smaller, and uncoordinated local action is not resolving matters.

Whether we welcome the situation or not, history, society, the media, and the academic community have validated the definition of Mennonite as ethnic, and all of these venues are popularizing and propagating that truth. The fact that the standard reference work, *The Canadian Encyclopedia*, introduces its extensive article on Mennonites by calling them a "religious-cultural group," reinforces perception and will help to maintain such views for a long time to come.[9] If we want to deal with the documented ethnic problem, then we must grapple with the reality, not ignore or minimize it.

In a lecture in July, 1986, the Anabaptist patriarch and elder "statesman," J. B. Toews, observed that, "Our forefathers did not distinguish between faith and culture." He is correct. In early years our forefathers' culture was continuous with the culture of North European society, at least most of the time. Then, especially in Russia, enclaves developed which had their own language and culture and were thus discontinuous with the surrounding society and language. That situation was later transplanted to North America where it persisted for several generations and in a few locales still does. But most of us now have a language and a fair bit of culture in common with our society. We should express our faith through our present culture which, for most of us, consists of a blend of ethnic Mennonite and generalized North American ways. We are no longer living in Russia, in enclaves surrounded by people with foreign language and culture. We should indeed express our faith through our culture, but it should be our present culture. In our time our conference must become a cross-cultural body because the Biblical norms require it, because Canada is multicultural, because our membership reflects it, and because the Great Commission assumes it. For earlier generations institutionalizing ethnicity as part of the faith made some sense. For us still to institutionalize that same ethnicity as part of our faith does not make much sense. We now have no language barrier. The time has come to build bridges rather than maintain walls. In adapting to change let us remember that flexibility on secondary questions is a virtue, not a vice.

In this connection I want to express great admiration for the thousands of older Mennonite Brethren in Canada and the U.S. who made major language adjustments in order to adapt to our present society. They have modelled what it means, in the church, to have language and culture be a means to an end but not a churchly end in itself.

Further, since we now have about 3% of our membership in French-speaking Quebec and also some other congregations functioning in additional languages and cultures, we should not, through the church and its designation, impose on them another culture or ethnic designation, namely, the Mennonite culture. Our increasingly multicultural membership should feel fully comfortable in the conference. The Mennonite Brethren conference should emphasize our oneness in Christ. It should recognize various individual and group fusions of ethnicity and culture. It should not officially bind itself to any one of those ethnicities and cultures. Our tradition is great and I am proud of my ethnic identity. For me, Mennonite heritage and anabaptist theology blend, and they always will. Thus I function as an integrated, whole person. But for others integration will involve a different heritage. They, too, wish to lead integrated lives. They have their own ethnic traditions. Shall they be denied anabaptism? Shall they be denied anabaptism in our conference? Let's not try to wiggle around that question. In sum, I want to be inspired by tradition not bound by tradition. Someone has said it well, "Tradition is the living faith of the dead; traditionalism is the dead faith of the living." It is folly and self-deception to affirm the absolute supremacy and authority of Scripture but then to plead traditionalism in order to escape the force and requirements of Scripture.

Gerald Zeeman, an astute observer of Mennonite/Anabaptist developments in Canada, has warned Mennonites that, "Unless you shed the ethnic image, you will have difficulty growing and eventually surviving."[10] Fortunately the shift away from a confusing *church emphasis* of a particular ethnicity has already begun.

It seems rather strange, indeed ironic, that we, who have historically so strongly opposed the fusion of church and state, should so easily accept, and sometimes insist on, the fusion of a vibrant, dynamic anabaptist conference with a particular, albeit good, ethnicity.

(3) *Should we "risk" a name change?*

Some people say "no." The July 16, 1986 *Gospel Herald* carried an interesting report by J. Nelson Kraybill, "The name does matter: 'Community' vs. 'Mennonite' churches."[11] This article is frequently cited as providing justification for retention of the Mennonite name and it does make some very useful points. But, in the end, for various reasons, its case is not convincing. The comparison in the article involves "Mennonite" versus "Community." It does not involve the renaming of an entire conference in the way that the Swedish Baptist Convention in the U.S. changed its name. Also, the community churches surveyed were, on average, only 8 years old and the Mennonite churches 14 years old. There are also other important variables. What this article tells me is that if we keep on drifting towards being a conference of Mennonite Brethren churches that actually call themselves community churches, or something like it, then we are headed for big problems. Those are the very problems which my proposal seeks to prevent!

In a 1985 issue of the *Mennonite Brethren Herald*, editor Harold Jantz raises some basic objections. He writes, "As a denomination we are respected across the country for our witness. Our name does not carry with it an unwelcome stigma."[12] But "respect" is not the major criteria. I respect many associations that I can not join or do not want to join. As for stigma, that's not the question either. I'm not suggesting that "Mennonite" carries a stigma. I'm simply saying that it's ethnic. So are "Chinese," "Vietnamese," "Ukrainian," and "Greek"! I cannot easily take on a Ukrainian or Greek identity and the others, for me, are utterly impossible — but not because of stigma. If we can keep those two issues apart — they are often confused — we will have made much progress. My point, I repeat, is not that the Mennonite label is an embarrassment to be denied or disguised. Rather, the point is that in our setting, as an ethnic name, it is no longer suitable for our denomination.

In discussing "the larger" Mennonite group and "witness," Jantz states that, "To drop the name 'Mennonite' is a way of easing ourselves away from this larger and very significant witness." Not at all, or at least not necessarily. The Brethren in Christ do not call themselves "Mennonite" and they're certainly a part of this "larger witness" to which Jantz refers. And, as stated above, while some Mennonite Brethren are dropping the name "Mennonite" for the reasons Jantz describes, my reason is precisely the opposite. I want to have the name changed so that we can simultaneously strengthen our anabaptist witness, together with other anabaptists, and prevent further erosion of anabaptism.

Jantz then asserts that, "advocacy of a change in name is also a serious challenge to the unity of the church."[13] Not necessarily. Again, given the present growing congregational rejection of "Mennonite" and the corollary theological disunity, my proposal might well arrest the present accelerating trends towards disunity. Or, to put it another way, we already have disunity (and it's worse in the U.S. Conference). The pressing question is — what are we going to do about it?

Why are we so hung up on the word "Mennonite"? It's not a Biblical term or concept. And if it's not Biblical it's not anabaptist. Let us not quietly slip ethnic values into the Biblical tent. Much that is ethnic masquerades as if it's theological. The word "Mennist" was, apparently, first used in 1544 as a nickname. It had no significance for the heroic and saintly early anabaptists. The early anabaptists "did not choose the name for themselves. They preferred to be called *Taufsgesinnt* (those who baptize on confession of faith)."[14]

Menno Simons would surely be aghast and perplexed if he could see how some people cling tenaciously to his name, as if the spiritual welfare of his followers depended on that name. Menno had other priorities. He placed the emphasis elsewhere. His favourite passage, placed on the title page of all of his writings, was I Corinthians 3: 11. "For no one can lay any foundation other than the one already laid, which is Jesus Christ." I'm impressed by the tenacity with which our spiritual forebears clung to the name of Jesus; I'm not particularly impressed by how some anabaptists cling to the name of Menno. Why have we made such a fetish, in the church, of this ethnic name?

Where did we get the notion that we should exalt denominational leaders or founders to positions that God never meant them to have? Leonard Vogt is right. "Some look at me as if taking the name Mennonite Brethren out of our conference is like taking Christ's name out of salvation. I seriously wonder if Menno Simons and the angels wouldn't rejoice if we got a more biblical name."[15]

Rodney Sawatzky, in a chapter devoted to showing, "the correlation between pacifism and Mennonite identity," discusses the 1947 name change of a small conference from "Mennonite Brethren in Christ" to, eventually, "Missionary Church." He raises some valid points. But there's surely a big difference between a name change which was intended to de-emphasize anabaptist theology, and my proposal which has the goal of increasing such an emphasis.[16] Significantly, when Sawatzky explains some key Biblical insights he says that, "This understanding of the Bible and the Christian faith came to the Mennonite tradition through the 'evangelical' Anabaptists of the sixteenth century."[17]

Mennonitism in Canada has had no more eloquent or stronger supporter than Frank H. Epp. But note his insightful comment in 1963. "It would be better for the Mennonite people to lose their name and keep the original meaning than to keep the name and lose the meaning."[18] A year later he wrote, "No, we need not fear to lose a name, as long as we do not lose the meanings the name originally meant to convey...."[19] In 1972 he reaffirmed his view. "Our essential Anabaptist character lies somewhat beyond the Mennonite name and culture as it also lies beyond Canadianism and popular evangelicalism."[20]

In 1977 Frank C. Peters, then moderator of the Canadian Mennonite Brethren Conference, said, "I'm at a point where I am asking whether the use of a name which has an ethnic connotation (as Mennonite Brethren) should not be reconsidered....It is the biggest issue we have faced in fifty years."[21] By now it is sixty years. Many people agree that the issue is very important, but virtually all seem unwilling to do so.

Let us now be willing to deal with it. A few specific points should be added. A denominational name should refer to the core of the Gospel, not something secondary. Does the "M" in MB, or MCC, or Mennonite Brethren Biblical Seminary, refer primarily to Biblical or to cultural values? We have kept this essentially ethnic name for our churches and then tried to downplay it. Surely it is better to change it to something we can always affirm. Furthermore, if Mennonite is an adequate name, then why do increasing numbers of writers and speakers add modifying words such as "evangelical," "religious," "anabaptist" or even, as in our case, "brethren"? True, "Mennonite" describes both ethnic and religious phenomena, but in doing so it obscures the very core of anabaptist theology, namely, that the community of the committed is always a separate and clearly distinct Christian community. Also, not every accommodation is a compromise of principle. Then, too, have we any mandate, as a church, to propagate a Mennonitism not rooted in the New Testament? Additionally, there are several meanings of the term "Mennonite"; if one major meaning is unsuitable for the church, then the others are thereby also rendered unsuitable because of the resulting confusion.

A name change does not change substance and, in itself, will not resolve the all too evident and well-documented ethnic problem, but it is necessary as a prerequisite in order for the ethnic problem to be resolved. It makes resolution possible. Granted, some churches advocate or "practice" a name change for wrong reasons but that does not invalidate the right reasons. Some people say that "Mennonite" is no different than Lutheran or Calvinist but they are wrong. Neither Lutheran nor Calvinist has taken on ethnic connotations anywhere, as far as I know.

There have always been pros and cons in retaining "Mennonite"; in recent years, I believe, the "con" side has gradually become much more weighty than the "pro." Also, over time it is impossible for one name, such as Mennonite, to include and describe an ethnic group, a church, a theology, and, for example, a variety of sausage. Eventually one or more usages will become distorted.

We must never forget that to change the name does not require nor involve a denial or rejection of the past any more than does a change of name at marriage. Rather, sometimes failure to change a name implies a denial of the present, a denial of the new reality.

Timing becomes an important question. The best time to change from an ethnic name to a more Biblical name is after some church-related sociological diversification has begun. The Mennonite Brethren, in Canada, are presently at such a juncture in their development as a people. However, this development cannot proceed much further without name modification. The only question is whether such change comes on an ad hoc fashion or whether it will be given direction and coordination by leaders.

There is no perfect name. Up to a point all names take on meaning. Wilfrid Laurier University, as a replacement for Waterloo Lutheran University, sounded strange but for only a few weeks. Then it took on the new meaning which it presently has. But some names, such as Mennonite, Hutterite, and Doukhobor, are so fraught with well-known ethnic content that it's hopeless to try to give them new meanings. Myron Augsburger seems to have understood that point rather well. Although he has said, time and again, that the Mennonite ethnic heritage should not be forgotten, and has strongly asserted, "I've never been embarrassed to be a Mennonite," which statement I heard him make,[22] it is both surprising and revealing that the record is not quite so impressive. Despite his fervent Mennonite affirmation at the Canadian national Mennonite Brethren convention in 1977, when it came to establishing an anabaptist church in another ethnic milieu, namely, among the Blacks in Washington, D.C., Myron Augsburger did not use the name "Mennonite." Myron Augsburger's anabaptist church in Washington was — maybe is still — called the "Washington Community Fellowship." Very interesting.

If, after a Mennonite Brethren conference name change, done partly for the reason that Augsburger set "Mennonite" aside, some of the present Mennonite Brethren congregations would wish to retain their present MB designation, they should, of course, be permitted to do so, provided that their conference affiliation is also clearly indicated. I am confident that after a relatively short time the new name would gain acceptance in virtually all congregations but the traditional name could well be kept locally if desired.

One final point must be stressed in answering this major question. The reason for my suggestion that anabaptist theology and our anabaptist church should be called something other than Mennonite does not arise from the fact that some Mennonites, by their own words, are not Christians, although that fact adds a further complication. (This "red herring" argument is often trotted out.) After all, some people who call themselves Christian are not Christian! It arises, as stated previously, from the fact that Mennonite, whatever else it may mean, refers to an ethnic group. One is born into an ethnic group; one is born again into the church. The two phenomena are profoundly different and, to avoid confusion and distortion as well as unbiblical designation, that difference should be reflected in the names. Concerning the one name we have no choice and need none. Some of us simply are Mennonites. Concerning the other one, the conference and church name, we have choice and, in my view, we do need a change.

(4) *Have there been other name changes?*

Yes there have been many successful religious and conference name changes. The illustrations can begin with the reminder that Saul's name was changed to Paul. In fact, one can go much further back in biblical history, for name change has a long and venerable tradition, from the time when Abram became Abraham, and Jacob became Israel, down through the ages. In modern times the Dunkers became the Church of the Brethren which resulted in a much more open church and major growth. Some decades ago the Molotschna Mennonite Brethren Conference in Ontario droped "Molotschna." Why was Molotschna dropped? To ask the question is to answer it.

In 1963 the Ontario Amish Mennonite Conference changed its name to the Western Ontario Mennonite Conference. It had gone by the previous name for 40 years but had come to realize that "Amish" created unnecessary problems.

I could cite many more examples but the point that name changes have been carried out successfully has been illustrated.

(5) *Is "Evangelical Anabaptist" the best alternative?*

If we ask only, "Do we like it?" then many people will probably respond with a negative answer. That's not surprising, since it is not altogether familiar. But if we think the matter through carefully, we may well find that "Evangelical Anabaptist" is not only a good alternative but an excellent designation.

A new name for our conference should, as much as possible, measure up to certain requirements:
   *It should draw attention to our denominational heritage. If we deny our heritage we deny who we are.

*It should state or infer a Biblical rather than a geographical or founder emphasis.

*It should not refer to a specific ethnicity. North American Mennonite Brethren are no longer uni-ethnic.

*It should remind people of our denominational emphases such as evangelicalism, biblicism, convenant community, service orientation, peace and an ethic of love, voluntarism, believer's baptism, Christo-centric peoplehood, discipleship, and separation from the world.

*It should permit Mennonites, as well as other ethnic groups, to be, or to become, fully comfortable with it. It must in no way be exclusivist.

*It should differentiate our conference from other Mennonite Conferences while still suggesting some common anabaptist traditions. It should facilitate future acceptance of churches and conferences with similar commitments.

*It should be as accurately descriptive as possible.

*It should, if possible, already have been introduced and widely understood so that we can avoid any sharp break or disconcerting disruption.

*It should be linguistically appropriate and idiomatic in at least English, German and French.

*It should be relatively short, readily recognizable, and easy to remember.

I reviewed scores of possibilities. In my judgement "Evangelical Anabaptist", with or without "Mennonite Brethren" in brackets, was the best choice. "The Kindred Church," "Gospel Brethren," "Bible Brethren," "Community Bible Churches," "Community Fellowships," "Anabaptist Christians," "Anabaptist Brethren," "Evangelical Community Churches," "Christian Disciples" and all the rest fell short on several counts. There may be a better alternative but it has not become obvious to me thus far. We should, however, weigh all the alternatives and make our choice very carefully. The consequences are substantial.

Abe Dueck has suggested that "Evangelical Anabaptism" "is less than adequate in defining our true theological position." [23] I find his reservations and criticisms unconvincing. First, simply to point out that on some anabaptist issues many Mennonite Brethren do not presently hold anbaptist views does not mean that the name should not incorporate them. Dueck shifts back and forth between the "is" and the "ought." According to his argument, if I understand it correctly, the term Mennonite, which Dueck tends to see as theological, would also be inappropriate. Many Mennonite church members do not subscribe to all of "Mennonite" theology either.

Dueck then explains several shortcomings associated with the term "evangelical." The first is that it includes six or more diverse types. He's right; one does encounter confusing usages. But the same thing applies to the term Christian — and not only in South Africa or Lebanon! But that does not mean we should stop calling ourselves Christians. Two points are important. The general thrust of evangelical is clear, and second, none of the other evangelical connotations is so strong that it undermines the validity of the meaning we wish to emphasize. Analogously, we do not stop calling Canada a democracy just because the dictatorial political regime of East Germany also calls itself democratic. Our definition of democracy is clearly understood and enjoys legitimacy and respect. Similarly with "evangelical"; a viable concept predominates. Using "evangelical" in an adjectival form, as in my suggested name, further aids us in minimizing any negative connotations associated with the term.

Dueck mentions three other problems with the term "evangelical": "acculturation," by which he means "accommodation to the values and goals of the world"; "anti-intellectualism"; and "ideological entanglement," by which he means identification with Marxism, or free enterprise capitalism, etc. The writer's comments warrant careful reading and heeding but it should be noted that all three problems involve particular misuses of the term, they do not derive from the actual meaning of the term. That difference must be emphasized. The problem with "Mennonite" is that its intrinsic dictionary meaning is ethnic and it is therefore unsuitable as an anabaptist Christian church name for Mennonite Brethren in North America today. The problems with "evangelical" include a variety of misuses of the term, but those problems do not prevent us from using it to good effect. We emphasize its standard, well-understood, dictionary meaning.

Some Mennonite Brethren in Canada, and more in the U.S., have trouble with the term "anabaptist" and we need to take those concerns seriously also. It is true, we know of some people who call themselves anabaptists but are probably unbelievers, as Mennonite Brethren have traditionally understood the term. Some of these people have quite candidly minimized or set aside the 16th century anabaptist, and New Testament, emphasis on Christian conversion. But, again, we must distinguish between abuse and essence. Dictionaries and history books clearly explain, and generally in similar ways, what anabaptist means. The term has no ethnic meaning, no cultural exclusiveness. Its imprecision is certainly less than the imprecision of "Mennonite," and it can, without much difficulty, be shaped and used to convey the meaning we want to emphasize. What most of the critics are actually complaining about involves actions of some people who call themselves anabaptists, not the well-established meaning of the term, that is, the well-known basic theological distinctives. Moreover, because "Mennonite" already includes much that is not religious, it seems more likely that an evangelical anabaptist church calling itself "Mennonite" will drift into culture-oriented or works-oriented liberalism than will one designating itself an anabaptist. We should review the options spelled out in my column "Peace — Six Expressions," in the *Mennonite Brethren Herald*, February 21, 1986, page 12. In both cases, concerning "evangelical" or "anabaptists," we must avoid accepting either misrepresentation or caricature as authentic.

Taken together the two terms modify each other and in combination they take on a distinctive meaning which neither has by itself. The designation emphasizes and integrates the two streams of our past and fundamental Biblical guidelines for the future. Our proposed new name links us unmistakably to our past, demonstrates our commitment to a peace theology (which originated not with Menno Simons but with Jesus), allows us to resolve most of our ethnic problem, signals our commitment to the atonement and the Great Commission and tells one and all that we're committed to the profound biblical truths which were rediscovered by the radical reformers of the 16th century.

Doubtless some Mennonite Brethren will not be enamoured by my proposed name. There may be good grounds for criticism but I suggest that in some cases the criticism actually grows out of a rejection of some of the doctrines stated in our Mennonite Brethren Confession of Faith, rather than a rejection of the name. Such problems cannot be addressed here, although they, too, need to be addressed. Valid criticisms must be weighed carefully.

In any event, as more of our pastors and other leaders receive their training in our "Evangelical Anabaptist Biblical Seminary" and our "Evangelical Anabaptist Bible College," difficulties with the name would decrease. [Incidentally, I believe that such a restatement, without ethnic labels, of identity and purpose would result in substantial growth in student body]. I think that the transition would go smoothly and that the name would gain acceptance rather quickly. We would then ask ourselves why we didn't make such a change much sooner!

Additional grounds for choosing "Evangelical Anabaptist" are that the label is already widely used by Mennonite writers, exactly in the sense that we would want it understood, and also by experts in various disciplines outside of our own ranks. A few examples must suffice.

I have already quoted Rodney Sawatzky's reference to "the 'evangelical' Anabaptists of the sixteenth century." In 1985 George Epp, director of the Mennonite Studies Centre at the University of Winnipeg, wrote the following. "There is only one Anabaptist theology and that is an Evangelical Anabaptist theology, using 'evangelical' in the best sense of that word — a theology based on Scripture and not on issues." [24]

E. K. Francis writes that "Mennonitism as a religious system," if one can separate it from the ethnic aspect, "is the direct continuation of Evangelical Anabaptism, one of the major reform movements of the sixteenth century." [25] He states later that, "In the Netherlands....Protestantism was almost identical with Evangelical Anabaptism." [26]

Thomas G. Sanders, one of the best scholars in comparative church-state studies, writes: "First appearing under the leadership of Conrad Grebel in Switzerland in 1523, those usually called Evangelical Anabaptists gained their most eloquent spokesman in Menno Simons...." [27] Thus "Evangelical Anabaptist," as a concept and as a designtion, predated Menno! In the subsequent 12 pages Sanders repeatedly refers to "Evangelical Anabaptists" as the most thorough reformers.

Many contemporary Mennonite and Brethren in Christ writers and spokesmen such as John Howard Yoder, Frank C. Peters, Ron Sider, and Harry Loewen have frequently used the term. And Harold Jantz, while urging that we not replace the name "Mennonite," does so partly on the ground that the Mennonite "witness...sincerely seeks to be both evangelical and anabaptist...." [28] Even James Coggins, who generally argues for the retention of the Mennonite label, cites both "anabaptist" and "evangelical" as two of the "Four Great Traditions" of Christianity in the Western World. [The other two are "Roman Catholic" and "Protestant." "Mennonite" is not mentioned.][29] While Coggins wishes to retain the Mennonite label, he also makes an excellent case for Evangelical Anabaptist substance. "Moreover, Mennonite Brethren added an Anabaptist emphasis to evangelicalism's emphasis...." In summation he asks:

Are we Anabaptists or evangelicals? The answer is that we are neither — or, rather, both. We are Anabaptists who insist that we are saved by faith and not by works of social action, that salvation is more of a gift than an achievement. We are evangelicals who believe that a conversion experience does not solve all problems and that we are called to a lifestyle that feeds the hungry, clothes the naked, and beats swords into ploughshares. It is impossible to eliminate either of our two traditions without a serious, painful and dangerous rupturing of our fellowship....

We must live with a duality....the tension can also be creative... we combine the strengths of both traditions.[30]

Coggins makes a good case for that which my proposal affirms.

A few disclaimers are in order. I have no problem with the emphasis on ethnic Mennonitism in relief sales, restaurants, art events, appropriate entertainment, service ventures, etc., provided that there are multi-ethnic options at the church and that we have no privileged ethnic caste there. Nor am I suggesting any retroactive separation of ethnicity and religion. Our history will always be Mennonite Brethren history and we should continue our historical research and writing. Our past must be preserved and appreciated. (Although we keep in mind that not every historical fact is universal truth.) Nor do I necessarily recommend an ethnic re-orientation and name change for all Mennonite Conferences. Each group must sort out its own priorities and set its own goals. My proposal involves particularly the Mennonite Brethren in Canada, though the analysis has wider validity.

If my proposal gains acceptance, then our conference would lose its ethnic designation but not its ethnic congregations. There should always be a large place for minorities, including various language minorities, in our conference. There are appropriate eras and places for these to function as separate, full-fledged, congregations within our conference. Although some ethnic groups will be much larger than others, we all remind ourselves that at the foot of the cross the ground is level.

If this proposal is accepted, we would thereby also resolve the slowly but steadily developing reaction to the gender bias in "Mennonite Brethren." We would thus nip a potentially serious problem in the bud. That could be another important reason for making the proposed change. We would resolve a problem without going through a major controversy about it.

John A. Toews has written that, "the tension between a particular culture and Christian ethics can never be fully resolved and no final solution of the problem is ever possible."[31] He is right, and we can extend his point to cover ethnicity and denominational identity, but we do have a

God-given mandate to do what we perceive to be necessary and what, with God's help, we can. Granted, there are some problems with the proposed option — there are problems with all options including doing nothing — but it seems to present fewer difficulties, by far, than any other.

We owe it to Canadian society, and to the larger anabaptist spectrum, to provide at least one authentically and avowedly evangelical-anabaptist conference which is not officially ethnic. The Mennonite Brethren are in the best position to become that option. Are we up to it? What is our first priority? The Great Commission or comfortable tradition?

A carefully and prayerfully arranged transition to the "Canadian Conference of Evangelical Anabaptist Churches", or some other alternative, could well be the occasion for a major denominational celebration — a recommitment and renewal. Beyond that, perhaps in closer cooperation with other evangelical anabaptists who would want to work with us, it could and should result in a far-reaching evangelical anabaptist resurgence, and in an evangelical anabaptist congregation in every city and town, as well as in many more rural communities, across this land.

Chapter 8 — FOOTNOTES

1. J. Howard Kauffman and Leland Harder, *Anabaptists Four Centuries Later* (Scottdale, PA: Herald Press, 1975), p. 77.
2. Elmer A. Martens, "Facing the Mission of the Church at Home," in A. J. Klassen, (ed.), *The Church In Mission* (Hillsboro, KS: Board of Christian Literature, 1967), p. 198.
3. Richard G. Kyle, *From Sect to Denomination: Church Types and Their Implications for Mennonite Brethren History* (Hillsboro, KS: Center for Mennonite Brethren Studies, 1985), pp. 181.
4. John E. Toews, "Theological Reflections," A Special issue of *Direction*, Fall, 1985, p. 62.
5. *Ibid.*, p. 64.
6. *Ibid.*, p. 68.
7. John E. Toews, *Christian Leader*, January 6, 1976, p. 4.
8. *Ibid.*, p. 2.
9. "Mennonites." *The Canadian Encyclopedia*, 1985, Vol. 2., pp. 1117-1118.
10. Quoted in *The Yearbook of the Canadian Conference of Mennonite Brethren Churches*, (Winnipeg: Christian Press, 1978), p. 154.
11. J. Nelson Kraybill, "The name does matter: 'Community' vs. 'Mennonite' Churches," *Gospel Herald*, July 16, 1985, pp. 494-495.
12. Harold Jantz, *Mennonite Brethren Herald*, January 11, 1985, p. 11.
13. *Ibid.*, p. 11.
14. *One Family of Faith*. A pamphlet. (Akron, PA: Mennonite Central Committee, n.d.).
15. *The Christian Leader*, November 21, 1978, p. 8.
16. Rodney Sawatzky, "Pacifism and Mennonite Identity," in H. Poettcker and R. Regehr, (eds.), *Call to Faithfulness: Essays in Canadian Mennonite Studies* (Winnipeg: Canadian Mennonite Bible College, 1972), p. 189-191f.
17. *Ibid.*, p. 191.
18. Frank H. Epp. Editorial, *The Canadian Mennonite*, August 6, 1963, p. 5.
19. An editorial, *The Canadian Mennonite*, January 7, 1964.
20. Frank H. Epp, "The Struggle for Recognition," in H. Poettcker and R. Regehr, (eds.), *Call to Faithfulness: Essays in Canadian Mennonite Studies* (Winnipeg: Canadian Mennonite Bible College, 1972), p. 172.
21. Frank C. Peters, *Mennonite Brethren Herald*, July 22, 1977, p. 2-4.
22. See the report in *The Christian Leader*, August 2, 1977, p. 8.
23. Abe Dueck, "Mennonite Brethren Definitions and Temptations," *Mennonite Brethren Bible College Bulletin*, Spring, 1985, pp. 3-5. The statement appears on page 4.
24. *Mennonite Reporter*, June 10, 1985, p. 7.

25. E. K. Francis, "The Russian Mennonites: From Religious to Ethnic Group," *The American Journal of Sociology*, September, 1948, p. 102.

26. *Ibid.*, p. 103.

27. Thomas G. Sanders, *Protestant Concepts of Church and State* (New York: Holt, Rinehart and Winston, 1964), p. 76.

28. *Mennonite Brethren Herald*, January 11, 1985, p. 11.

29. James Coggins, "Where do Mennonite Brethren fit in?" *Mennonite Brethren Herald*, May 17, 1985, p. 2-3.

30. *Ibid.*, p. 3.

31. John A. Toews, "Cultural Change and Christian Ethics: A Historical Perspective," *Voice*, vol. xv (November-December, 1966), p. 1.

CHAPTER NINE

QUESTIONS COMMONLY ASKED

1. *Why talk about Mennonitism? There is no problem.*

Many people see no problem. Even though the local paper was point-
ing out that Mennonite meant ethnic, a Fraser Valley pastor asserted that
the problem which had existed in his previous pastorate "doesn't exist
in this community."[1] Subsequently I interviewed a number of people in
that community and discovered that for a significant percentage it was
a problem. That pastor probably got his impression from "non-ethnics"
attending his church. But such a thoroughly biased sampling of opinion,
an approach often used, is akin to asking residents of the Yukon if it's too
cold to live there.

Many prominent Mennonite leaders see no ethnic problem, at least not
with the name. Having described the historical meaning of "Mennonite,"
and Mennonite church, Katie Funk Wiebe writes: "If the name doesn't
mean that today, the problem is not with the name, but with us, its members."[2] James Pankratz writes from Winnipeg: "The association of ethnicity with the name 'Mennonite' does occur occasionally today, and
especially in some regions of southern Manitoba and Ontario; but I do not
encounter it very often.... The label on the church is not the issue...."[3]
He then asserts that the problem involves ethics, not ethnicity. I have
demonstrated that it involves both.

My survey results support certain views. Most respondents associate
"Mennonite" with ethnicity, and most MBs think that Mennonite ethnicity constitutes a problem at the local level. No less than 79% of Canadian MB pastors and other leaders believe that it constitutes a problem
nationally. It's not easy — nor wise — to ignore such data.

Frequent spokesman Dave Hubert writes: "You will no doubt agree
that from the perspective of the global village, Mennonitism is not an ethnic phenomenon."[4] Yes, but we do not live in a global village. We live

in particular villages, in cities, towns, and rural areas in North America. We may think of the world as a village, but even the privileged 6% which lives in Canada and the US does not really interact, in anything other than a sporadic way, with Mennonites who are part of the other 94%, most of whom couldn't even speak a common language with us. Our perspective must be primarily North American and there Mennonite does mean ethnic. I thought that's what Hubert also believed when he accepted membership, as a representative of Alberta Mennonites, on the ethnic Alberta Cultural Heritage Council.[5] The ethnic evidence has often been denied because its not universal, but in Canada it's overwhelming.

The "global perspective" can be very misleading. Averaging calorie consumption, there is no malnutrition on earth. And seasonally adjusted, Canada has no winter. Sometimes the larger view obscures truth.

"It is easy, in a situation where ethnic and ecclesiastical affiliations often coincided, for cultural attachments to mask themselves as theological principles."[6] Let us beware.

Some will keep on insisting that there is no ethnic, specifically name, problem. I wish that it were thus. To be sure, the ethnic problems can be suppressed, but the evidence can not be denied.

2. *Would not a name change constitute a betrayal of our anabaptist traditions and beliefs?*

No, it would not. Our religious founders did not call themselves Mennonites and did not establish an ethnicity. Both of those items came later. Waldo Hiebert put it correctly at the 1978 Mennonite World Conference in Wichita. In his sermon entitled, "One Greater Than Menno (Matthew 12:38-42)," he said, "For a proper identification of Mennonites we must speak of Jesus.... Today we must say, the answer is not Menno but the answer is the person to whom he pointed, even Jesus...." Essence is not at issue in the proposed name change.

Further, replacing the term Mennonite with a more suitable label does not mean that we would thereby succumb to, or be acculturated into, some sort of North American "common denominator" or "evangelical mainstream." Often the two options, Mennonitism and "mainstream evangelicalism" are simplistically and erroneously posited as the only two options. Paul Toews says that "to reject 'any linkage between faith and a particular culture'... implies an uncritical assimilation into the surrounding culture of our day."[7] It does not necessarily imply such uncritical assimilation! It does not necessarily imply any assimilation. That stance illustrates the simplistic analysis I sometimes encounter.

In his powerful message on Sunday, July 6, 1986, the Brethren in Christ preacher, Ron Sider, addressing a huge centennial rally in Kitchener, Ontario, demonstrated very convincingly that one does not have to wear a Mennonite badge in order to be a thorough-going evangelical anabaptist. Many people have believed this simplistic myth for too long. It's time that the matter be clarified. A name change would involve a change in some denominational distinctiveness, but not of any that ultimately count.

Gordon Harland of the University of Winnipeg put the matter in proper perspective. "To repeat what our fathers and mothers in the faith said in the same way in which they said it, is to fail to say what they said."

For many of us anabaptism comes via the 16th century; for others not. Nor should it. The key element is the acceptance of the Biblical norm, not how people discover it. Or have we been seduced into believing that "the way" is as important as "The Way"?

Anabaptists stress that the Bible is the final authority — to that we call all people. All who join with us form a united, equally valued, people of God. In our Canadian communities we must not bind our theology to any one ethnicity.

3. *Would not a formal name change from Mennonite Brethren to something else create a loss of identity?*

No, it would not. Our most important identity involves our Christian essence and that, of course, would remain unaffected. Beyond that, we would retain all local and congregational bonds. The key aspect which would be affected is church reinforcement of Mennonite ethnicity. Perhaps a diagram will help us to understand our identity.

Diagram 1. Canadian Categories of Mennonites

A = secular Mennonites. e.g. Patrick Friesen, a highly regarded Mennonite poet and playwright.

B = Christian Mennonites who attend non-anabaptist churches. e.g. Peter Penner, a highly regarded Mennonite professor in Sackville, NB. He is associated with the United Church.

C = Christian Mennonites who attend Mennonite/anabaptist churches. e.g. Harold Jantz, well-known Mennonite editor who belongs to an M.B. church. People in this category form a Mennonite anabaptist peoplehood.

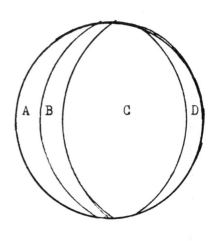

D = non-Mennonite Christians who attend "Mennonite"/anabaptist churches. e.g. Carlin Weinhauer, well-known pastor of an M.B. church. This category also includes French-speaking, Chinese-speaking, Hindi-speaking, and other "Mennonite" churches where the dominant ethnicity is not Mennonite.

The three categories — A, B, C — constitute the Canadian Mennonite ethnic community, an ethnic Mennonite peoplehood.

The two categories — C and D — constitute the Canadian "Mennonite"community, a Christian anabaptist peoplehood.

People represented by section A are Mennonite only in ethnic terms. People represented by section B are Mennonite in ethnic terms and are also religious. Many identify personally with the anabaptist part of Canadian "Mennonitism" but for various reasons do not attend Mennonite/anabaptist churches. People represented by section C are Mennonite in both ethnic and religious terms. They form the traditional Mennonite/anabaptist peoplehood. People represented by section D are Christians of non-Mennonite ethnicity who attend Mennonite churches. Many of these Christians accept anabaptist theological emphases. Christians represented by sections C and D form the contemporary Christian/anabaptist peoplehood.

In recent years individuals in section A have become more prominent than they used to be. Simultaneously, Christians represented by section D have become more numerous. Most people represented by section D do not get involved in Mennonite ethnic activities or causes. Many do not know how to respond to ethnic activities and causes which celebrate or emphasize Mennonite ethnicity.

Diagram 2. Global Categories of Mennonites

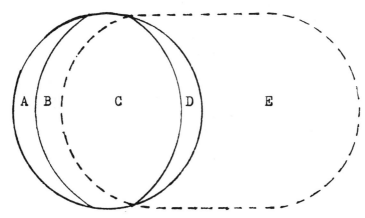

A = secular Mennonites. These people are ethno-cultural Mennonites without a religious emphasis. They are found only in countries such as Canada, the US, the USSR, Brazil, Paraguay, etc., where the term Mennonite has both a religious and an ethnic meeting.

B = Christian Mennonites who attend non-anabaptist churches. (e.g. Baptist, Christian and Missionary Alliance, United, Methodist, Presbyterian, Pentecostal, etc.) These people are Mennonite in both ethnic and religious terms although some do not accept anabaptist emphases. They are found in countries where the term Mennonite has both a religious and en ethnic meaning.

C = Christian Mennonites who attend Mennonite/anabaptist churches. These people are Mennonite in both ethnic and religious terms. They are found in countries, such as Canada and the US, where the term Mennonite has both a religious and an ethnic meaning.

D = non-Mennonite Christians who attend "Mennonite"/anabaptist churches. In Canada and the US we also have some individual churches, such as "Bethel Chinese Christian," "Greek Evangelical Christian," "Hindi Punjabi Gospel," "Templo El Calvario," and "El Faro," as well as a few small M.B. conferences in Quebec, North Carolina, etc., which belong to this category. Because the Canadian and US Mennonite Brethren conferences are dominated by people represented by section C, such ethnically non-Mennonite churches and conferences tend not to be fully involved in Canadian and US conference events and activities. Because these churches and conferences are linguistically/culturally separate — and sometimes geographically distant — this lack of full involvement and integration has not, thus far, become a major problem. In the future these ethnically "different" churches and conferences will either remain marginalized, or we will be forced to acknowledge and then clarify our identity and name problems. If we deal positively with these issues, all churches and conferences can be successfully integrated.

E = Mennonite/anabaptist churches in countries where Mennonite has only a religious meaning. Theological emphases range from conservative to liberal.

A + B + C = an ethnic Mennonite peoplehood spanning various countries. This kind of peoplehood exists in countries where the term Mennonite has both a religious and an ethnic meaning.

D + E = anabaptists have various non-Mennonite ethnic backgrounds. Section E represents the Mennonite/anabaptist churches in countries such as India, Zaire, Japan, Indonesia, etc., where the term Mennonite has only a religious meaning. Section D represents ethnically non-Mennonite Christians, churches, and conferences in countries such as Canada and the US where the term Mennonite has both a religious and an ethnic meaning.

C + D + E = the world-wide Mennonite/anabaptist peoplehood, or church. Only the C section possesses Mennonite ethnicity as well.

Area "C" is a comfortable place to be, since there a person's ethnicity and faith are fused. But a church rooted in "C," but still calling itself by a name shared with "A," will have very great difficulty extending itself and having any local evangelical success other than in area "A."

Now let us assume for a moment that Mennonite Brethren in North America were mainly Swedish. Then "A" would represent Swedish culture and ethnicity and, in a sense, Sweden. I submit that if we were mainly Swedish we would have an easier time replacing the name "Swedish" than we do replacing the name "Mennonite." As Swedes we would still have a clearly secular Swedish culture and, importantly, a Sweden with which to identify. But if we let go of "Mennonite" in our church name, we have only a quasi-secular culture and no land of Menno at all, with which to identify. Thus our problem is greater and our emotions become more intense. And that's one reason why it is so difficult for us to comprehend what needs to be done, and then do it!

That also partially explains why so many of us, thousands of us, including secular Mennonites, make pilgrimages to Mennonite "root regions" in The Netherlands, in Switzerland, in Austria, and especially in Russia. We are yearning for a homeland. I suggest that's why we now have college ad university courses on the Mennonite Russian experiences, many paintings of our Russian sojourn, a growing stream of reminiscences and other books on the topic, and a growing business in Russian Mennonite artifacts and antiques. We also have numerous films on our Russian era, Russian Mennonite cookbooks and restaurants, Russian Mennonite dramas, and assorted other expressions of Russian Mennonite nostalgia. Interestingly, Soviet Intourist guides are now using first-rate Mennonite-made Canadian maps to help tourists by the busload find their way around in the Ukraine. I actually helped Intourist to revise one of their maps.

Yes, as Mennonites, especially Russian Mennonites, we have a group identity problem. We never quite accepted Russia as our motherland and yet we have no other. Our centuries of wandering have left us with a social and psychological void, and this void becomes greater as the anabaptist church "covenant community" weakens. But surely this consequence of historical migrations, accentuated by our current neglect of the close community of Christian brothers and sisters, does not give us the moral right to make the church, as ethnic entity, fill that secular void! History and contemporary social-religious developments in Canada explain how the Mennonite Brethren church came to fill a secular identity need, but that does not mean that the perpetuation of such a practice is right.

The solution involves strengthening the church community, making that primary "covenant brotherhood" our key reference point, and looking to national citizenship and assorted ethnicities, including Mennonite, to fill additional personal and group needs.

A truly Christian peoplehood, as we read in the book of Acts, does not require a homogeneous ethnicity in order for its members to have a full sense of identity and worth. We need to read and reread Acts chapter 2, very carefully and very thoughtfully. In coming to the faith and in living in the Christian "brotherhood," there is no such thing as a right history or a right pedigree.

It is true, "He who has no people has no God," but "people" here obviously refers to church, not to ethnicity. Often certain Mennonite scholars use this Biblical concept to justify ethnic clanishness — and most hearers, swayed by the seemingly sound logic, nod approvingly. Let us not lose sight of the Church as the body and people of Christ.

The carriers of Mennonite culture have already begun to shift from the church to other vehicles. Those are healthy developments. Let us consciously move in that direction.

4. *"But I don't want a name change. I don't want to let go of "Mennonite."*

About 50 respondents to my questionnaire expressed such sentiments. I cannot deny their personal feelings but I can point out that to hang on to a name just because it makes me feel good can be an expression of personal or corporate self-centredness and pride. What did the Apostle Paul say about his own grand ethnicity? He gladly counted it as "loss," in order to achieve a greater gain. (Philippians 3:7-11)

Ultimately reason cannot override will. I cannot imagine any arguments or evidence which could convince those people who have decided to let their will have the last word.

5. *Does not Mennonite diversity in the global scene prove that "Mennonite" does not mean a particular ethnicity?*

Many otherwise well-informed people misread the evidence and then make this argument. "Last summer's Mennonite World Conference, where thousands of Mennonites from 44 different national and ethnic backgrounds were celebrating their spiritual commonality, was vivid proof that no particular tribe or culture can be equated with the 'Mennonite Way.' *Zwieback* and *Plumamousse* are no more Mennonite than Indian curry or Zairian luku."[8] Try telling that to Multiculturalism Canada, or the publishers of Mennonite cookbooks, or the organizers of Mennonite cultural tours in Ontario, or to the operators of the Mennonite Village Museum at Steinbach, or to the peddlers of Mennonite paintings and quilts. Ask Kathy and Reg Good whether they explained the diet and folkways of the large French-Canadian MB conference in Quebec when they applied for a Multicultural travel grant. Ask David Hubert if he explains native Alberta Mennonite Indians' ethnic values when he speaks at sessions of the Alberta Cultural Heritage Council.

Do Mennonites in India, Nigeria, Japan, Zaire, or Ethiopia operate Saturday language and heritage schools? Do they teach their children about the educational agricultural innovation of Johann Cornies in Russia? Do they consider their non-Christian family members to be Mennonite? Do their neighbors consider such non-Christian family members to be Mennonite? Do they apply to their governments for cultural grants for their Mennonite tribe? Do they apply for publishing subsidies to preserve their Mennonite cultural heritage? Do they form a (non-church) Mennonite orchestra or drama troupe? Are they compiling a Mennonite dictionary? Would they know what to put into it?

In most of the world "Mennonite" means a religion, a faith. That fact must be readily acknowledged and affirmed. But in certain countries such as Canada, the US, the USSR, Mexico, Brazil, Paraguay, Uraguay, Belize, and a few others it also has a very powerful ethnic meaning. Indeed, this ethnic image exists even in parts of Europe. This fact was underscored by comments made by a Wilfrid Laurier University colleague lecturing in Marburg, Germany. In a personal letter sent in January, 1987, he describes some of his lectures. "One was on the Mennonites in Canada.... The image the Germans have of Mennonites relates to horse and buggies, dark clothes, hats and meeting houses. My constant reminder that the Old Order only represent a small portion of the Mennonites I believe went unheeded."

An April 13, 1985 letter written by George Wiebe, a prominent Canadian Mennonite musician, captures the dilemma, I presume unintentionally. "In keeping with the multi-cultural nature of the world-wide Mennonite church, THE ABIDING PLACE has several spoken and musical items from non-ethnic Mennonites." Some months later, when I carefully watched many concert-goers in a very large audience of ethnic-Mennonites read this statement on their concert programs, hardly a one apparently noted the logical contradiction in this printed comment.

Moreover, not all anabaptists in other countries call themselves Mennonite. The PIPKA Conference in Indonesia is a classic example.

On this question, in particular, it's high time that we acknowledge reality and face the facts.

6. *Would not a change of name confuse people?*

Hardly. Many people, including many Mennonites, are now very confused about what "Mennonite" means. A clear statement of what we believe, of how we relate our Mennonite ethnicity to our faith, and of why we let go of an ethnic denominational name in favour of a theological name, would help to clear the atmosphere. It would help clear up, not create, confusion.

Granted, some of our members might become disturbed. Established patterns are not changed easily. We might lose some members and even some congregations. But that's happening now! Besides, the main question is not "What is most popular?" but, "Which option is ethically and theologically best?" We must give most weight to the merits of the arguments.

An important step we should take to clarify matters in our own ranks is to make sure that all pastors and denominational leaders accept unequivocally our entire Confession of Faith. To the extent that we believe a better understanding of the Word warrants revision of our Confession of Faith, we should, of course, revise it.

7. *Is not the situation already improving?*

Almost all evidence indicates that Mennonite ethnicity in Canada continues to be vigorous and resilient. Nurtured by affluence, a search for roots, multicultural policies, the emergence of a growing Mennonite intelligentsia, and the proliferation of ethnic awareness, Mennonitism will likely, and fortunately, thrive for many years to come, especially in Manitoba.[9] Ed Unrau is right when he writes thus about Mennonites. "In Manitoba they lived more like an ethnic group than in any other place in their history."[10] Mennonite ethnicity in Canada is not declining but, in part, it is changing its expression. We should note, in this regard, that while in earlier times recognized regional, national, and international Mennonite spokesmen were all church people, that is no longer the case. Now some, an increasing number, are secular.

Even if some MBs are in a partial ethnic transition, many Mennonites in Canada are not. It's not "only a problem for this generation," as one respondent put it. The Old Order and many other components and aspects will maintain both the reality and the perception of Mennonitism as ethnic for generations to come. And as more Mennonite museums are built; literature written; dramas performed; and good, sound Mennonitism taught on campuses, it may even increase. James Urry has suggested that since 1955 the practice of Mennonites referring to themselves as ethnic has increased markedly.

And if, perchance, our conference really becomes substantially "de-ethnicized" that's an additional reason to replace a name that then would no longer fit.

Yes, there will always be a few who manage to jump the ethnic hurdles, but we should not assume that they symbolize the solution to the problem. They illustrate it! Besides, many of these people report that they have experienced serious problems as they encountered the various ethnic aspects in our churches more fully. Our minority-language congregations will soon feel that way as well, unless we change. For now they remain largely isolated and sheltered.

8. *What's wrong with being an ethnic church? Aren't all people ethnic?*

Religious-cultural integration is very important. If we do not achieve it or seek to achieve it, we will lead fractured lives. But the dynamics of integration involve the individual, the family, and the church in a generic or catalytic sense but not in the sense of a conference promoting itself as the embodiment of a specific ethnicity. Exceptions because of special linguistic or transitional reasons have already been noted.

Yes, all people are ethnic, but there is a right and a wrong way to handle our ethnicity. Eric Mierau has addressed some of the aspects involved. "But ethnicity is a very special problem for Mennonites — a problem compounded by confusion between theological and non-theological perceptions of peoplehood."[11] He describes how events in history "forged that ethnic Mennonite identity that continues to confuse us today.... We continue to see ourselves as an ethnic group called Mennonite."[12] He then adds, "The Anabaptist vision, however, must survive in continuously updated, reinterpreted, contemporary forms."[13] Indeed, that is the challenge. He continues. "To be a true church of Jesus Christ, our time to lose a particular ethnicity is long overdue." And again, "No church that identifies itself with a particular ethnic strain is fulfilling its calling as a reconciling community of Christians.... Ethnic traps will always lure the church, and they must always be guarded against."[14] Other than making a case for immigrant and certain kinds of minority churches, or those which use a state name as a general identification (e.g. American Baptist, British Presbyterian), I agree with the comments as quoted.

We need both to accept our ethnicity and break the boundaries of ethnicity. We need to remember that nostalgia is not a suitable basis for the church of Jesus Christ and that, if the church is equated with an ethnic group, especially a smallish minority, then, over time, that church will almost assuredly be redefined in terms of ethnic peoplehood.

Understanding someone's ethnic background, including our own, is always important. Affirming ethnic diversity in the church is biblical, defining Christianity in ethnic terms is wrong. One is born into an ethnic group; one is born again into the church. Christians have a perpetual mandate to think in terms of "they and us," but such a distinction must always be Gospel-related, not ethnic-related.

We take ourselves too seriously and our Lord not seriously enough. Some MBs say, as one questionnaire respondent put it: "We are no more exclusive or cliquish than Baptists, etc." That has not been my experience. But even if that assessment is partially or totally valid, the fact remains that Baptist and Methodist cliquishness can be overcome by change of attitude and by education; Mennonite not, because Mennonite signifies an authentic, and in many ways natural and justifiable, clanishness.

9. *Are not the ethnic churches in North America growing rapidly?*

Some are. There is a place for ethnic congregations, especially if a language barrier exists. But such congregations must then reach out to the non-Christians who speak that language. Christian missionaries use such an approach all the time. But if a church or conference has "language access" to other ethnic groups, it must not create a barrier by fusing its ethnicity with the Gospel.

The ethnic churches which are growing rapidly are those ministering to immigrant peoples who still have their own closed communities. Most Mennonites in Canada, and certainly the Mennonite Brethren, can no longer claim to be such a church or conference. Our mandate must at least match our secular penetration of society.

10. *Would any other name not produce the same problems?*

Not necessarily. Names do make a difference. Commercial advertisers very carefully craft brand names and then jealously guard them. They know the importance of a particular name.

In this connection two news items caught my attention. "What's in a name? Apparently quite a bit, as the University of Manitoba found out recently."[15] When the university changed the name of its Home Economics faculty to the Faculty of Human Ecology, in an attempt to erase what is called the "unfavorable stereotype created by the old name," the "first-year enrolment promptly jumped almost 55 per cent."[16] Names do make a difference.

The second story carried the headline, "Having the name Clifford Olson made life tough for the salesman."[17]

If we can honestly say that our present Mennonite Brethren conference would be no less effective in its Christian witness if it were called "Serbian Brethren," or "Doukhobor Church," or "Sons of Freedom Church," then I will gladly state that my proposal is irrelevant.

11. *Can't we educate the public?*

It's one thing to minimize ethnicity in our churches; it's something entirely different to try to counteract the massive output of the national media and of the ethnic Mennonite voices. Frankly, the effort is futile. Those who think that the solution lies in better public relations and education are whistling in the dark. Besides, we have more important things to do. The better solution involves removing from the church the focus of the ethnic emphasis. To think that MBs can educate Canadians to think of Mennonite Brethren as non-ethnic constitutes a grand delusion.

12. *How would a name change affect our relations with other Mennonite conferences and inter-Mennonite agencies?*

Mennonite Brethren now participate in approximately 55 of the 70 or so major inter-Mennonite and inter-anabaptist agencies in North America and beyond, and I see no reason why a name change should affect such participation.[18] We would follow the practice set by the Brethren in Christ. The Evangelical Anabaptists would be no less committed to MCC, Mennonite Disaster Service, Mennonite Mutual Aid, etc., than are the Mennonite Brethren. Instead of "Mennonite and Brethren in Christ," we would say. "Mennonite, Brethren in Christ, and Evangelical Anabaptist."

13. *How would a Canadian Conference name affect our mission work overseas?*

There would be some ramifications but nothing serious. After all, as John B. Toews tells us, "For years Third World Mennonites have told Western Mennonites of their difficulties with our ingrained ethos perhaps derived more from ethnicity than from some purer religious-ideological source. They are prepared to accept Anabaptism as an ideal, but contemporary Western Mennonitism is another matter."[19] The problems would lie with us, not with them.

Significantly, the Japan Anabaptist Centre in Tokyo has launched a series of lectures on anabaptist themes. The anabaptist theology evokes much interest.[20] A recent seminar in Cachipay, Columbia brought together four groups "for the first national seminar on Anabaptism." The Mennonite Brethren were involved. The discussions dealt with the "common background stemming from the Radical Reformation of the 16th century...."[21] There seems to be a broad Third World interest in the tenets of evangelical anabaptism. I foresee no problems in explaining the situation and then letting overseas conferences decide whether to change to "Evangelical Anabaptist" or stay with Mennonite Brethren. Such interaction as I've had with missionaries and MB "internationals" leads me to conclude that they would be delighted with the new name. Naturally, local situations vary. Just as "Christian" is presently an inappropriate label for missions and relief activity in Lebanon, because one of the "armies" calls itself Christian so there might be isolated problems with any name. Incidentally, MCC's wise decision not to proclaim itself as "Christian" in Lebanon at present, illustrates again that the argument about a name making no difference is seriously flawed. In most countries, "In the Name of Christ" is a good slogan; in a few, for the present, it is not. Similarly, in most countries "Mennonite" can be an appropriate church and denominational label, in some, including Canada, it is not.

14. *How would the proposed name change affect our denominational institutions?*

The answer consists of three parts.

In the first place, many Mennonite Brethren agencies and institutions, both official and unofficial, have already dropped the MB label. For example: Kindred Press, Christian Press, Columbia Bible College, Bethany Bible Institute, Winkler Bible Institute, Camp Crossroads, Columbia Camp, Eden Christian College, and many more.

In the second place, almost all of those ventures now calling themselves Mennonite, or Mennonite Brethren could keep their names. For example: "Mennonitische Rundschau," Mennonite Educational Institute, Mennonite Brethren Historical Society, and many others. Of course, nobody is suggesting any change for MCC, MDS, and other inter-Mennonite organizations or for private ventures, often combining culture and religion, such as singing and musical groups.

In the third place, it would seem reasonable, although there are presently some postal restrictions,to expect a renaming of the *Mennonite Brethren Herald* to *Evangelical Anabaptist Herald*, or something similar, and of the Mennonite Brethren Biblical Seminary. The Mennonite Brethren Bible College could choose to go either way. Denominational colleges frequently use historical names.

15. *Would Mennonite Brethren cease to be Mennonite?*

Not in an ethnic sense. Those who, like myself, would still want to be known as ethnic Mennonites would be thus known. The "non-ethnic" MBs would decide for themselves. Likely they would want to live and function in their natural ethnicities. Those who had managed to think of themselves as transformed into ethnic Mennonites would celebrate their new identity — borscht, vereniki, Mennonite Museum, and all. Only in the sense that membership in Evangelical Anabaptist churches would not involve an attempt automatically to make people Mennonite, would MBs cease to be Mennonite.

16. *Would a conference name change not make us appear dishonest?*

One respondent in my national survey wrote: "I'm sure there are people who do not join the MB church because they do not want to be 'Mennonite', but I do not think we should drop the word from our conference name — it would seem dishonest to me." Numerous respondents expressed similar sentiments.

If we were truly a Mennonite ethnic church, and intended to be only a Mennonite ethnic church, then it would be dishonest not to make that stance known. But, since we have decided not to be strictly an ethnic Mennonite church, then, it seems to me, it is misleading, or even dishonest to keep the ethnic element in our name.

17. Could a name change be undertaken without a similar change occurring in our sister MB conference in the US?

Technically yes. Component parts of a larger entity need not all have the same name. It would, of course, be desirable if the US conference would simultaneously make the change but such action is not essential.

Whether the US conference or the North American Mennonite Brethren General Conference undergoes a name change would not affect our close relations or joint ventures.

18. Would keeping the name Mennonite not help us to retain our theological distinctives?

Probably not. In Europe, in North America, and in a few other places, there are groups which have kept the name but lost the theology. Biblical orthodoxy will not be ensured by retaining the name of a human leader.

Chapter 9 — FOOTNOTES

1. Don Balzer, *Abbotsford, Sumas & Mastqui News*, January 4, 1978, p. 9B.
2. Katie Funk Wiebe, *Who Are The Mennonite Brethren?* (Winnipeg: Kindred Press, 1984), p. 6.
3. James Pankratz, "Mennonite Identity," *Mennonite Brethren Herald*, October 18, 1985, p. 21.
4. In a personal letter to the writer, August 27, 1985.
5. *Alberta Cultural Heritage Council 10th Anniversary Report, 1972-1982* (Edmonton: Alberta Cultural Heritage Council, 1982), p. 14.
6. John W. Grant, *The Church in the Canadian Era; The First Century of Confederation* (Toronto: McGraw-Hill Ryerson, 1972), p. 20.
7. *Mennonite Reporter*, January 5, 1987, p. 4.
8. Wally Kroeker, *The Christian Leader*, June 5, 1979, p. 24.
9. See Leo Driedger, Roy Vogt, and Mavis Reimer, "Mennonite Intermarriage; National, Regional and Intergenerational Trends," *Mennonite Quarterly Review*, April, 1983, vol. 57, pp. 132-144.
10. *Mennonite Mirror*, October, 1980, p. 22.
11. Eric Mierau, "Rehabilitating Ethnicity," *Direction*, April, 1983, p. 4.
12. *Ibid.*, p. 4.
13. *Ibid.*, p. 5.
14. *Ibid.*, p. 6. See also Rudy Wiebe, "For the Mennonite Churches: A Last Chance," in *A Voice in the Land: Essays By and About Rudy Wiebe*, J. W. Keith, (ed.), (Edmonton: NeWest Press, 1981).
15. *University Affairs*, December, 1981, p. 9.
16. *Ibid.*, p. 9.
17. *Kitchener-Waterloo Record*, August 17, 1982, p. 13.
18. See *Mennonite Quarterly Review*, July, 1983, p. 257.
19. *Mennonite Quarterly Review*, April, 1984, p. 82.
20. *Mennonite Reporter*, October 13, 1986, p. 2.
21. *Mennonite Reporter*, January 20, 1986, p. 2.

CHAPTER TEN

CONCLUSION

Eventually we must take a stand on the matter. I shall be so bold as to suggest that this lengthy analysis is not totally wide of the mark. But I am always open to more light and correction. Whichever view prevails, on such an important question we must listen to minority views very carefully and record them.

For me the evidence has become convincing and conclusive. I believe that this volume has made a persuasive case for my three-fold "modest proposal" and for a whole-hearted recommitment to a Biblical stance which I have called anabaptism.

Why have we not acted sooner? Because we were not fully aware. Because, as Diagrams 1 and 2 of chapter 9 indicate, the situation is complex and has perhaps not been clearly explained. Because being at the heart of the situation we were comfortable. Some people have reacted and questioned. However, often they did not fully understand and did not accurately describe. Besides, they had been conditioned to believe that a fused ethno-religious Mennonitism was proper and normative. They simply sensed that something was wrong.

Now we can choose either of two responses. We can take the easy road and try to live with the problem, try to minimize the problem, rock no boats. There is some merit in such an approach. An ethno-religious fusion produces certain benefits. Or we can try to do something concrete about the problem. We can decide that because we now know that, by and large, in North America Mennonite means ethnic, or at least ethno-religious, we will cultivate such attitudes, undertake such actions, and implement such a name change, as is required to make it clear to one and all that our ethnicity is not on a par with our Christian faith.

If we wait too long, if we do not act while there is still some ethnic and theological glue which holds our Mennonite Brethren conference together, then there may be no denominational base, no general consensus, which will enable us to launch and carry through the needed redefinition, renewal, and name-related redirection. We will than have the problem which the Evangelical Mennonite Brethren conference seems to be having. That fine group seems to have waited so long for a redirectional, redefinitional consensus to build, that in the end there may be only disagreeing segments left. If we decide to wait until consensus comes, until everybody is ready for change, until a time comes when we will lose no members by changing, then we will never change. Such a time will never come. To wait for such a time is not to give leadership.

I acknowledge that the task at hand will not be easy. The temptation is to make the best of the present and, if necessary, to escape into individualism, local activism, or mere academic discussion. But we must not settle back too easily. We must persevere with patience and diligence and sensitivity. The present time of conference introspection can yet become a time of great opportunity and rediscovery. It is to such an outcome that I call our conference and particularly our leaders and pastors. We want to be sensitive to one another. We want to hear one another but we must not be afraid to move ahead.

Paul Toews has written that "The last stage in the process is an assimilation into the national religious system."[1] All who are in conference leadership must make sure that such a succumbing and dilution does not occur.

If we cannot be sure about the answer to fundamental questions, then tradition should be our guide. Often the status quo is the best option. However, if we know of a better way, then that knowledge should, indeed must, inform our leadership.

We should, above all else, reject the notion that, "It can't be done." It can be done.

I conclude with these summary propositions.

1. Mennonite Brethren in Canada now face a serious problem because Mennonites are widely perceived as being ethnic.

2. While there are some advantages in retaining our official ethno-religious emphasis, there are more advantages in changing that emphasis.

3. We can do something about our triple-faceted ethnic problem without weakening our theological stance. In fact, carefully led correction can strengthen our theological stance.

4. We want to do something about the problem.

5. Accepting basic Biblical teaching, we agree to put Christian matters first.

6. The solution can be achieved without creating greater problems.

If the basic recommendations, as spelled out in this book, are accepted, then I, and many thousands with me, will end up being more authentically Mennonite, since we no longer will need to minimize our ethnicity, and also, hopefully, more authentically Christian, as we maximize our faith and our multi-ethnic Christian peoplehood.

The "genie" is out of the bottle. I have released it. I had no choice. In calling for reassessment and reaffirmation I had to present the evidence. Non-ethnic Mennonite Brethren have been shown what, in fact, most of them already knew or suspected. Mennonite ethnicity is a fact in North America and, in general, most of them can not expect to become full-fledged Mennonites. Given the evidence, most of them cannot become full-fledged Mennonites any easier than I could become a full-fledged Jew. Of course, there are some exceptions.

If my analysis is valid, then we must move ahead courageously. The "non-ethnic" Mennonite Brethren now have informed reasons to enquire what the Mennonite Brethren, in general, and Mennonite Brethren leaders, in particular, are going to do about our problem. We must address the problems not because our churches will then necessarily grow faster, or we will feel better, or we will look better, but because it is the right thing to do, at least as I see it.

In all things, may this truth guide our reflection, decision and any subsequent action. The issue is not faithfulness to tradition, but faithfulness to God.

Chapter 10 — FOOTNOTES

1. Paul Toews, "Faith in Culture and Culture in Faith." A paper read at Mennonite Brethren Bible College, Winnipeg, November, 1986, p. 18.

POSTSCRIPT

The advance circulation of more than twenty copies of this manuscript has produced considerable response. Most was favourable, some was mixed, and a few written responses were critical. Given the dialogue which publicity about this work has already generated, it may be useful to comment on some of the issues raised.

Several readers wondered whether the research is "balanced." Naturally I have tried to be balanced in the sense of being fair, but I did not intend to look at all sides of the main question. I assumed at the outset that the word Mennonite had a religious meaning and that such a meaning was self-evident. My intent was to find out if it also had a specific ethnic meaning and, if it did, what such a situation meant for the Mennonite Brethren Conference. Therefore this book does not describe the obvious religious meaning of the term Mennonite.

Similarly, while acknowledging the positive role of ethnicity in supporting our Anabaptist beliefs, especially while we or our forebears lived, or still live, in relatively closed communities, this work does not dwell at length on these positive aspects. Clearly, a fused ethno-religiousity provides certain advantages, especially to immigrant groups. I readily acknowledge that fact but my concern in this regard was to question the theological propriety of perpetuating ethnic exclusivity, especially in a changed social situation.

One reviewer inferred that I believed that "The confusions that presently exist can be eliminated by a change of the denominational name." I do not hold to such a view and must obviously keep on emphasizing that fact. While I consider a name change to be prudent, I strongly believe and repeatedly state that any name change, by itself, will not get us very far. It would marginally reduce the ethnic Mennonite reality and image in the church. It would also make possible additional openness towards other ethnic groups but if we really are prepared to move in that direction then we will consciously have to initiate additional church-based changes involving attitudes and practices.

One reader stated that "ethnicity emerges out of a people's experience. It is a historic category." Yes indeed, he is right. I do not question the ccuracy of such sociological or historical statements. My intent is not to minimize or redefine historical experiences but to suggest that the faithful church, especially one that has entered a multi-ethnic phase, should not be constrained by ethnic history or ethnic boundaries. Ethnic groups are properly concerned with cultural peoplehood and purity, at least up to a point. But the church has a different agenda. My analysis places priority on the church, not the ethnic group. This means that the lesson which Peter learned at Joppa (Acts 10 and 11), has continuing relevance for us.

Several readers wondered whether ethnic diversity among Mennonites should not be seen as being analogous to having "Irish Catholics, Italian Catholics, and Mexican Catholics" in our society. Obviously they assumed that the word Mennonite was analogous to the word Catholic. In one sense they are right but in another sense not. I suggest that the major point which this book has documented is that in North America, and in some other regions, the term Mennonite is also, if not primarily, analogous to Irish, Italian, and Mexican. Accordingly, if we want to retain both usages of the word Mennonite, and if we also want to be consistent, then we should speak not only of Japanese Mennonite Brethren, Chinese Mennonite Brethren, French-Canadian Mennonite Brethren, and East Indian Mennonite Brethren, but also of Mennonite Mennonite Brethren. If this book has presented a convincing argument evidence that in Canada "Mennonite" is the name of an ethnic group, and if we want to retain Mennonite in our name, then logic pushes us to such confusing and inappropriate usages. If this book has not proven that in Canada, at least, "Mennonite" is the name of an ethnic group, then the critics' point is valid.

One reader insisted that ultimately all denominations are ethnic. I doubt it. I have had extensive involvement with specific Baptist, Nazarene, as well as Christian and Missionary Alliance congregations which could hardly be described as ethnic. In several instances, even after six months of fellowshipping as part of a closely knit congregation, I sensed no emphasis on any specific ethnicity. Of course, if by ethnicity one means the national language and some attitudes found in society at large, then, I suppose, all people are ethnic. But that is not the usual meaning of the term. I think of a church as not being ethnic if substantial numbers of Hispanics, Germans, white Americans from various ethnic backgrounds, and Canadian Mennonites with roots in Russia can all participate as equals in a vibrant and integrated Christian community. I have been part of such a community. Many such congregations exist.

Additionally one can identify a somewhat more ethnic category of churches and denominations such as Presbyterian, Evangelical Free, and Missouri Synod Lutheran. All of these had or still have a recognizable dominant ethnic group. But these churches and denominations do not label themselves as ethnic. In fact, they all practice full acceptance of people from other ethnic groups. I have been involved in several such congregations and have found that the presence of a dominant ethnic group, when seen and treated as nothing more than a secondary designation in the church, constitutes no barrier. I suppose that would be my preferred model for the Mennonite Brethren church in the future. The crucial element here involves the relative emphasis placed on the dominant ethnic group.

In this connection I should answer the queries of two readers. Let me state emphatically that I have no desire to separate ethnicity fully from faith in any operational sense. They will, and should, remain linked, but not in a way which explicitly or implicitly causes people of other cultures to feel like second-class participants.

Several people referred me to Martin Marty's article, "Ethnicity: The Skeleton of Religion in America." Marty's main point is that American religious pluralism has its roots in American ethnic pluralism. No one would disagree with his analysis. He is obviously right. But that is not the issue. The question is how the various denominations and local congregations should handle their ethnicities in the future. Significantly, Marty nowhere suggests that a denomination which has committed itself to live according to New Testament guidelines should give preferred place to a particular ethnicity.

Concerning the question about being born into the Mennonite ethnic group, one critic asserted that "If one were to ask the same question about Presbyterians, Anglicans and Catholics, the responses would be the same. Most church memberships are determined by the faith allegiances of the parents." The second sentence is true but the first, I suggest, is not. The data in Graph B3 and the large number of candid written comments by non-Mennonites respondents clearly indicate that this critic's first assertion is flawed. Non-Mennonites do not perceive Mennonite churches as being as readily accessible as Presbyterian, Anglican or Catholic churches.

A few readers invoked the old adage, "A rose by any other name is still a rose." One added, "Changing the name will deceive nobody," and continued, "people in communities are not fooled by these name changes." Two comments are in place. First, surely deception is not at issue when a denomination openly and with public explanation chooses to modify or change its name, especially as part of a general clarification of emphasis. Such action has occurred many times, even among Mennonites. Deception occurs not when a name is reviewed and altered but when we have a name which we believe is inappropriate and we try to hide it. Such "deception" is now commonplace. I suggest to my critic that certain name changes, as in the New Testament case of Saul becoming Paul, are not intended to try to fool anyone but to reflect and to reinforce a changed situation.

Second, the adage or proverb about the rose applies only if there has been no change other than in the name and if that change of name has no intrinsic significance. On both counts the proverb would not apply to the Mennonite Brethren if we changed our name. We must note that not only has our conference composition already changed — the former ethnic Mennonite rose is no longer a purely ethnic Mennonite rose — but also that the name change, together with the other two parts of my "modest proposal," would itself constitute a significant shift in emphasis.

A few respondents pointed to successes in ethnic evangelism and wondered why I would want to abandon such ventures. They seem to have misread what I wrote. I am totally supportive of ethnic evangelism and of ethnic churches resulting from ministries in ethnic communities. Christians have a mandate to proclaim the Good News among the full spectrum of racial, linguistic, and ethnic peoples, including secular Mennonites or Mennonites who are only nominally associated with any church. Often within local congregations and always within evangelical denominations there must be room for diverse ethnic groups to worship in their own language and their own culture. We need to expand and reaffirm ethnic evangelism and support ethnic churches but, as I see it, we have no Biblical basis for requiring minority ethnic congregations to take on our majority ethnic label. Christian majorities should not treat minorities that way.

Some readers implied or specifically stated that they prefer to stay with the present situation. I am therefore compelled to repeat that the present situation is changing rapidly and that the status quo, whatever its merits, is simply not an option. Significantly, in recent months virtually no new Mennonite Brethren church has called itself Mennonite Brethren and additional established Mennonite Brethren churches have been dropping the name.

Finally, I wish to emphasize that while "Evangelical Anabaptist" remains for me the best option among the scores of alternatives which have been suggested thus far, I do not see it as the only option. More suitable designations may yet emerge. Some current suggestions may gain support. In any event, if we decide to reconsider our conference name, then we will naturally want to study all options prayerfully and carefully.

SUBJECT INDEX

A

Abbotsford BC 86
Abbotsford, Sumas and Matsqui News 86
admiration for elders 156
Alberta 69,92
Alberta Cultural Heritage Council 88,168, 174
Alberta Mennonites 168
Alberta survey 95f
alienation from God 15
Altona MB 73
Amish 58,70,85f,160
anabaptism 13f,15f,63,68,77,81,90,97,132, 144f,147,148,185
  in judgement over Mennonite ethnicity 132
anabaptist, definition of 13,14
anabaptist distinctives 13,14,121,147f
anabaptist essentials
  wanted by Chinese Mennonites 132
anabaptist, problematic term for some 162f
anabaptist theology 2,13,14,20,156
  erosion 154
  reaffirmation 153,154
  some rejection of it 20
anabaptist tradition, importance of 13
Anabaptist-Mennonite heritage 2
"And When They Shall Ask" 124f
Anglicans 85,187
"Anthology of Mennonite Writing in Canada" 89
Antioch 133
Arab 88
Argentina 70
art 65f,71f,80f,88f
Arts Festival 87,88f
atonement 13,163
attitudes and habits 20,152
Austria 172
author's purpose 157,158,185
author's stance 8,90f,148,151f,155,156
avoidance of modernity 15
axe analogy 54

B

Baptists 3,85,171,176,186
becoming a Mennonite 32f
  MB response 32f
  student views 32f
believers church 4,14
Belize 89,174
Bethany Bible Institute 24f
Bethel Chinese Christian Church 171
bias in questionnaire 25
Bible 13,14,18,147,148,169
  and ethnicity 132f
  supremacy over tradition 156
  we must obey clear teaching 135
Biblical guidelines 12,20
Blacks 71,159
Blumenort MB 89
Board of Reference and Counsel 2
Bolivia 89
borscht 74,78,90,179
Braeside Evangelical Mennonite Church 83
Brazil 171,174
"brethren" 12,119
  gender bias 164
Brethren in Christ 16,65,87,157,160,178
British 91
British Columbia 16,72,83,86,88,89,92
  Mennonite data 16
  Mennonites fully ethnic 89
Brubacher Hause 79
buggy 29,39,58,61,81,84,85,87,174
Burnaby BC 83

C

cabaret, Mennonite 88,133
Calgary 75
California 77,81,83
Calvary Mennonite Church 83
Calvinist 159
Canadian categories of Mennonites 170f
Canadian Census 16
Canadian Conference of Evangelical Anabaptist Churches 153
Canadian Conference of Mennonite Brethren Churches 62
Canadian Consultation Council on Multiculturalism 87
Canadian Encyclopedia, The 155
Canadian Ethnic Studies 95
Canadian government view 112
Canadian Mennonite, The 61,87
Canadian Mennonite Bible College 24f,89
Catholic, not analogous to Mennonite 185
Catholic Mennonite 90
Catholics 86,164,187
census data 16
centennial celebrations 15,64,89,92
Centennial Concert Hall 68
Central Mennonite Brethren Church 75
Chair in Mennonite Studies 80f
Chilliwack BC 79
Chinese 58,79,88,145,157,170
Chinese Mennonite Church 132
Christian and Missionary Alliance 3,171,186
Christian Leader, The 77,81f
Christian renewal 131,182
Christianity, four traditions 63
church 4,8,14,15,16,35f,58,136,144f, 173,176
  and ethnicity 134

place of ethnic church 134
Church of God in Christ (Holdeman) 153
Clearbrook BC 24,76,86
clothing 70f
Coaldale AB 6
Collected Works of Arnold Dyck 74
Columbia anabaptist seminar 178
Columbia Bible Institute (College) 24f
Committee for the German Language,
    The 6,75
community, sense of 74f
Confession of Faith 13,175
Confession of Faith (1902) 8
congregations changing name 1
Conrad Grebel College 3,65,74,79,81,
    86,88
cookbooks 75f
Cord Weekly 85
cornball humour 68
corpus culturum 122
1986 Conference 3
Council of Boards 22,23
counterculture 14
covenant community 14
conversion 162
cultural events 65f
culture 4,6
    as means to an end 156
    should not be imposed on others 156

D
Dalmeny Church 1
"Das Kommittee fuer die deutsche
    Sprache" 6
de-emphasis of "Mennonitism" 52,53
decision 15
Der Bote 59
Detroit 79
Diagram 1 170
Diagram 2 171
difficulty in joining Mennonite
    church 35f
discipleship 14,15
Doon Pioneer Village, ON 85
Dordrecht Confession 136
Doukhobors 58,86,92f,145,159
Driedger survey 96f
duck analogy 64
Dunkers 160
Dutch 58,59,91f,131,137
Dutch-German 71
Dutch-German-Russian 66,76
"Dutch va. Mennonite" 86
"Dynamics of Faith and Culture in
    Mennonite Brethren History"
    conference 3

E
ease in joining Mennonite church 35f
East Indians 59

Eastern Manitoba Travel Guide 84
Eden Christian College 24f
educating the public 19,41f,177
    not realistic or successful 41f,54
    wasted effort 177
El Faro Church 171
Elmira ON 58,76,86
en Route magazine 84
enchiladas 84
enclavement 122f,155f
Ethiopia 174
Ethnic Almanac, The 58
ethnic and non-ethnic 126f
ethnic church, place of 134,145f,187
ethnic communities 18
ethnic cooking 64,76f
ethnic dominant group 186
ethnic heritage 90,123f
    need not reject 20,66
ethnic identity, increasing awareness 2,
    79f,175
    resurgence of 81,92,94f,97,175
ethnic list 112
ethnic Mennonites, one group 43f
ethnic need not mean secular 57
ethnic problem 7,12,19,20,46f,77,81f,
    83,90,97,113,119,121f,128,131,145,151f,
    155f,167,176
    resolution of 20,77,148,176f
    the biggest problem in fifty years,
        F.C. Peters 158
ethnic traditions 4,57,75f
ethnicity 4,77f,186
    and faith 8,122,186
    and religion 6,57,60,122f,186
    as identity 67,81,90,185
    definition 5,6,77,90,186
    denial of 137
    denial of a problem 146f
    denominational problem 48f
    development 137f
    faulty analysis 138f
    importance of 5
    increasing 175
    local problem 46f,77
    Mennonite Brethren want it studied 50f
    positive contributions 18,81,144,164,
        177,185,187
    rediscovery of 61,78f,175
    six identification factors 6
ethnocentrism 4,87,134
    definition of 123f
Ethnocultural Directory 93
ethno-religious 4,5,19,57f,65,69,78,80f,
    93,121f,146
"ethnos" 133,136
    inconsistent usage 133,136
Europe 3,14,66
"evangelical," problematic term for
    some 161f

Evangelical Anabaptist 187
  advantages of 160,162f,164f
  alleged problems with the name 161f
  already used widely 163f
  appeals to overseas Mennonites 178
  early usage 135,158,163
  predates Mennonite name 163
Evangelical Anabaptist Bible College 163
Evangelical Anabaptist Biblical
  Seminary 163
Evangelical Free 3,186
Evangelical Mennonite Brethren 182
evangelicalism 17,77
evangelism 12,14,60,61,84,143f,172,186
  and ethnic boundaries 127
  ethnic problem 128
  problems in 36,54,131f

F
FM 96 84
facilitation of ministries 20
failed efforts 134
faith and culture 4,60,187
  faith expressed through culture 155
  fusion 155
  importance of 5
  should be linked says Paul Toews 143
"Faith and Culture" conference 3
Faith Today 61
family names 60f,125
"faspa" 86
Festival Quarterly 61,94,136
Filipino 88
film 73
folk art 80
Folk Arts Council 66
folk festivals 90
Folklorama 66,67,68,133
Four Great Christian Traditions 164
Fraser Valley BC 59,167
Fraser Valley College 59
French 91,96,145,161,170
Fresno CA 94,125
Friesen Alberta survey 95f
fundamentalism 14
fusion of faith and ethnicity 8,20,57,
  58,61,65,77,81,122,139,143,172
  some major benefits 181

G
General Conference of Mennonite
  Brethren Churches 77,180
German 6,12,16,18,64,74f,82f,93f,126,
  131,137f,161
German-Canadian Congress 89
Germans 58,97
Germany 93
global categories of Mennonites 171,173
global village 167f
Globe and Mail 80,124

Golden Age Society 76
Goshen IN 6
Gospel Herald 156
Great Commission 57,65,131,163,165
Greek 157
Greek Evangelical Christian Church 171
Guide to the Mennonite Bicentennial,
  A 68,69
  multicultural funding for 69

H
Halifax 87
handicrafts 64,65f
Harbourfront Mennonite Festival 64,69
hats 71
Harvard Encyclopedia of American
  Ethnic Groups 58
Hepburn SK 24
Herald Press 65
Herbert SK 1
heritage 2,64,65f,81f,156
Hillsboro KS 6
Hindi 170
Hindi Punjabi 171
Hispanic 71
historic situation and opportunity 18
history 83,92,94,97,122
  affirmation of the past 152,164
  central for Mennonites 94
Holy Spirit 133
Hutterites 58,92f,145,159
hymns as entertainment 73

I
Icelandic 145
identity 5,81,94,129,131
  author's 8,147,148,156
  crisis 7,60
  Mennonites have the highest rating 96f
  no crisis 96
identity problem 3,4,63,64,93,157,176f
immigrants 18
India 172,174
Indians, native 71,74,85
Indonesia 172,174
Inglewood CA 83
integration 176
Intourist 172
Inuit 58
Irish 83
Italian 58,60,145

J
Japan 174
Japan Anabaptist Centre 178
Jerusalem 133
Jews, Jewish 16,57,60,77,90,92,133,
  155,182
  in Winnipeg 96f
  statistics 16

Joseph Schneider Haus 79,86
Journal of Mennonite Studies 80f
"Just Plumb Hollow Group" 88

K
Kansas 90
Kauffman-Harder study 154
"Kernlieder" 68,72
Kitchener-Waterloo 84,87,89,168
Kitchener-Waterloo Record 78,85,86,88,
112
knowledge of Mennonites 26f
"Koop en Bua" 68,69,73f

L
Lancaster County PA 6,85
language
no longer a problem 155
transition 18
leaders, responsibility of 17,18,50f,97,
152,159,182
leadership requested to act 50,51
Lebanon 178
letters received from agencies 98f
"Licht Auf dem Weg" 60
Lieutenant-Governor 69
lifestyle 38f
"limitless love" 15
Lincoln Glen CA 122
literature 74f
Lithuania 88
"Locusts and Wild Honey" 67,68
London ON 16,80
Lordship of Christ 134
Low German 60,67,68,72f,75,76,78
dictionaries 75
menus 76
New Testament 75
parody of sermons 88
love ethic 14,15
Lutheran 159
Lutheran Church (Missouri
Synod) 153,186

M
"Man Alive" 84
Manitoba 59,61,69,70,72,86,167,175
Manitoba "Ethnic Mosaic" survey 91
Manitoba Festival of Art and Music 68
Manitoba Intercultural Council 98
Manitoba Mennonite Historical
Society 78
Manitoba Mennonites 16,68,91,92
Manitoba Parents for German
Education 89
Marburg Germany 174
Members of Parliament, ethnic
designation 60
Menno Simons Centre, Vancouver 81
Menno Singers 68,72
MennoVan 64,70,87

multicultural funding for 174
Mennonite
as denomination 43f,63f,120
as race 132
as religion 87f,174,185
as strongest ethnic group 97
as tourist attraction 69,71,72,78f
becoming a 32f,54
by birth 32,33,34,54,84,94,120,126,
139,160,176
census data 16,60
centennial project 78
definition 5,6,13,29,63f,68,83,90,91f,
119f,147,155
denial of 146f
double meaning 11,19,30,31,54,62,64,
67f,77f,84,86,87,92,112,137,145f,162
emphasis on ethnicity 15,60,66,87f,95f
ethnic connotation 11
family names 70,90
kinds of 16,84,120
meaning of 2,5,15,65
positive conotation of 12,18,81,112,
144,164
secular 68,72,74,88,133,136,187
similarity and diversity 41f
total numbers 16,74,87
why is "Mennonite" so important for
the church? 157f
Mennonite art 69f
Mennonite Book Club, The 74
Mennonite Brethren
are ethnic 121,122f,186
as church 63,91,119f,125,186
as multi-ethnic 120
as sub-category of Mennonites 41f
blurred image 151
call for renewal 131,165,182
changing the name 1,113,120,148,153,
159f,177f
dual membership among MBs 123f
ethnic brotherhood 123f
ethnic traits 125
ethnicity as a problem 90,121
ethnicity "more important" 123f
ethnicity not a problem 120
historical centres 94
one ethnic group 41f,122f
part of one ethnic group 43f
sense of superiority 124f
two communities in the church 123f,
144f
United States 2,122f,180
wanted to separate religious affiliation
from ethnic in 1860 140,152
Mennonite Brethren Bible College 24f,84
Mennonite Brethren Biblical
Seminary 94,132,158,163,179
"Mennonite Brethren Church Membership
Profile", 1982 2f,121,154

Mennonite Brethren Collegiate
Institute 24f
Mennonite Brethren Conference 58,70,
134,152f,157,159,164,177,185,187
developments in Canada since 1980 18
Mennonite Brethren Herald 62f,67,84,
121,136,157,179
editorial philosophy 63,64,157
ethnic advertising 62
Mennonite Brethren identity 2,119f,147
Mennonite Brethren renewal, a three-
part proposal 152
Mennonite Brethren theology 2
Mennonite Catholic 61,62,90
Mennonite Central Committee 12,84,87f,
112,178
MCC Relief Sales 77,79f,87,88,125
MCC Selfhelp 12
Mennonite Centre in Toronto 81,89
Mennonite Children's Choirs 72
Mennonite choirs 63,65
Mennonite church, ease in joining 35f
Mennonite church should not have
ethnic label 165
Mennonite clothing 70f
Mennonite Commonwealth 139
Mennonite Community Orchestra 72
Mennonite cookbooks 63,65,75,76,77,
172,174
"Mennonite country" 84,85
Mennonite cuisine 68,76
Mennonite culture 2,3,5,61,64f,68f,81,
88,90f,94f,126f,144f,174
wrongly described as being
German 125,139
Mennonite dictionary 75,174
Mennonite Disaster Service 12,86,178
Mennonite distinctives 17
Mennonite Drama Company 63
Mennonite Educational Institute 24f
Mennonite Economic Development
Associates 12
Mennonite Encyclopedia 3
Mennonite ethnicity 4,54,72,77,78f
as a problem 19,20,46f,54,60,68f,
87f,90
members want it studied 51f
problems in recognizing it 46f,54f
Mennonite Festival of the Arts 66
Mennonite foods 63,75f,79,85,88,123f,
133
Mennonite German Society of Canada 89
Mennonite German Socity of Winnipeg 89
Mennonite global perspectives 120
Mennonite Historical Society of BC 79
Mennonite Historical Society of
Canada 80,89
Mennonite identity 2f,60f,96f,123f
"Mennonites in Canada, 1920-1940" 89
Mennonite language 75

Mennonite lifestyle, way of life 38f,66,
133
Mennonite Literary Society 60
Mennonite literature 74f
Mennonite Low-German Dictionary 75
Mennonite Media society 68,73
Mennonite memory 80
Mennonite Mennonite Brethren 186
Mennonite Mirror 60,66,68,70,136
editorial philosophy 61
ethnic advertising 61
Mennonite museum 62,63,78f,133,175,
179
Mennonite music 72f
Mennonite Mutual Aid 178
Mennonite name 17
Mennonite names 60f,125
Mennonite needlework 65,71,88
Mennonite Observer 121
Mennonite Pavilion 66f
Mennonite pilgrimages 172
Mennonite People, the 59
Mennonite peoplehood 146
Mennonite periodicals 16,59f,95
Mennonite Piano Concerto 68,72,124
Mennonite Publishing Service 89f
Mennonite religion 16,77f,128
Mennonite Reporter 58,59,61,62,68,
70,85,89,136
inconsistent assertions 133
Mennonitische Rundschau 59f
ethnic advertising 59,60
ethnic data 60
pastoral letter 60
Mennonite restaurants 76,78,172
Mennonite sausage 76,88,159
Mennonite self-understanding 3
Mennonite Studies 80f,93
Mennonite Studies Centre (Menno
Simons College) in Winnipeg 81
"Mennonite Studies in North America:
The State of the Art" conference 93
Mennonite versus Mennonite
Brethren 43f,54
Mennonites
German-speaking but not German 137
in school curricula 97
leaving Mennonite church 81,90
lived in Russia but were not
Russian 137
recognizable anywhere 66
unique identity 137
Mennonites, Third World 2
Mennonitism 2,4,8,15f,87,90f,137,143,
146f,154,158f,164,168,175
became secularized 139
has its place 164
in Russia 137f
some see no problems 167f

unrelated to Menno Simons'
  teachings 136
Methodist 171,176
Metis 74,88
Mexican 76
  food 76
Mexican Mennonites 74
Mexico 89,174
militarism 17
military 15
Minister of State for Multiculturalism 60,
  63
"Missing Mennonite Cabaret" 89
Mission BC 1
Missionary Church 158
missions 14,60,61,131
  and ethnicity 132
  name change 178
"Modest Proposal", three parts 152
  we need to address all three 153f
Molotschna 160
Molotschna Mennonite Brethren
  Conference in Ontario 160
Moral Majority 17
"Morningside" 73
Mountainview Gospel Chapel 1
Multicultural History Society of
  Ontario 93
multiculturalism 2,3,87,90,93f,174
Multiculturalism Canada 59,63,174
  advertisements 59,60,61,62,67,93
  announced by Trudeau 62
  funds Mennonite projects 59,62,64,69,
  73,88,89
multi-ethnic 5,77,136,182,185,188

N
name change 158f, 177f,185,187
  as part of a larger proposal 153f
  extent of present support 52,53
  inadequate by itself 153
  not very useful alone 20,185
  other name changes 160
  other options 161,188
  reasons for past failures 153f
  requirements for a new name 160
  should retain Mennonite name 156f
  trends 1,12,63,179,188
names 60,69,70f,90
national dishes 59
Nazarene 186
New Brunswick 170
New Hamburg ON 79
"new" Mennonites 81f,83,175
New Testament 14,16f,72,97,133,144,153,
  155,159,187
New York Times 71
Niagara-on-the-Lake ON 24
Nigeria 66,174
non-Mennonite ethnics 16,19,81,84,144f,

154,170f
  leaving the Mennonite church 81f
non-Mennonites 16,63,95f,123f,127,132,
  143,170
North Carolina 171
Norwegian 145

O
Old Order 25,39,70,84,86,174,175
Old Testament 14,97
Ontario 72,84f,87f,167f,174
Ontario ethnocultural directory 93
Ontario Living 85
Ontario Ministry of Culture 69,73
Ontario Multicultural Information 111
Ontario, Yours to Discover 85
options for dealing with the Mennonite
  ethnic problem
  "the fusers" 143
  "the elitists" 144
  "the overlappers" 144
  "the parallelists" 145
  "the ethnicists" 146
  "the anti-ethnics" 146
  "the double denyers" 147
  "the separators-reaffirmers" 148
orientals 71
Ottawa Office of MCC 112
"outsiders" 15,90

P
pacifism 15
paintings 71f
Paraguay 61,89,171,174
"Pastoral Letter" in the Mennonitische
  Rundschau 60
peace emphasis 8,14,15,17,84,154
  erosion of 17
  not only for the military 154
Pennsylvania 65,76,90
Pennsylvania Dutch 69,75
Pentecostal 171
peoplehood 4,12,62,81,91,122,128,136,
  139,146,170f,176,182,185
perception of Mennonites 3,19,20,29,30
  33,36,41,48,54,58,63,64,78,87,96f,
  112,175,187
PIPKA 174
"Plautdietsch" 67,74,75
"ploome mouse" 66,174
Plum Coulee MB 88
Polish 58,145
Portuguese 58,145
Portage Ave. Mennonite Brethren
  Church 72
press coverage 86f
Presbyterian 171,186,187
pride 173
Prince of Peace 15
Prussia 137

public relations problem 64
Punjabi 145

Q
Quebec 171,174
Quebec Mennonite Brethren
  Conference 2,18,156
  acceptance of 2
  not of Mennonite extraction 120
questionnaire bias 25
questionnaire sample 22f
quilt 64,69,71,79,87

R
redemption 15
rediscovery of ethnicity 61
Regional Municipality of Waterloo 70
Reedley CA 6
Reinland MB 89
relief 15
relief sale 77,79f,87,88,125
religion and ethnicity 6
religion, functions of 6,123f
religious symbols 6,57
  role of 6,57
Rockway Mennonite School 66,69,87
"rollkuchen" 64,66
"rose by any other name, a" 187
Rosthern Junior College 89
Royal Commission on Bilingualism and
  Biculturalism 87
  Mennonite brief 87
Russia 6,58,64,119,120f,125,138f,171f
  Russians 88,92
Russian Mennonites 69f,79f,86,89,93f,
  122,131,137,155,172
  difficulties in Quebec 120
  food 76,172
  studies 81
Russian Mennonite Church 140,155

S
Sackville NB 170
salvation 15
San Jose CA 77,122f
San Jose survey 122f
  "And When They Shall Ask" 124f
  definitions 123,125
  dual membership 123f
  ethnic brotherhood 123
  ethnic traits 125
  ethnic value system as dominant 124,
  126,129
  ethnicity as obstacle to evangelism 127
  ethnicity not fully recognized 127,128
  importance of Mennonite names 125
  Mennonite by birth 126,128
  MCC Relief Sale 125
  purpose of research 123
  three key questions asked 125

views of non-ethnics 127f
Saskatchewan 69,72
Saskatoon SK 75,84
Scandinavians 97
school curricula 58f
Scottish 85,145
Secretary of State, Canada 59,69
secular Mennonites 68,72,74,89,170,
  171,175,187
seminary 18
Serbian 88
shalom 13
Shalom Synagogue 16
social science research/approach 7
socialogical evidence 57
South Africa 133,161
South American Mennonite
  Brethren Conference 60
Spanish 145
Sparetime 85
Springfield Heights Mennonite
  Church 89
St. Jacobs ON 72,76,85
state 14
Steinbach MB 6,75,78
Steinbach Mennonite Brethren
  Church 76
stereotypes 58,71,87,177
stigma, not an issue for MBs 157
Strassbourg 4
summary propositions 182
Surrey BC 76
Swedish, Sweden 172
Swedish Baptist Convention 156
Swiss-German 71,76,77,79,94,131
Switzerland 163,172
symbols 5
Symposium on Mennonite Studies in
  North America 80

T
Templo El Calvario church 171
"The Abiding Place" 174
The Christian Leader 5,77,81f
The Meeting Place, St. Jacobs, ON 72
The Mennonite Book Club 74
The Mennonite Centre, Toronto 72
"The Shunning" 73,89
The Western Producer 70
theological diversity 2,151,153
theology 2,4,13,17,20,35f,52,97
  and church membership 35f
Third World 2
  and name change 178
threefold challenge 132
Three Hills AB 4
  1978 convention 4
Tokyo 178
Toronto 64,79,81,87,89
Toronto Star 86

tortillas 76,77,79
tourism 69,71,72,78f,84f,87
"Toward a Mennonite Self-
  Understanding" conference 3
trends in name change 1
"tweeback" 68,78
two communities in the church 123f,144f

U
Ukrainian 58,60,80,97,157,172
United Church 91,171
United Mennonites 70
United States 65,77,79,87,120,123f,
  156,162,164
  Mennonite data 16
United States Mennonite Brethren
  Conference 157,180
University of Alberta 24f
University of Calgary 24f
University of Manitoba 24f,177
University of Toronto 80,93,121
University of Waterloo 24f,79
University of Winnipeg 24f,80,109
"Unter dem Nordlicht: Anthology of
  German Writing in Canada" 89
Uraguay 174

V
Vancouver 80,81
Vancouver Art Gallery 80
verenike 66,78,179
Vietnamese 69,79,145,157
Vineland ON 69
Virgil ON 6
Vistula Delta 137
Volk 60

W
Wall Street Journal 75
Washington D.C. 159
Washington Mennonite Fellowship 159
Waterloo ON 6,69
Waterloo Inn 85
Waterloo Lutheran University 159
Waterloo Regional Tourist Guide 79,85
Western Producer, The 70
Whitehorse, Yukon Territory 4
"Who Are The Mennonite
  Brethren?" 112,120,139
Wichita KS 168
Wilfrid Laurier University 24f,85,159,174
Willingdon Mennonite Brethren
  Church 83
Winkler MB 24,89
Winkler Bible Institute 24f
Winnipeg 24,68,76,81,83,84,96f,121,
  132,143,167
Winnipeg Free Press 78
Winnipeg 1986 Consultation 5
Winnipeg Mennonite Theatre 73
World War II 12,92
writers 74
Wycliffe Bible Society 75

Y
Yarrow BC 6,86
Yukon 4,167

Z
Zaire 66,172,174
"zwieback" 76,77,174

NAME INDEX

A
Abram 160
Alexander, Lincoln 69
Augsburger, Myron 159

B
Baerg, G.G. 92
Beatty, Perrin 112
Berg, Wesley 72
Bizet 72
Bonisteel, Roy 84
Born, Floyd 131
Brown, Hubert 83
Brubacher, Ray 85
Burdett, Nelda 81

C
Chieu, David 84,132
Clark, Joe 72
Coggins, Jim 63,64,65,163,164
Cornies, Johann 174
Cosens, John and Brenda 83
Cooper, Charlotte Sloan 59

D
Detweiler, D.B. 66
Doelman, Jim 74
Driedger, Leo 6,92,96f,139
Dueck, Abe 161f
Dueck, Al 94
Durksen, Martin and Kathe 70
Dyck, Arnold 74,75
Dyck, Cornelius J. 4
Dyck, Peter 88

E
Enright, Robert 74
Epp, Frank H. 4,61,62,89,92,158
Epp, George K. 89,163
Epp, Jake 91
Ewert, David 3

F
Falk, Gathie 80
Fast, Peter 75
Francis, E.K. 69,90,92,135,138,163
Fretz, Winfield 92,94
Friesen, David 80
Friesen, Eric 90
Friesen, Patrick 69,73,74,89,133,170

G
Gingerich, Melvin 71
Good, Kathy 70,87
Good, Kathy and Reg 87,174
Good, Merl 73
Graybill, Beth 90
Grebel, Conrad 136,163

Groen, Rick 124
Gzowski, Peter 73

H
Hamm, Peter M. 121
Harland, Gordon 169
Hiebert, Bruce 89
Hiebert, Frances 139
Hiebert, Waldo 168
Hubert, David 88,167,168,174
Hughes, Selwyn 133

I
Isaac, Frank 89

J
Jacob 160
Janacek 72
Jantz, Harold 63,67,68,119,157,163,170
Jantz, B.B. 4
Janzen, Edmund 77
Janzen, William 112
Jellinek, Otto 60,61
Jesus 5,8,13,14,15,64,132,135,136,155,
    157f,163,168,176
    as example 135,152f
Juhnke, James 147

K
Kauffman, Don 88
Kauffman, Ivan J. 90
Kelly, Dan 84
Kempel, Brenda 85
Klaassen, Walter 13,15,16,90
Klassen, Doreen 72
Klassen, William 5
Kraybill, Donald 5,57,94f,138
Kraybill, J. Nelson 156
Kroeker, Allan 73
Kroeker, Wally 5,83,84,134
Kyle, Richard 137,154

L
Lefever, David 88
Lehman, Louis Paul 81
LeMessurier, Mary J. 88
Letkeman, Jacob 112
Loewen, Harry 74,80,88,163
Loewen, Jacob A. 17
Loewen, Royden 89
Lohrentz, John H. 120

M
Marty, Martin 186
Mierau, Eric 176
Mohl, Hans 93
Mulroney, Brian 60

197

N
Neufeld, John J. 75
Neufeld, Peter Lorenz 91
Neufeld, Woldemar 71
Nikkel, James 131,132

O
Olson, Clifford 177

P
Pankratz, James 63,167
Parson, Talcott 5
Patterson, Nancy-Lou 71,80
Paul 134f,152,173
Pellman, Kenneth 71
Pellman, Rachel 71
Penner, Fred 72
Penner, Jacob 86
Penner, Peter 170
Penner, Roland 86
Peter 133,185
Peters, Alan 70,125
Peters, Catharine 83
Peters, Frank C. 158,163
Peters, Jacob 96
Postma, Johan Sjouke 70
Prince Philip 72

R
Rabbi Howard Hoffman 16
Reddig, Ken 119f
Redekop, Calvin 136
Reimer, Al 61,66,68,74,81
Reimer, Margaret Loewen 71
Reimer, Viola 75
Regehr, Rudy 67
Rempel, Herman 75
Rempel, Jake 67
Rempel, John D. 89
Rempel, Ron 58,133
Ruth, John L. 65,74

S
Sanders, Thomas G. 13,163
Saul 160,187
Sawatzky, Rodney 137,158,163
Schlegel, Ray 112
Schmidt, Charlene 82
Sewell, Ken and Bev 83
Shakespeare, William 73
Sider, Ron 163,168

Siebert, Allan J. 88
Siemens, Louise 76
Simons, Menno 6,119,135,136,158,163,168
    would be unhappy with the name
    "Mennonite" 134,157
Snyder, Peter Etril 71,72
Staebler, Edna 75
Stobbe, Leslie 121

T
Thielman, George 92
Tiessen, Hildegarde Froese 74,80
Tiessen, Paul 89
Thiessen, Jack 88
Thiessen, John 75
Toews, David Waltner 74
Toews, J.B. 155
Toews, Jacob John 121
Toews, John A. 4,78,122,135,164
    questionable interpretation of
    Mennonite history 138,139
Toews, John B. 88,138,178
Toews, John E. 2,4,5,121,132,154
Toews, Paul 5,122,139,143,168,182
Turdeau, Pierre Elliott 2,62

U
Unrau, Ed 175
Urry, James 93,137,139,175

V
Vogt, Leonard 158

W
Waltner-Toews, David 74
Warner, Miriam 77,122f,140,144
Weaver, Laura H. 93
Weinhauer, Carlin 170
Wiebe, Gayle 67
Wiebe, George 174
Wiebe, Heinrich 89
Wiebe, Katie Funk 12,70,112,120,139,167
Wiebe, Menno 146f
Wiebe, Rudy 74,90,121
Wiens, Delbert 8

Y
Yoder, John Howard 163

Z
Zeeman, Gerald 156
Zorilla, Hugo 4,5